Multilevel Business Processes

Christoph G. Schuetz

Multilevel Business Processes

Modeling and Data Analysis

With a foreword by Prof. Dr. Michael Schrefl

Springer Vieweg

Christoph G. Schuetz
Linz, Austria

Dissertation Johannes Kepler Universität Linz, 2015

ISBN 978-3-658-11083-3   ISBN 978-3-658-11084-0 (eBook)
DOI 10.1007/978-3-658-11084-0

Library of Congress Control Number: 2015947820

Springer Vieweg

Printed on acid-free paper

Springer Vieweg is a brand of Springer Fachmedien Wiesbaden
Springer Fachmedien Wiesbaden is part of Springer Science+Business Media
(www.springer.com)

Foreword

The multilevel modeling approach has gained prominence during the last couple of years, highlighted by high-quality contributions in various fields, such as database modeling and software engineering, as well as the emergence of the MULTI workshop series co-located with the MoDELS conference. Multilevel models more naturally reflect the reality of many information systems. In this respect process-aware information systems are no exception. Multilevel models capture interdependencies between business processes at different organizational levels and allow for a convenient representation of business process variability which, in turn, facilitates the analysis of business processes across different organizational units.

In his dissertation, which is now published in this book, Christoph G. Schuetz proposes a multilevel modeling approach for the artifact-centric representation of business processes. The proposed approach towards multilevel business process modeling extends an existing object-oriented data model, the multilevel object, for the representation of data at multiple levels of abstraction. This extension, the *multilevel business artifact*, describes, in a single object, a process instance as well as data-centric process models at multiple, iterative instantiation levels. Multilevel business artifacts are arranged in concretization hierarchies, which allows for the specialization of business process models in different sub-hierarchies of an organization. The resulting business process model is hetero-homogeneous: A globally homogeneous model interspersed with heterogeneities in individual sub-hierarchies.

This book, on the one hand, examines the conceptual modeling aspects of multilevel business processes without neglecting, on the other hand, the implementation aspects. An XML-based logical representation allows for the automation of multilevel business processes. Furthermore, this book investigates the advantages of hetero-homogeneous models for quantitative business process analysis.

Linz, June 2015 *Michael Schrefl*

Preface

Tennis, like any activity, can be mastered
if one knows the principles behind it.
— Alexander McCall Smith, "Portuguese Irregular Verbs"

This book with the title "Multilevel Business Processes: Modeling and Data Analysis" is a revised version of my business informatics dissertation of the same name [117], submitted to the Johannes Kepler University (JKU) Linz, Austria, for the doctorate program in social and economic sciences in January 2015. As such, the book is the result of my research activities with Michael Schrefl and Bernd Neumayr at the Department of Business Informatics – Data & Knowledge Engineering (DKE) of JKU Linz started in March 2010. Michael Schrefl and Werner Retschitzegger served as reviewers of the dissertation and members of the defense committee. Josef Küng complemented the defense committee as third member. Preliminary results were published at various international conferences and workshops [115, 111, 114] as well as in a technical report [110]. This book features revised and extended versions of these preliminary results.

The fundamentals for the modeling part of this book were developed together with Lois M. L. Delcambre during my research stay at Portland State University (PSU) in Portland, Oregon, USA, from 1st March to 31st August 2012; this research stay was supported by a Marshall Plan Scholarship awarded by the Austrian Marshall Plan Foundation. The fundamentals of the XML-based logical representation and the data analysis part of this book were developed during my research stay with Marc H. Scholl's database group at the University of Konstanz, Germany, from 1st March to 31st August 2014; this research stay was supported by a Marietta Blau Grant awarded by the Austrian Federal Ministry of Science and Research. My research was further supported by a study grant awarded by the Faculty of Social Sciences, Economics and Business at JKU Linz, partly financing conference visits. My doctoral studies were also sponsored by Pro Scientia, which contributed towards literature expenses.

In addition to my main contributors, thesis supervisors, committee members, and host professors, special acknowledgments are due for my colleagues Michael Huemer, Michael Karlinger, Dieter Steiner, Stefan Berger, and Felix Burgstaller at DKE for their support. Margit Brandl provided invaluable administrative support and patiently listened to my explanations of various research topics. Many thanks go to Scott Britell, Jeremy Steinhauer, and David Maier at PSU who were open for discussion during the weekly 'slim meetings' at PSU and beyond. Leonard Wörteler from the BaseX team provided highly useful advice on XQuery and the BaseX database management system. Andreas Weiler from the University of Konstanz, with whom I shared an office during my research stay, helped create an enjoyable workplace. Last, but not least, Michael Grossniklaus at PSU and later at the University of Konstanz gave invaluable advice on various matters.

My time as a doctoral student and research assistant at DKE was a rich and interesting experience. Although hard at times, I had a wonderful time conducting the research that underlies this book, meeting many great people on the way. I publish this book in the hope that it will be useful and that readers will find the topic as interesting as I did while conducting the research for this book. The interested reader is also referred to my personal website[1], which contains links to source code and other material.

Linz, June 2015   *Christoph G. Schuetz*

---

[1] http://christoph.schuetz.ws/

Contents

List of Figures

List of Tables

List of Consistency Rules

List of Code Listings

1 Introduction

In this book we introduce the notion of multilevel business process which has its origins in the hierarchical organization of companies; the multilevel business process pyramid serves as the business-theoretic model. The formal representation of multilevel business processes is a pre-requisite for their (semi-)automated execution using information technology. The multilevel business artifact (MBA) serves as the conceptual modeling construct for the representation of multilevel business processes, putting emphasis on the data objects involved in the business processes.

1.1 Multilevel Business Processes

The hierarchical organization is arguably the most popular organizational structure for companies. Many, if not most, companies are hierarchical organizations in some way or another. Top management steers the course of the company, defining vision and goals. Middle management puts into practice the objectives set by top management. The lower-level operatives, on the other hand, are concerned with handling everyday business cases. In general, these generic hierarchy levels are referred to as the strategic, tactical, and operational layers of a company [124]. The specific implementation of these levels, including the number of hierarchy levels, varies between industries and companies.

Using the extended event-driven process chain (eEPC) notation, Figure 1.1 illustrates the *multilevel business process pyramid*, a generic value creation process across the various hierarchy levels of an organization. In eEPC notation [107], hexagons denote events, rounded boxes denote functions (or activities), ellipses denote organizational units (or actors), and rectangles denote data objects. The multilevel business process pyramid mirrors the hierarchical organization which traditionally comprises strategic, tactical, and operational layers, although the specific implementation of these levels, including the number and appellations of the individual hierarchy levels, may differ between companies. At each level, different actors conduct different, value-creating activities using different data objects. The higher levels in the

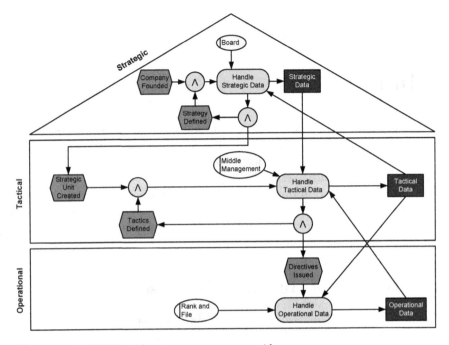

Figure 1.1: Multilevel business process pyramid

organization coordinate the lower levels, the lower levels provide feedback to the higher levels. The different data objects play a central role for the interactions between these levels. The strategic data produced by top management constrains middle management which, in turn, produces tactical data that constrains lower-level operatives but also provides feedback to top management which can adjust corporate strategy accordingly. The multilevel business process pyramid should not be confused with the BPTrends business process pyramid [42, p. xxvi et seq.] which describes concepts and methodologies related to business process management at different levels of concern with different participants.

The multilevel business process pyramid is orthogonal to the different levels of detail which are inherent to any business process architecture [27, p. 42]. Typically, business process model abstraction refers to the reduction of complexity in business process models by grouping individual activities into sub-processes [119], thereby providing a more general view on the underlying business process. The recursive grouping of sub-processes into more general processes produces a *process hierarchy*, each recursion step yielding a different level of detail in the description of the overall business process [42, p. 80 et seqq.]. Similarly, the notion of *function hierarchy* in the object-process methodology allows for the stepwise refinement of the activities associated with an object into sub-activities involving component objects [26, p. 267 et seqq.]. A multilevel business process model, however, describes the activities conducted at the different hierarchy levels within a company, involving different actors and data objects at each level. The business processes at the different hierarchy levels interact with each other. In this sense, the relationships between the processes at different hierarchy levels correspond to the "consumer–producer relation" pattern [27, p. 42], where the output of one process serves as input for another. Still, the activities at each hierarchy level may be grouped into sub-processes which, in turn, may themselves be grouped into more general processes, and so forth, yielding a separate process hierarchy at each level.

The *multilevel business artifact* (MBA) applies the artifact-centric approach to multilevel business process modeling [111, 114]. Artifact-centric business process management organizes business processes around a company's data objects and the operations that manipulate these data, yielding business artifacts which encapsulate, in a single object, the data model along with the corresponding life cycle model [82, 55]. It is common to model object life cycles with variants of finite state machines [47], describing the legal execution order of a data object's operations. The MBA approach extends this principle to the realm of multilevel modeling. An MBA encapsulates, in a single object, data and life cycle models at various levels of abstraction which are hierarchically ordered. For each level, an MBA defines a class and the corresponding life cycle model; for its top level, an MBA also represents instance data. Then, a level's class is in a one-to-many relationship with the child level's class.

Figure 1.2 illustrates an MBA model for the generic value creation process of the multilevel business process pyramid, focusing on strategic, tactical, and operational data objects, describing their data and life cycle models. In practice, these generic levels are replaced by levels that reflect the specific business case, for example, product categories, brands, models, and physical entities in a manufacturing company. The graphical illustration of MBAs consists of several boxes, linked by dotted lines, with different compartments. Each box represents a level of abstraction, the boxes being top-down ordered according to the position in the level hierarchy. The top compartment of each box contains the name of the level in angle brackets (⟨*level*⟩), the

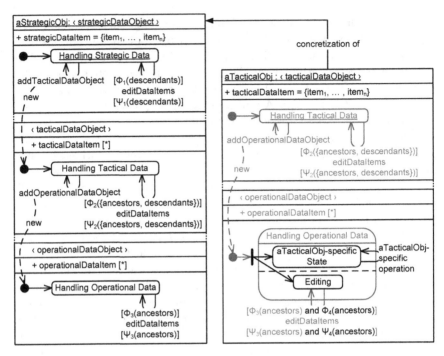

Figure 1.2: An MBA model for a generic multilevel business process with an extended life cycle model for operational data objects in the aTacticalObj subhierarchy

middle compartment describes a data model using UML notation, and the bottom compartment contains a UML state machine diagram [88, p. 535 et seq.] describing a life cycle model. In UML state machine diagrams, rounded boxes denote states, a filled black circle denotes the initial state, arrows between states denote transitions which are labeled with the name of the triggering operation and possibly pre- and post-conditions in square brackets before/above and after/below the event name, respectively. The top compartment in the top-level box contains, underlined, the name of the MBA followed by the level name separated by colon, signifying instantiation of the top-level data and life cycle models. Figure 1.2 thus depicts two MBAs, namely aStrategicObj at the strategicDataObject level and aTacticalObj at the tacticalDataObject level.

MBA aStrategicObj in Figure 1.2 represents an individual data object at the strategic level of the multilevel business process pyramid and also describes the common schema for the tactical and operational data objects underneath it. For each of these levels, strategicDataObject and tacticalData-Object, MBA aStrategicObj therefore defines both data model and life cycle model which other MBAs at the respective levels may then instantiate. In this sense, aStrategicObj is an aggregate of the data objects at the various levels, namely those data objects that directly or indirectly instantiate the respective data and life cycle models defined by aStrategicObj.

The feedback and coordination interactions between the different levels of the multilevel business process pyramid translate into synchronization dependencies between the life cycle models of the different levels of an MBA. Pre- and post-conditions of transitions over states and attributes of descendants and ancestors describe such synchronization dependencies between levels. Figure 1.2 employs generic logic predicates, denoted by Greek letters Φ and Ψ with a subscripted number, over ancestors and descendants as pre- and post-conditions. These predicates may refer to those attributes and states of descendants and ancestors that occur in the data and life cycle models for the respective levels as defined by the same MBA. In this book, we propose specific predicates for various cases of synchronization.

The *concretization* relationship between MBAs indicates instantiation of a level and thus, at the same time, membership to a particular aggregate. Concretization, however, is not arbitrary but follows specific, well-defined rules. First, the concretizing MBA's top level must be second level of the more abstract parent MBA. For example, MBA aTacticalObj is a concretization of aStrategicObj, with the top level of aTacticalObj, that is, tacticalData-Object, being a second level of aStrategicObj. Then, the concretizing MBA inherits from its parent all levels underneath this second level. Finally, the concretizing MBA's data and life cycle models for the inherited levels are specializations of the models that the parent defines for the respective levels; for the specialization of life cycle models, some form of behavior-consistent specialization (see [108]) applies. For example, MBA aTacticalObj refines the inherited life cycle model at the operationalDataObject level, adding sub-states to inherited states with additional operations as well as strengthening pre- and post-conditions for inherited operations. Note that Figure 1.2 depicts inherited model elements in gray color. The concretizing MBAs with their specialized data and life cycle models may themselves be subject to concretization. Thus, a concretizing MBA represents an individual data object at a particular level underneath its parent MBA and, at the same time, an entire sub-hierarchy with its own set of concretizations at each level, resulting in a kind of hierarchy/instance duality.

The MBA model in Figure 1.2 is hetero-homogeneous. The hetero-homogeneous approach for the representation of hierarchical information grounds on the following principle: a homogeneous global schema interspersed with heterogeneities in well-defined partitions of the hierarchy. MBA aStrategicObj describes the common schema for all descendant MBAs at the tacticalDataObject and operationalDataObject levels. MBA aTacticalObj is such a descendant at the tacticalDataObject level, following the common schema but introducing a behavior-specialized life cycle model for the descendants of aTacticalObj at the operationalDataObject level. Other descendants of aStrategicObj at the tacticalDataObject level might themselves introduce heterogeneities relevant for their own descendant MBAs while satisfying the common schema.

1.2 Contributions

In this book we investigate multilevel business processes. We extend the multilevel object (m-object) for artifact-centric business process modeling, thereby introducing a hetero-homogeneous approach towards the representation of variability. We further investigate the automation of multilevel business processes, providing a logical representation and outlining the design for a multilevel business process management system. Finally, we provide the fundamental for multilevel business process intelligence and leverage the advantages of hetero-homogeneous business process models for data analysis.

We propose a core metamodel for m-objects which contributes towards a more holistic understanding of m-objects. The core metamodel is a generalized formalization based on UML which abstracts from the details of the various application domains of m-objects. The core metamodel may serve as the formal foundation for future extensions of m-objects as well as an improved, UML-based representation of the metamodels for existing application domains of m-objects.

We introduce the multilevel business artifact (MBA) as a special kind of m-object which associates data and life cycle models with its abstraction levels. The proposed MBA modeling approach employs UML state machines for the representation of life cycle models. A set of OCL syntax macros – multilevel predicates – and the corresponding graphical notation allow for the explicit representation of synchronization dependencies between the data and life cycle models at the various abstraction levels. Thus, the MBA makes explicit the interactions between the various hierarchy levels within an organization, potentially leading to a better alignment of lower-level operational processes with higher-level management processes.

The MBA, in conjunction with multilevel concretization, introduces the concept of hetero-homogeneous models, known from data warehousing, to business process modeling. An MBA represents the homogeneous schema of an abstraction hierarchy of processes. Multilevel concretization allows for the introduction of heterogeneities into sub-hierarchies which comply with the homogeneous global schema. The life cycle models in the sub-hierarchies are variants of the homogeneous global schema. Multilevel concretization grants liberties to business process modelers in tailoring the business process models to the particularities of individual departments or local branches of a company, accounting for the variability of real-world processes. On the other hand, in order to allow for the enforcement of organization-wide business practices, multilevel concretization consciously limits the degree of freedom of modelers in modeling variants for sub-hierarchies. In particular, the life cycle models defined by the more concrete MBAs must extend and refine the homogeneous schema according to well-defined rules of behavior-consistent specialization. The precise semantics of behavior consistency may differ with the application scenario but influences the degree of freedom for the modeler. The hetero-homogeneous approach overcomes the dichotomy between flexibility and compliance with standard operating procedures.

We investigate the possibility of the MBA-based, (semi-)automated execution of multilevel business processes. To this end, we introduce an XML representation for MBAs and the concept for a multilevel business process management system working with the XML representation of MBAs. A thus constructed multilevel business process management system will produce event logs which may serve as the basis for business process performance analysis, allowing for the calculation of quantitative performance measures such as cycle time. Multilevel synchronization dependencies may then refer to the calculated performance measures.

We further investigate the advantages of hetero-homogeneous business process models for performance analysis, leveraging observation consistency for data analysis. The existence of a generally homogeneous schema allows for the calculation of organization-wide performance indicators. The preservation of heterogeneities in the schemas of sub-hierarchies, on the other hand, allows for a more detailed analysis of the business situation in certain departments or local branches of the company.

1.3 Outline

The remainder of this book is organized as follows.

Background. In Chapter 2 we review related work and briefly introduce existing technologies that serve as the basis for the development of a methodology for the conceptual and logical modeling of multilevel business processes as well as their automation and analysis. This book builds on previous work from multilevel domain modeling, business process modeling, business process automation, and business process intelligence. The presented approach employs standards such as UML, OCL, XML, XQuery, and SCXML.

Multilevel Object Core. In Chapter 3 we describe the fundamentals of the hetero-homogeneous approach to data modeling and introduce a generalized metamodel which identifies the very essence of m-objects, abstracting from the details of the manifold application domains that m-objects have been successfully applied to. This core metamodel roots the presented approach for multilevel business process modeling in the broader context of multilevel modeling. The subsequent chapters extend the core metamodel which provides a framework for the formal definition of general consistency rules for multilevel business process models.

Multilevel Business Artifacts. In Chapter 4 we present the multilevel business artifact (MBA), an extension of the m-object for artifact-centric, conceptual modeling of multilevel business processes. An MBA encapsulates, in a single object, data and life cycle models of data objects at various levels of abstraction. Multilevel predicates describe synchronization dependencies between the data and life cycle models of the different levels of an MBA.

Hetero-Homogeneous Business Process Models. In Chapter 5 we present a hetero-homogeneous approach towards the representation of variability in artifact-centric business process models. A hetero-homogeneous business process model features a homogeneous, global schema for data and business processes which all parts of the hierarchy are conforming with. Different parts of the hierarchy may specialize the global schema, following the rules for behavior-consistent specialization. The specialized schema becomes the homogeneous schema of a well-defined sub-hierarchy. Sub-hierarchies of this sub-hierarchy may again specialize the schema, and so on.

XML Representation. In Chapter 6 we introduce a logical representation of MBAs using XML. In order to allow for the (semi-)automated execution of multilevel business processes using information technology, the conceptual model must be converted into a logical model which serves as the input for the business process execution engine. The logical representation of MBAs models object life cycles using State Chart XML (SCXML), an XML-based state machine language.

Multilevel Business Process Automation. In Chapter 7 we propose a design for a multilevel business process management system. The core components of this system are an MBA database and an XQuery-based SCXML interpreter. The (semi-)automated execution of multilevel business processes produces event logs which may serve as the basis for quantitative business process analysis.

Multilevel Business Process Intelligence. In Chapter 8 we introduce an approach for quantitative business process analysis using multilevel models. We investigate the definition of multilevel synchronization dependencies over performance data. We further investigate the advantages of hetero-homogeneous business process models for performance analysis. Due to observation consistency, hetero-homogeneous models enable data analysts to leverage additional data which would otherwise be lost for the analysis.

We conclude with a summary, a discussion of the MBA-based modeling approach, and an outlook on future work.

2 Background

In this chapter we review related work and briefly present approaches and technologies used in the development of the presented approach for multilevel business process modeling and data analysis. Multilevel business process modeling builds on existing research on multilevel domain modeling, especially multilevel objects [76]. The proposed modeling approach qualifies as data- or artifact-centric business process modeling [82] and relies on the notion of behavior-consistent specialization of life cycle models [108]. Multilevel business process models are executable in an automated way, the resulting traces being subject to business process intelligence. The multilevel business process modeling approach relies on UML (with OCL) as modeling language and for the definition of the formal metamodel; XML serves as the format for logical representation.

2.1 Multilevel Modeling

A plethora of multilevel modeling approaches exists in the literature [10]. A common feature of these approaches is the support for arbitrary-depth instantiation/classification hierarchies. For a multitude of use cases, multilevel modeling approaches lead to a more accurate representation of reality than "traditional" modeling approaches with two-level instantiation/classification hierarchies [59].

The *multilevel object* [77] (m-object) is a versatile approach to multilevel modeling. The m-object combines elements of other multilevel modeling approaches, most notably powertypes, materialization, and deep instantiation (see [81] for a detailed comparison). A mapping of m-objects to OWL [79] renders multilevel modeling accessible to ontology engineers. The design of data warehouses using m-objects leads to an improved representation of heterogeneities in OLAP cubes [80]. In this spirit we extend the m-object modeling approach to the realm of business process management.

The notion of powertype derives from powersets in set theory [20] and has since been included in the UML standard [88, p. 54]. The instances of a powertype are subtypes of another object type, thereby providing metamodeling capabilities [85, p. 28]. Gonzalez-Perez and Henderson-Sellers [33] propose a powertype-based approach without strict separation of traditional two-level instantiation with classes and objects, using instead the notion of "clabject". In this approach, the powertype pattern consists of "a pair of classes in which one of them (the powertype) partitions the other (the partitioned type) by having the instances of the former be subtypes of the latter" [33, p. 83]. The relation of the m-object modeling approach to powertype-based approaches [29] is as follows. A level of an m-object may act as partitioned type and powertype at the same time. In an MBA's level hierarchy, a parent level is the powertype of the child level.

Other concepts related to m-objects are materialization and deep instantiation. Materialization [95, 25] blurs the boundaries between aggregation and instantiation. Deep instantiation [11] introduces potencies to multilevel instantiation hierarchies. Attributes of a class may have potencies assigned. An attribute's potency specifies the number of instantiation steps to be taken until the assignment of a value to this attribute happens. Dual deep instantiation abandons the strict metamodeling confinements of deep instantiation and distinguishes between source and target potencies [78].

2.2 Business Process Modeling

In large parts of this book we deal with business process modeling. More specifically, we propose an artifact-centric modeling approach for multilevel business processes. In this context, variability and flexibility are important aspects, with the notion of behavior consistency being closely related. Orthogonal to multilevel business processes is the traditional notion of business process model abstraction.

2.2.1 Data- and Artifact-Centric Modeling

A *business artifact* [82] encapsulates, in a single object, a data model along with the corresponding business process model for working with the data, referred to as the object life cycle model. Object life cycles are commonly modeled using variants of finite state machines [47]. Object behavior diagrams [55], for example, employ Petri nets for the representation of object life cycles. Other work [66, 72] leverages the expressive power of the BPMN standard for artifact-centric business process modeling. The guard-stage-milestone approach [48, 49], on the other hand, produces a more declarative representation of object life cycles. Various existing approaches towards business process management put their emphasis on the data objects involved in a process. The object-process methodology [26] defines the notions of objects, processes, and states as the main modeling primitives. States describe objects and processes change the states of objects. The PHILharmonicFlows framework [57, 56] supports object-aware business process management and distinguishes between micro and macro process modeling, the former capturing the behavior of individual objects, the latter representing interactions between objects. Proclets [5, 6] are an object-oriented representation of business processes, where a proclet corresponds to an object that is attached with an explicit life cycle model. The proclet modeling approach especially emphasizes the interaction between objects, rather than considering objects only in isolation.

The UML standard describes model types that may be employed for artifact-centric business process modeling. In such a UML-based approach [30], a UML class diagram represents the data model of business artifacts and UML state machines typically represent the life cycle model of artifacts. UML-based artifact-centric business process models are accessible to methods for the formal verification of correctness [19]. In this book, we employ UML state machines for representing object life cycles.

2.2.2 Variability and Flexibility

Central to the notion of variability is the concept of *process variant*. Different process variants may exist for achieving the same goal. These process variants have the same underlying core process but may differ from the core process with respect to the exact type and sequence of conducted activities [98, p. 45]. Configurable process models make explicit the variation points between different process variants [105]. Questionnaire-based approaches may reduce the complexity of handling multiple configurable process variants and facilitate the tailoring of a configurable process model to the specific needs of individual users [58, p. 105]. The operational approach towards the management of process variants performs change operations on a base process model, allowing for the insertion/deletion and modification of process fragments at specified variation points [40, 41]. Business process families [37] adapt the principle of software product lines for the representation of business processes. A business process family comprises a reference business process model and a set of features. The features relate to elements in the process model and serve as the basis for customization. Process owners may customize the reference business process by using different selections of features. A business process family may also be characterized as a "collection of processes meeting a common goal but in different ways" [102].

Real-world business situations often necessitate dynamic adaptations of business process models [99]. Change patterns may guide modelers through the adaptation of process models and instances, thereby ensuring correctness of the resulting adaptation [138]. Flexible approaches towards business process management allow for the quick implementation of new processes and on-the-fly adaptation of process instances [97]. Business processes may also be flexible by design, providing process owners with different choices [98, p. 59 et seq.]. Meta-processes may allow for the dynamic construction of business process models, resulting in a business process model that optimally fits the needs of the current situation [104]. For artifact-centric business process modeling, the representation of a process design entity along with the actual business process model supports the handling of flexibility [65].

2.2.3 Behavior-Consistent Specialization

The notion of behavior consistency realizes variability in data- and artifact-centric business process models. A life cycle model that is a behavior-consistent specialization of another, more general life cycle model is a variant of this more general life cycle model. Different frameworks for behavior-consistent specialization rely on various different modeling languages, for example, Petri nets [3], UML state machines [125], or object/behavior diagrams [108]. More recent work [141] has investigated the observation-consistent specialization of synchronization dependencies. In the context of process views, behavior-consistent specialization assists with the propagation of local changes to a central process model [67].

Two flavors of observation consistency may be distinguished, namely *observation consistency* and *invocation consistency* [108]. Observation consistency applies to situations where the specialized life cycle model is observable in the same way as the more general life cycle model. In this case, any execution of a specialized life cycle model must be a valid execution of the more general life cycle model, when disregarding the refinements and extensions of the specialized life cycle model. The notion of invocation consistency is stronger than observation consistency, additionally demanding that any sequence of activities that is valid in the more general life cycle model must also be a valid in the specialized life cycle model.

2.2.4 Business Process Model Abstraction

In business process modeling, abstraction commonly refers to the description of the same process at different levels of granularity. A process may thus be composed by several sub-processes. For example, the negotiation and signing phase sub-processes constitute the conclusion of a contract. Most business process modeling languages allow for the representation of such abstraction hierarchies. UML state machines allow for the nesting of states under composite states [88, p. 560]. BPMN allows for the representation of sub-processes, the notation allowing for both a collapsed and expanded presentation in order to hide unnecessary details from the user [16, p. 118].

Business process model abstraction is essential to handling complexity of large-scale models [119]. Typically, business process model abstraction refers to the reduction of complexity in business process models by grouping individual activities into sub-processes [118], thereby providing a more general view on the underlying business process. Business process model abstraction is part of the broader research field on well-structuredness of business process models [96]. This whole field is orthogonal to multilevel business process modeling: Rules for well-structuredness may be applied individually to each of the business process models at the different levels in a multilevel business process model.

2.3 Business Process Automation

Business process management systems support modeling and execution of business processes [27, p. 298 et seq.]. In particular, business process management systems ensure the valid execution order of the activities of a business process and provision the appropriate resources needed for the completion of these activities. Some of these activities may even be completed autonomously by the software system, without human intervention. An automated business process may be referred to as *workflow* [27, p. 298]. The automation of business processes requires a suitable representation language [94]. For example, BPEL is a widely-supported modeling language for business process automation [84, 62]. The modeling language YAWL also comes with an execution environment, its formal foundation in Petri nets making it accessible to formal verification [44]. The Genesys Orchestration Server [32] employs State Chart XML, an XML-based representation language for state machines. For artifact-centric business processes, the Siena system [23] was among the first prototypes (cf. [24]) for the execution of artifact-centric business processes. The Siena system employs XML for the representation of business artifacts, similar to the approach for business process automation as presented in this book, which also adopts an XML representation in order to allow for the execution of multilevel business processes. The Barcelona system [43] supports the design and execution of business processes using guard-stage-milestone models.

2.4 Business Process Intelligence

Following a review of BPI literature, Felden et al. [31, p. 200] define BPI as "the analytical process of identifying, defining, modelling and improving value creating business processes". In the chapter on business process intelligence of their comprehensive book about the fundamentals of business process management, Dumas et al. present tools and techniques for "intelligently using the data generated from the execution of the process" [27, p. 353]. Business process intelligence (BPI) comprises a multitude of tools and techniques related to the analysis, monitoring, control, and optimization of business process execution [36]. An important aspect of business process intelligence is the discovery of processes through the mining of event data [21]. Other authors [74] use the term "business process analytics" as an umbrella term for various techniques for the analysis of event log data generated during the execution of business processes.

A data warehouse may organize the base data for business process analysis. In that case, the data warehouse is then often referred to as process data warehouse [36] or simply process warehouse [64, 63]. Process models may serve as the starting point for the definition of the schema for such a data warehouse [126, 70, 69]. Other work [122] investigates how knowledge about the life cycle models of the analyzed business objects may enrich a data warehouse schema. Furthermore, business processes may also require access to the data in a data warehouse and adjust further processing accordingly, based on the contents of the data warehouse [121, 123].

In business process analysis, measures may either refer to the models of business processes or the execution thereof [106]. Business process models may be analyzed with respect to their complexity and understandability, for example. A popular measure of interest for process execution is the cycle time, that is, the amount of time needed to complete a process instance [27, p. 219 et seq.]. In this book, we focus on the analysis of measures related to business process execution, in particular cycle time.

2.5 Modeling Languages

Conceptual models describe the domain of an information system [86]. The Unified Modeling Language (UML) defines model elements for both static and behavioral modeling [88], state machine diagrams and activity diagrams being the most notable for the modeling of behavior. Protocol state machines define the legal execution order of the methods of a class [88, p. 535 et seq.]. In this book, we rely on UML state machine diagrams in order to model artifact-centric business process modeling, in conjunction with UML class diagrams for representing the data elements.

Conceptual data models translate into database schemas [28]. The Extensible Markup Language (XML), although introduced as a web technology, has gained prominence for the specification of semi-structured logical database schemas. Examples for available XML database management systems are BaseX[1] and eXist-db[2]. In this book, we employ an XML database for the storage of business artifacts.

For business process automation, modelers must translate business process models into executable models, or workflow models [94]. State Chart XML (SCXML) is a W3C proposed recommendation for the representation of state machines using XML [136]. We use SCXML in the logical representation of business artifacts since its model elements and their semantics are very similar to UML state machines, allowing for an easy translation of conceptual multilevel business process models that use UML state machines into a corresponding logical representation. We differ from the SCXML specification in employing the XPath data model as described by the candidate recommendation [129] and last call working draft [130] since it neatly integrates into XML and XQuery; the feature was dropped due to lack of implementation [129].

XQuery is the standard query, manipulation, and programming language for XML data [134, 128]. The XQuery Update Facility (XQUF) [128] introduces data manipulation operations for XML documents. The concept of node identity from the XQuery and XPath data model [135] allows for (a sort of) object-oriented programming style. In this case, XML elements may be regarded as objects and passed to functions under preservation of their identity. Manipulation operations on these elements then propagate directly to the database.

---

[1]http://basex.org/
[2]http://exist-db.org/

Part I

Modeling

3 Multilevel Object Core

The multilevel object (m-object) is a versatile construct for modeling multilevel abstraction hierarchies with applications in domain modeling [77], ontology engineering [79], data warehousing [80, 116, 112], business model intelligence [113], and business process modeling [111, 114]. The employment of m-objects in the design process allows for the representation of heterogeneities while preserving advantages of homogeneous models, yielding *hetero-homogeneous models*. In this chapter we summarize the hetero-homogeneous modeling approach and present a core metamodel for m-objects which generalizes the specializations for different application domains. We formally define the metamodel using UML; we employ OCL for the definition of consistency criteria and derivations. Although based on the foundational work on m-objects [76] we present an independent, generalized formalization which itself contributes towards a holistic understanding of m-objects.

3.1 Hetero-Homogeneous Data Modeling

The origin of m-objects and the hetero-homogeneous modeling approach lies in domain (or conceptual) modeling. The purpose of a conceptual model is twofold [93]. On the one hand, a conceptual model describes the expected instance data in all variants, serving as a documentation for application developers of what is to be expected. On the other hand, a conceptual model prescribes the structure of the data, acting as a schema, thereby constraining application developers. For homogeneous instance data, modelers easily represent the application domain using classes and associations. For heterogeneous instance data, however, domain modelers resort to inheritance, increasing the complexity of the resulting model and entailing other, application-dependent issues, for example, summarizability problems in data warehousing.

Consider, for example, the UML object diagram in Figure 3.1 which illustrates data associated with a company's rental business; the example derives from the EU-Rent use case [90]. In this example, the rental business manages individual rentals in different countries and markets these rentals to different

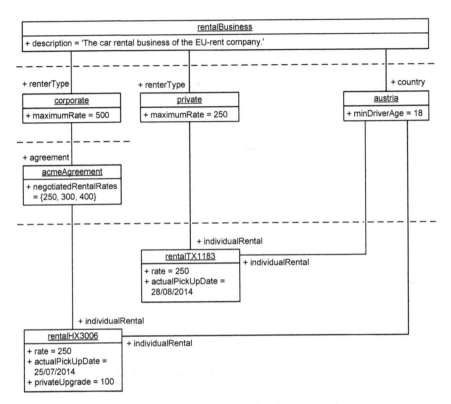

Figure 3.1: A heterogeneous object diagram for the representation of data about car rentals

renter types. In addition, for corporate renters, each individual rental falls under a corporate rental agreement. The example object diagram assumes no schema information, that is, omits stating classes for the illustrated data objects. Still, the role names at the link ends allow for the clustering of the different objects into abstraction levels which allow for the observation of the rental business at varying granularities. The rentalBusiness object links to corporate and private under the renterType role as well as to austria under the country role. Objects corporate and private then constitute the renterType level whereas austria constitutes the country level. Similarly, objects rental-HX3006 and rentalTX1183 constitute the individualRental level as they are linked to other objects under the individualRental role. The acmeAgreement object constitutes the agreement level.

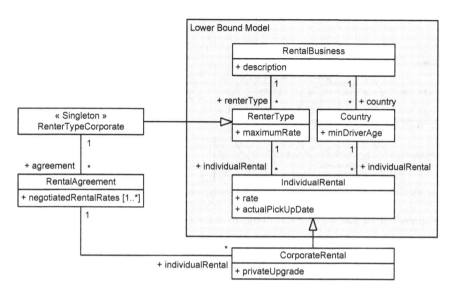

Figure 3.2: The upper bound model as an extension of the lower bound model for the objects in Figure 3.1

The clustering of the data objects in Figure 3.1 into abstraction levels may serve as a starting point for the definition of a UML class diagram as the conceptual model for the EU-Rent use case. In this case, however, one may notice the inherent heterogeneity of the object diagram. The rental-HX3006 object has an additional attribute privateUpgrade with respect to the rentalTX1183 object, both objects being at the same abstraction level individualRental. Furthermore, whereas the private object directly links to an object at the individualRental level, the corporate object links transitively, via the acmeAgreement object, to the individualRental level. Thus, in order to accurately represent the objects in a class diagram, taking into account the variability between the different abstraction levels, modelers must resort to the specialization mechanism.

The lower bound model [17, 93] fulfils the conceptual model's purpose of constraining the stored data, describing only the common elements of the data objects at the different abstraction levels. For example, Figure 3.2 defines classes RentalBusiness, RenterType, Country, and IndividualRental as the lower bound model for the data objects in Figure 3.1. An instance of the RentalBusiness class associates multiple instances of the classes RenterType

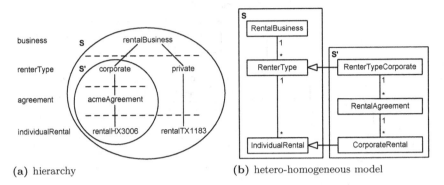

(a) hierarchy   (b) hetero-homogeneous model

Figure 3.3: A hierarchy of data objects and its hetero-homogeneous model

and Country which, in turn, associate multiple instances of the Individual-Rental class. The lower bound model omits the description of objects at the agreement level as well as an inclusion of the privateUpgrade attribute in the IndividualRental class since the lower bound model represents a "least common denominator".

The upper bound model [17, 93] fulfils the conceptual model's descriptive function, employing specialization in order to represent additional features of data objects at some abstraction levels. Using specialization, Figure 3.2 defines the upper bound model for the objects in Figure 3.1, which consists of the lower bound model extended with classes RenterTypeCorporate, Rental-Agreement, and CorporateRental. The RenterTypeCorporate class specializes RenterType by introducing an association to the RentalAgreement class which associates the CorporateRental class. In turn, the CorporateRental class specializes the Rental class by introducing the privateUpgrade attribute.

Given hierarchically-organized information, the hetero-homogeneous modeling approach stipulates the stepwise definition of lower bound models for hierarchies, sub-hierarchies, sub-hierarchies of sub-hierarchies, etc., the model for each sub-hierarchy extending the more general hierarchy using specialization. The ensemble of these lower bound models for the various sub-hierarchies then constitutes the upper bound model for the entire hierarchy. Each hierarchy is homogeneous with respect to its lower bound model but heterogeneous in the sense that sub-hierarchies may specialize the homogeneous, lower bound model by introducing additional features. The same principle recursively applies to sub-hierarchies.

Consider, for example, the hierarchical organization of data objects in Figure 3.3a which derives from the object diagram in Figure 3.1 and consists of levels business, renterType, agreement, and individualRental but omits attributes as well as the country level for presentation purposes. The abstraction levels are ordered from most abstract to most concrete. Lines between the data objects establish inter-level links between data objects. The set S of data objects, which comprises rentalBusiness, corporate, private, acme-Agreement, rentalHX3006, and rentalTX1183, constitutes the main hierarchy. The subset S' of S, which comprises corporate, acmeAgreement, and rental-HX3006, constitutes a specific sub-hierarchy. For each of these sets of objects, S and S', Figure 3.3b defines a lower bound model. The abstraction levels translate into classes, the inter-level links between data objects translate into associations between the respective classes. The lower bound model for the main hierarchy over the set S consists of classes RentalBusiness, RenterType, and IndividualRental. The lower bound model for the sub-hierarchy over the set S' consists of classes RenterTypeCorporate, RentalAgreement, and CorporateRental. Together, these lower bound models constitute the upper bound model for the entire hierarchy. Subsequently, a modeler may define further lower bound models for other sub-hierarchies as well.

Each individual lower bound model in Figure 3.3b already represents a sort of proto m-object, encapsulating the model of an entire (sub-)hierarchy of data objects. The data objects in the sub-hierarchy are homogeneous with respect to this lower bound model, they conform at least to this model but may have additional features not captured by the lower bound model for this particular hierarchy. After all, the lower bound model prescribes only a minimal structure and does not account for each and every case. The hetero-homogeneous approach demands a stepwise, recursive definition of a lower bound model for each sub-hierarchy specializing the more general hierarchy's model.

3.2 Multilevel Objects

A multilevel object (m-object) represents, in a single object, an entire hierarchy of abstraction levels. With each abstraction level in this hierarchy, an m-object associates a set of arbitrary model elements. Furthermore, an m-object may be the concretization of other m-objects. The thus directly or transitively related m-objects constitute a concretization hierarchy. In such a hierarchy, a concretization inherits from its abstractions a subset of their levels, including the associated elements. On the other hand, a concretization may also introduce new levels and elements with respect to its abstractions. Modeling with m-objects is an incremental, top-down approach for the representation of hierarchical information, always from more abstract to more concrete m-object.

In the graphical representation of (core) m-objects (Figure 3.4), each level is a box with two compartments. The top compartment of each box contains the name of the respective level between angle brackets (‹ *level* ›). The other compartment contains the model elements that the m-object associates with the respective level. Gray color denotes inherited levels and model elements. The boxes are arranged according to their hierarchical order and linked by dotted lines joining the left and right corners of the boxes. The top compartment of the top level's box contains the name of the m-object in addition to the level name, underlined and separated by a colon.

Figure 3.4 illustrates an m-object model for the hierarchical organization of car rental data; the example adapts and extends the EU-Rent use case [90]. The EU-Rent company's rental business manages primarily data about individual rentals, such as rental rates and car pick-up dates as well as information about authorized drivers. Each individual rental is offered to a particular type of client, that is, renter type, and occurs in a particular country. The renter type determines the individual rental's maximum rate, the value of which is a management decision based on market studies. The country, on the other hand, imposes legal regulations such as the minimum age for driving.

For particular renter types and countries, EU-Rent might capture additional information due to different business practices and/or legal regulationss. First, corporate clients could negotiate a set of rental rates under a framework rental agreement between EU-rent and the client company. Employees of corporate clients may, however, choose to upgrade their car for a personal fee. Second, in Austria, due to legal requirements and/or particular policies, for example, by local insurers, EU-Rent might store the issue dates of the authorized drivers' licenses in addition to the driver information commonly captured by local branches in other countries.

Using UML classes and instance specifications (objects) as the model elements attached to the different levels, the m-objects in Figure 3.4 represent the extended EU-Rent use case with heterogeneities in specific parts of the business. The model consists of m-objects Rental at the business level, Corporate at the renterType level, Austria at the country level, ACMEAgreement at the rentalAgreement level, and RentalTX1183 at the individualRental level.

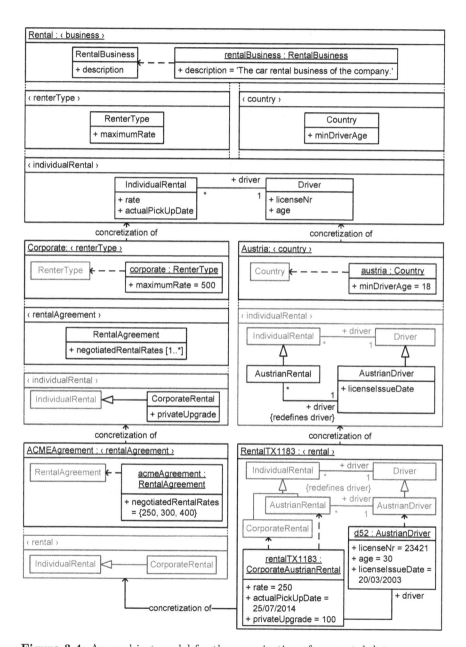

Figure 3.4: An m-object model for the organization of car rental data

The presented example basically follows the rules for m-objects in multilevel domain modeling [76, p. 97 et seq.], although for illustration purposes some specifics differ from the original formalization in order to keep the model more understandable. Thus, in this example, each m-object associates a number of classes with each of its levels; for the top level, an m-object also defines instance specifications (objects) for the top-level classes.

The Rental m-object organizes levels business, renterType, country, and rental in a hierarchy where rental is under both country and renterType, each of these two levels having, in turn, business as parent level. For the business level, Rental defines the RentalBusiness class and a corresponding instance specification which assigns a value to the description attribute. For the renterType level, Rental defines the RenterType class which represents different renter types each having a maximum rental rate (attribute maximum-Rate). For the country level, Rental defines the Country class representing the company's different local branches with each country having a certain minimum age for driving (minDriverAge). For the individualRental level, Rental defines the IndividualRental class which represents individual car rentals with a specific rental rate (rate), a particular pick up date (actualPickUpDate), and one or more authorized drivers, represented by an association from IndividualRental to the Driver class at the driver association end; a driver has a specific license number (licenseNr) and age. The Rental m-object represents the homogeneous model for the entire rental business.

The Austria m-object, as a concretization of Rental, represents both a node at the country level in the hierarchy as well as an entire sub-hierarchy. For its top level country, Austria defines an instance specification for the Country class inherited from the abstraction, Rental. The country level is a second level of Rental and Austria inherits all levels from Rental that are underneath country, in this case, individualRental. For the individualRental level, the Austria m-object defines the AustrianRental and AustrianDriver classes as specializations of the classes inherited from the Rental m-object, namely IndividualRental and Driver, respectively.

The other (direct) concretization of the Rental m-object, Corporate, at the renterType level, represents the corporate renter type. The Corporate m-object introduces an additional level rentalAgreement between renterType and its inherited level individualRental. The rentalAgreement level stores information about the framework agreements that companies may negotiate with EU-Rent over corporate rentals. For the individualRental level, the Corporate m-object defines the CorporateRental class as a specialization of the inherited IndividualRental class.

Whereas m-objects Rental, Austria, and Corporate introduce both schema and instance data, ACMEAgreement and RentalTX1183 introduce only instance data of data objects. When using m-objects for conceptual modeling, modelers may omit these instance-only m-objects and include them only in cases when clarification is necessary, similar to the use of instance specifications in UML. An implementation that uses m-objects, however, may also choose to represent instance data as m-objects [109]. Furthermore, what is instance data at one level may be considered schema information at another, more specific level. For instance, the maximum rental rate is instance data at the renterType level whereas it constrains the possible rental rates, and thus represents schema information, at the individualRental and rentalAgreement levels. Although omitted in Figure 3.4, such dependencies between levels are an essential feature of multilevel models and should be made explicit using OCL constraints. Special applications of m-objects, for example, in business process modeling [114], may provide dedicated predicates for the representation of dependencies between abstraction levels.

In the core metamodel, an m-object is little more than a collection of hierarchically ordered containers for arbitrary model elements. The ensemble of m-objects, which are themselves hierarchically ordered, constitutes a hierarchical model; each m-object both is a node and represents a sub-hierarchy in the hierarchical model. The concretization of m-objects allows for the introduction of additional levels in well-defined sub-hierarchies provided this introduction does not violate the previously defined level order. Similarly, an m-object may introduce additional model elements while inheriting the model elements defined by more abstract m-objects. The core metamodel, however, does not prescribe any particular rules for the relationships between inherited and introduced model elements. For particular modeling purposes, the core metamodel for m-objects may be specialized by restricting the attached model elements to particular types of model elements and demanding special relationships between the inherited and introduced model elements. For example, a specialization of the core metamodel for artifact-centric business process modeling may restrict the attached model elements to classes and state machines. Furthermore, introduced classes and state machines must be consistent specializations of inherited classes and state machines.

We formalize the basic characteristics of m-objects in a generalized core metamodel. Figure 3.5 defines, using UML, the elements of this core metamodel for m-objects. An m-object (abstract metaclass MultilevelObject) has several levels of abstraction (association end level to abstract metaclass Level). With each of these abstraction levels an m-object associates, represented by

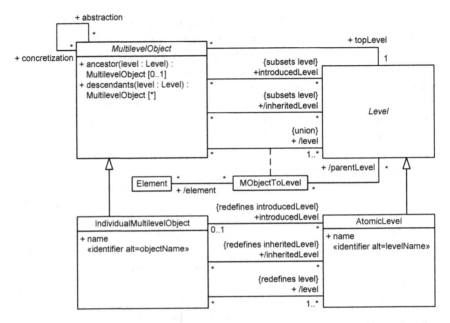

Figure 3.5: The core metamodel for multilevel objects in UML. Note that for the definition of explicit identifiers we use the notation proposed in the Ontology Definition Metamodel [87, pp. 290-293]. The «identifier» stereotype marks attributes or association ends as part of the explicit identifier of the respective class. The optional alt attribute allows for the distinction of alternative identifiers.

association class MObjectToLevel, a number of parent levels (association end parentLevel) – thereby establishing the hierarchical order of the abstraction levels – and, in the general case, a number of arbitrary model elements (association end element to metaclass Element). Furthermore, m-objects are typically arranged in a *concretization* hierarchy. An m-object may have multiple concretizations (association end concretization to metaclass MultilevelObject) and, conversely, may be an abstraction (association end abstraction) of several other m-objects.

The MultilevelObject metaclass generalizes the characteristics of individual m-objects and multilevel relationships. An individual m-object (metaclass IndividualMultilevelObject) is an m-object with a unique name, the levels of which are named and atomic (metaclass AtomicLevel), as opposed to relationship levels which consist of several levels (see Section 3.3). A multilevel relationship (m-relationship), on the other hand, connects a number of other m-objects at multiple levels of abstraction. With each relationship (or connection) level, an m-relationship may associate a number of model elements. An m-relationship is thus a kind of m-object. This section focuses on m-objects in the general case as well as the particularities of individual m-objects. Section 3.3, on the other hand, is dedicated to a more detailed discussion of m-relationships.

In the remainder of this section we define additional consistency rules for m-object models according to the core metamodel. Using OCL, we define these consistency rules over the core metamodel for m-objects (Figure 3.5). The consistency rules, in part, derive from Neumayr's formalization of m-objects [76], thereby adapting the original formalization for the UML context. Unlike this original formalization, which defines consistency rules mainly over fully specified m-objects, the presented OCL formalization also defines derivation rules for inherited model information, which potentially enables the construction of more intuitive modeling tools. With derivation rules for inheritance in place, modelers may more easily concretize an m-object by specifying only the information "delta" with respect to the abstraction. The derivation rules then determine an m-object's full specification.

The ensemble of an m-object's MObjectToLevel links (Figure 3.5) constitutes the m-object's level hierarchy. Within the m-object's level hierarchy, a particular level's set of ancestor levels corresponds to the transitive closure of this level's set of parent levels («OclHelper» ancestorLevel in Rule 3.1), that is, includes the parent levels, parent levels of parent levels, and so forth; ancestorLevel refers to «OclHelper» transitiveParentLevel which defines transitive parent levels of a level's parent level. The thus resulting level hierarchy is acyclic (Rule 3.2) with a single top level; an m-object is said to be *at* its top level. An m-object's top level (association end topLevel) refers to the single level which has no parent level within the m-object's level hierarchy (Rule 3.3). In order to avoid level skipping, a level's parent level must not, at the same time, be part of the transitive closure of the parent level's parent levels (Rule 3.4). Furthermore, a parent level must always belong to the same m-object as all of its child levels (Rule 3.5).

A level may belong to multiple m-objects. Therefore, a level's parent and child levels, as well as the model elements associated with the level, are defined local to a particular m-object, as described by association class MObjectToLevel in Figure 3.5. Different m-objects may thus associate with the same level different parent and child levels as well as different model elements. These variations, however, are not arbitrary but depend on the

Rule 3.1: A level's set of ancestor levels is the transitive closure of parent levels

```
1 context MObjectToLevel
2  def: transitiveParentLevel : Set(Level) =
3    self.parentLevel->closure(p |
4      p.MObjectToLevel->select(l |
5        l.MultilevelObject = self.MultilevelObject
6      ).parentLevel
7    )
8  def: ancestorLevel : Set(Level) =
9    self.transitiveParentLevel->union(self.parentLevel)
```

Rule 3.2: The level hierarchy of an m-object is acyclic

```
1 context MObjectToLevel inv:
2  not self.ancestorLevel->includes(self.level)
```

Rule 3.3: An m-object has a single top level with no parent

```
1 context MultilevelObject inv:
2  let mobjectToTop : Collection(MObjectToLevel) =
3    self.MObjectToLevel->select(parentLevel->isEmpty())
4  in mobjectToTop->size() = 1 and
5     mobjectToTop->any(true).level = self.topLevel
```

Rule 3.4: A level's parent level must not be a transitive parent level

```
1 context MObjectToLevel inv:
2  not self.parentLevel->exists(l |
3    self.transitiveParentLevel->includes(l)
4  )
```

Rule 3.5: A level's parent levels must belong to same m-object

```
1 context MObjectToLevel inv:
2  self.parentLevel->forAll(p |
3    self.MultilevelObject.level->includes(p)
4  )
```

hierarchical organization of m-objects. The variations are governed by the semantics of the concretization relationship which presents characteristics of inheritance and specialization as well as a kind of aggregation. Different applications of m-objects may, however, provide varying interpretations of the exact nature of the concretization relationship. In particular, an application may require inherited and introduced model elements to be in a specific relationship with each other, as illustrated in the previous example from the adapted EU-Rent use case which employs semantics from multilevel domain modeling for the concretization relationship.

M-objects are themselves hierarchically organized: An m-object may be the concretization of multiple other m-objects (association end concretization in Figure 3.5). Conversely, an m-object may also be the abstraction of multiple other m-objects (association end abstraction). The concretization relationship is also transitive. A transitive abstraction of an m-object is referred to as ancestor. An m-object's set of ancestor m-objects («OclHelper» ancestors in Rule 3.6) corresponds to the transitive closure of the m-object's abstractions. At any given level, an m-object has at most one ancestor m-object (Rule 3.7). The ancestor method takes an abstraction level as argument and returns the m-object's single ancestor at the argument level (Rule 3.8), provided there exists an ancestor at the given argument abstraction level. Likewise, a transitive concretization of an m-object is referred to as descendant. An m-object's set of descendant m-objects («OclHelper» descendants in Rule 3.9) corresponds to the transitive closure of the m-object's concretizations. An m-object's descendants method, in turn, takes an abstraction level as argument and returns all of the m-object's descendants at that argument abstraction level (Rule 3.10).

The hierarchical order of m-objects mirrors the level hierarchy: An m-object's top level must be a second level in the level hierarchies of this m-object's abstractions (Rule 3.11). Then, from its abstractions, an m-object inherits (association end inheritedLevel in Figure 3.5) all levels underneath this second level (Rule 3.12), that is, the concretizing m-object's own top level. Besides inheriting levels from its ancestors, an m-object may also introduce additional levels into the level hierarchy (association end introducedLevel) with respect to its abstractions. The set of levels (association end level) of an m-object is a derived union of this m-object's pairwise disjoint (Rule 3.13) subsets of introduced levels and inherited levels. Introduced levels must not change the relative order of (inherited) levels with respect to the abstractions (Rule 3.14). Thus, a concretization represents a sub-hierarchy, possibly with additional levels, of the level hierarchy described by the abstractions.

Rule 3.6: An m-object's set of ancestors is the transitive closure of abstractions

```
1 context MultilevelObject def:
2   ancestors : Set(MultilevelObject) =
3     self->closure(abstraction)
```

Rule 3.7: An m-object has at most one ancestor at a particular level

```
1 context MultilevelObject inv:
2   Level.allInstances()->forAll(l |
3     self.ancestors->select(topLevel = l)->size() <= 1
4   )
```

Rule 3.8: The ancestor query retrieves an m-object's ancestor at a level

```
1 context MultilevelObject::ancestor
2   (level : Level) : MultilevelObject body:
3     self.ancestors->any(o | o.topLevel = level)
```

Rule 3.9: An m-object's set of descendants is transitive closure of concretizations

```
1 context MultilevelObject def:
2   descendants : Set(MultilevelObject) =
3     self->closure(concretization)
```

Rule 3.10: The descendants query retrieves an m-object's descendants at a level

```
1 context MultilevelObject::descendants
2   (level : Level) : Set(MultilevelObject) body:
3     self.descendants->select(o | o.topLevel = level)
```

Rule 3.11: An m-object's top level must be second level in all abstractions

```
1 context MultilevelObject inv:
2   self.abstraction->forAll(o |
3     o.MObjectToLevel->select(l |
4       l.level = self.topLevel
5     ).parentLevel->includes(o.topLevel)
6   )
```

Rule 3.12: An m-object inherits its abstractions' levels from top level downwards

```
1 context MultilevelObject::inheritedLevel :
2 Set(Level) derive:
3   self.abstraction.MObjectToLevel->select(l |
4     l.ancestorLevel->includes(self.topLevel) or
5     l.level = self.topLevel
6   ).level->asSet()
```

Rule 3.13: An m-object's sets of introduced and inherited levels are disjoint

```
1 context MultilevelObject inv:
2 self.introducedLevel->forAll(l |
3   not self.inheritedLevel->includes(l)
4 )
```

Rule 3.14: The relative order of levels does not change during concretization

```
1  context MultilevelObject inv:
2  let commonLevels : Set(Level) =
3    self.level->intersection(self.abstraction.level)
4  in commonLevels->forAll(l1, l2 | (
5    self.abstraction.MObjectToLevel->exists(m |
6    m.level = l1 and m.ancestorLevel->includes(l2)
7  ) implies self.MObjectToLevel->exists(m |
8    m.level = l1 and m.ancestorLevel->includes(l2)
9  )
10 ) and (
11   self.MObjectToLevel->exists(m |
12   m.level = l1 and m.ancestorLevel->includes(l2)
13 ) implies
14   self.abstraction.MObjectToLevel->exists(m |
15   m.level = l1 and m.ancestorLevel->includes(l2)
16 )
17 )
18 )
```

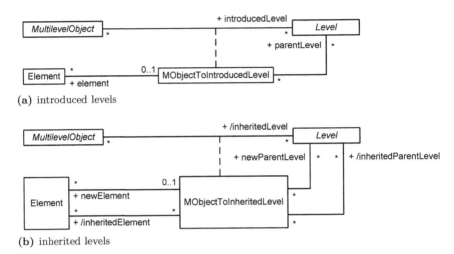

(a) introduced levels

(b) inherited levels

Figure 3.6: The data attached to an m-object's introduced and inherited levels in the core metamodel for m-objects in Figure 3.5

In the particular case of individual m-objects, that is, instances of the IndividualMultilevelObject metaclass, a *unique introduction rule* for levels requires that each level is introduced by a single m-object only. The 0..1-multiplicity at the IndividualMultilevelObject end of the redefined introduced-Level association (Figure 3.5), in conjunction with the disjointness condition for the sets of introduced and inherited levels (Rule 3.13), enforces this unique introduction rule for levels. Therefore, any two individual m-objects (IndividualMultilevelObject instances) that share a level must either be in a concretization relationship or have a common ancestor that introduces the shared level. The unique introduction rule for levels ensures semantic equality of levels across sub-hierarchies. With the unique introduction rule in place, a level shared by different m-objects carries the same meaning in each m-object's level hierarchy. The unique introduction rule for levels, however, does not apply to all kinds of m-objects. In particular, m-relationships have no unique introduction rule: The semantic equality of relationship levels derives from the individual levels (see Section 3.3).

An m-object's level hierarchy as well as the set of elements associated with each of the levels in the level hierarchy derive from the data that are attached to an m-object's introduced and inherited levels. The MObjectToIntroduced-Level and MObjectToInheritedLevel association classes, which are not shown in Figure 3.5, connect the MultilevelObject class with Level. Figure 3.6 defines MObjectToIntroducedLevel and MObjectToInheritedLevel as part of the core metamodel for m-objects. These association classes describe the data that an m-object attaches to its introduced and inherited levels, respectively. In the case of the MObjectToIntroducedLevel association class the attached elements are asserted. In the case of the MObjectToInheritedLevel association class some of the attached elements are asserted, others are derived. In the following, we define, using OCL, the corresponding derivation rules for the inheritance of elements.

For an introduced level, an m-object (association class MObjectToIntroducedLevel in Figure 3.6a) asserts a number of parent levels (association end parentLevel) and model elements (association end element). A model element (metaclass Element) may belong to at most one MObjectToIntroducedLevel instance, that is, a particular model element may be introduced by a single m-object only (unique introduction rule for elements). Note, however, that multiple m-objects may, through inheritance, associate the same element with the same level. Consequently, two m-objects that share a given model element are either in a concretization relationship or have a common ancestor m-object.

For an inherited level, an m-object (association class MObjectToInheritedLevel in Figure 3.6b) derives from its abstractions a number of parent levels (association end inheritedParentLevel) and model elements (association end inheritedElement). An inherited level's inherited parent levels correspond to the union of the parent levels that the m-object's abstractions associate with the respective level (Rule 3.15). Parent levels that are not in the concretization's level hierarchy are omitted (Rule 3.15, Lines 6-8). An inherited level's inherited model elements correspond to the union of the model elements that the m-object's abstractions associate with the respective level (Rule 3.16).

For an inherited level, an m-object (Figure 3.6b) may also assert a number of parent levels (association end newParentLevel) and model elements (association end newElement). Then, the parent levels and elements of an inherited level derive from the inherited data and the newly asserted data. The inherited level's set of parent levels («OclHelper» parentLevel in Rule 3.17) corresponds to the union of the newly asserted parent levels and a subset of the inherited parent levels: only those inherited parent levels are included that are not already in the transitive closure of any newly asserted parent level's set of parent levels (Rule 3.17, Lines 6-14) in order to avoid skip levels, that is, optional levels which in some paths through the hierarchy

Rule 3.15: An inherited level inherits the parent levels from abstractions

```
1 context MObjectToInheritedLevel::
2  inheritedParentLevel : Set(Level) derive:
3    let obj : MultilevelObject = self.MultilevelObject
4    in obj.abstraction.MObjectToLevel->select(l |
5      l.level = self.inheritedLevel
6    ).parentLevel->asSet()->select(l |
7      obj.inheritedLevel->includes(l)
8    )
```

Rule 3.16: An inherited level inherits elements from abstractions

```
1 context MObjectToInheritedLevel::inheritedElement :
2  Set(Element) derive:
3    let obj : MultilevelObject = self.MultilevelObject
4    in obj.abstraction.MObjectToLevel->select(l |
5      l.level = self.inheritedLevel
6    ).element->asSet()
```

Rule 3.17: An inherited level's set of parent levels derives from the union of new parent levels and inherited parent levels

```
 1 context MObjectToInheritedLevel def:
 2  parentLevel : Set(Level) =
 3    let obj : MultilevelObject = self.MultilevelObject
 4    in self.newParentLevel->union(
 5      self.inheritedParentLevel->select(i |
 6        not self.newParentLevel->includes(n |
 7          let objToN : Set(MObjectToIntroducedLevel) =
 8            obj.MObjectToIntroducedLevel->select(m |
 9            m.introducedLevel = n
10          ) in objToN.parentLevel->closure(p |
11            p.MObjectToIntroducedLevel->select(
12              l | l.MultilevelObject = obj).parentLevel
13            )->union(objToN.parentLevel)->includes(i)
14        )
15      )
16    )
```

have no associated instances. Note that only an introduced level can serve as newly asserted parent level. Otherwise, the resulting m-object would violate the requirements of non-skip levels only (Rule 3.4) and/or stable level order (Rule 3.14). The inherited level's set of elements («OclHelper» element in Rule 3.18) corresponds to the union of the newly asserted elements and the inherited elements. Depending on whether a level is introduced or inherited by the m-object, the level's parent levels (Rule 3.19) and elements (Rule 3.20) derive from the m-object's introduced level links (MObjectToIntroducedLevel) and inherited level links (MObjectToInheritedLevel), respectively.

The unique introduction rule for model elements requires that each model element be introduced only once. First, an m-object must not associate a previously introduced model element with a newly introduced level (Rule 3.21). Second, an m-object must not associate a previously introduced model element with an inherited level (Rule 3.22). The unique introduction rule for model elements, much like its counterpart for levels, ensures semantic equality between different sub-hierarchies: any two m-objects that share a model element must either be in a concretization relationship or have a common ancestor that introduces the shared model element. Unlike the unique introduction for levels, the unique introduction rule for model elements also applies to the general case and, consequently, m-relationships.

In Rule 3.21, A_MObjectToInheritedLevel_newElement refers the association in Fig. 3.6b between MObjectToInheritedLevel and Element, where Element assumes the newElement role. The OCL standard [92, p. 19] specifies the default name of an association that the modeler has not explicitly named as being composed of a capital A, followed by an underscore, followed by the lexically first association end name, followed by an underscore, followed by the other association end name. In case the modeler has not explicitly named an association end, the name of the class constitutes the respective association end's name.

Alternative paths in an m-object's level hierarchy are possible. These alternative paths, however, constitute mandatory rather than optional paths, that is, the hierarchy supports navigation along each of these paths. Therefore, an m-object must have an ancestor m-object at each of its top level's ancestor levels as defined by any ancestor m-object (Rule 3.23). This rule guarantees a certain homogeneity within the level hierarchy of an m-object, which is particularly important for data warehousing; optional paths would result in a fully heterogeneous hierarchy. An m-object's level hierarchy, however, defines a least common hierarchical schema that descendants must follow although they can extend the least common schema.

Rule 3.18: An inherited level's set of elements derives from the union of new elements and inherited elements

```
1 context MObjectToInheritedLevel def:
2   element : Set(Element) =
3     self.newElement->union(self.inheritedElement)
```

Rule 3.19: A level's parent levels derive from introduced or inherited level links

```
1  context MObjectToLevel::parentLevel : Set(Level)
2  derive:
3  let obj : MultilevelObject = self.MultilevelObject
4  in if obj.introducedLevel->includes(self.level)
5  then obj.MObjectToIntroducedLevel->select(l |
6    l.introducedLevel = self.level
7  ).parentLevel
8  else obj.MObjectToInheritedLevel->select(l |
9    l.inheritedLevel = self.level
10 ).parentLevel
11 endif
```

Rule 3.20: A level's elements derive from introduced or inherited level links

```
1  context MObjectToLevel::element : Set(Element)
2  derive:
3  let obj : MultilevelObject = self.MultilevelObject
4  in if obj.introducedLevel->includes(self.level)
5  then mobject.MObjectToIntroducedLevel->select(l |
6    l.introducedLevel = self.level
7  ).element
8  else obj.MObjectToInheritedLevel->select(l |
9    l.inheritedLevel = self.level
10 ).element
11 endif
```

Rule 3.21: An introduced level's new element must not already have been introduced

```
1 context MObjectToIntroducedLevel inv:
2   self.element->forAll(e |
3     e.A_MObjectToInheritedLevel_newElement->isEmpty()
4   )
```

Rule 3.22: An inherited level's new element must not already have been introduced

```
1 context MObjectToInheritedLevel inv:
2   self.newElement->forAll(e |
3     e.MObjectToIntroducedLevel->isEmpty()
4   )
```

Rule 3.23: For all ancestor levels of an m-object's top level there must be an ancestor m-object at this ancestor level

```
1 context MultilevelObject inv:
2   self.ancestors.MObjectToLevel->select(l |
3     l.level = self.topLevel
4   ).ancestorLevel->asSet()->forAll(l |
5     self.ancestors->exists(o | o.topLevel = l)
6   )
```

3.3 Multilevel Relationships

A multilevel relationship (m-relationship) connects m-objects at various levels of abstraction. The connected m-objects are referred to as the m-relationship's coordinates. Furthermore, an m-relationship has a label. An m-relationship also has multiple, hierarchically ordered relationship levels, each representing a connection between levels of the coordinate m-objects. Being a kind of m-object itself, an m-relationship may associate a set of arbitrary model elements with each relationship level. Likewise, m-relationships are arranged in concretization hierarchies.

In the graphical representation (Figures 3.7-3.10), diamonds represent m-relationships. An m-relationship's label is in the center of the diamond, solid lines lead from the diamond to the boxes that represent the m-relationship's coordinate m-objects. Dotted lines running through the diamond and connecting the boxes that represent the coordinate m-objects' individual levels represent relationship levels. For the representation of the attached model elements, the graphical representation of m-relationships adopts the notation for m-objects, a dashed line graphically linking the joined boxes that represent the relationship levels of the m-relationship. Rather than names of individual levels, however, the top compartment of each box contains a comma-separated pair of level names inside angle brackets; the level names refer to the connected levels from the coordinate m-objects.

Figure 3.7 illustrates the use of m-relationships for the representation of context-specific, business-related knowledge in the adapted EU-Rent use case by means of the REA business model ontology [45]. The main elements of the REA ontology are Resources, Events, and Agents. Business model ontologies formalize the value-adding processes at a higher level of abstraction than business process models. Typically, a business model ontology documents the exchange of goods and money between different actors, thereby abstracting from individual tasks and activities [34]. Business model ontologies also allow for the formalization of business policies and practices. Business modeling using a business model ontology may be regarded as a precursor to business process modeling. Note that even though the illustrations use a UML-like notation for the representation, REA models are not UML models.

The m-relationship in Figure 3.7 between m-objects Rental and Car expresses the fact that the EU-Rent company's rental business is concerned with renting cars to customers. The company offers a variety of car models to the different renter types, as expressed by the ⟨ renterType, model ⟩ relationship level, and provides individual renters with physical car entities, as expressed by the ⟨ renter, physicalEntity ⟩ level. With each of these relationship levels, the m-relationship between Rental and Car associates REA model elements which constitute the vocabulary for the more concrete m-relationships. Thus, for the ⟨ renterType, model ⟩ level, the m-relationship demands from its concretizations the definition of policies that apply to a renter type and a car model. For the ⟨ renter, physicalEntity ⟩ level, the m-relationship demands from its concretizations the recording of individual transactions, capturing the reception of rental services by individual renters in exchange for payments. Note that possible attributes of the RentalPolicy policy as well as the attributes of the Payment and Rental events are omitted in Figure 3.7. For example, a rental policy might have a description detailing the policy, a payment might record the paid amount, the rental might record the rental duration.

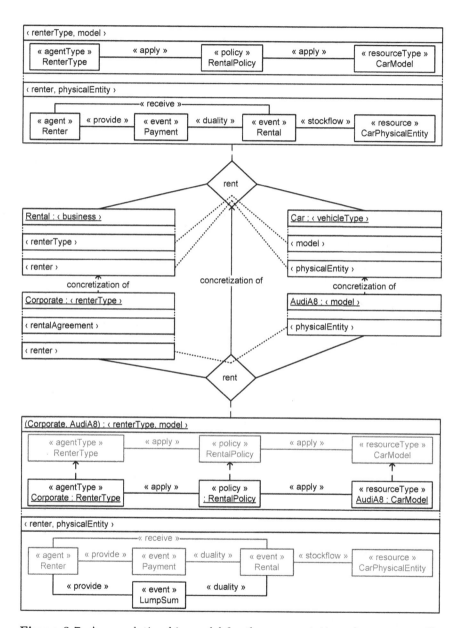

Figure 3.7: An m-relationship model for the representation of context-specific knowledge expressed in the REA ontology using a UML-like syntax

The m-relationship in Figure 3.7 between m-objects Corporate and AudiA8 is a concretization of the m-relationship between Rental and Car, instantiating the REA model at the ⟨ renterType, model ⟩ level, extending the REA model at the ⟨ renter, physicalEntity ⟩ level. At the ⟨ renterType, model ⟩ level, the m-relationship between Corporate and AudiA8 introduces a policy which applies to the corporate renter type and the Audi A8 car model; the specifics of this policy are omitted in the illustration. At the ⟨ renter, physicalEntity ⟩ level, the m-relationship introduces the LumpSum event. Thus, for the Corporate renter type and the AudiA8 car model, the company accepts compensation by lump sum, which covers a group of individual rentals and might not depend on driven distance and rental duration, rather than having an individual payment for each individual rental. Note that the inclusion of the LumpSum event as a possibility for payment applies only for the Corporate renter type and only for the AudiA8 model. In reality, the EU-Rent company might rather allow payment by means of lump sum for corporate renters regardless the car model. In this case, the LumpSum event would have to be introduced at the ⟨ renter, physicalEntity ⟩ level by an m-relationship between the m-objects Corporate and Car.

The m-relationship between m-objects TX1183 and AudiA8-KN45 in Figure 3.8 describes an individual rental transaction by associating as model elements the involved agent, event, and resource instances. Renter TX1183 rents the AudiA8-KN45 in the course of rental RentalTX1183 paid for by means of the ACMEPayment2014 lump sum payment. The m-relationship follows the inherited REA model for the ⟨ renter, physicalEntity ⟩ level as defined by the more abstract m-relationships in Figure 3.7, the inherited elements being depicted in gray color.

Assume now the EU-Rent company wishes to extend its business model for the Corporate renter type, the extension of the business model applying to rentals of all car models by any corporate renter. Corporate renters, unlike other renter types, such as private renters, conclude a rental agreement with EU-Rent which defines general conditions for all future rentals of the corporate renter. In the agreement, a client company and EU-Rent may then detail rental conditions for specific car models. In this case, an m-relationship between the m-objects Corporate and Car must define these additional rental terms and policies. For example, in Figure 3.9, such an m-relationship between the m-objects Corporate and Car introduces for the ⟨ rentalAgreement, model ⟩ level an REA model for the formalization of rental terms agreed upon by a client enterprise for rentals of a particular car model. In this example, such a rental agreement between the EU-Rent company and

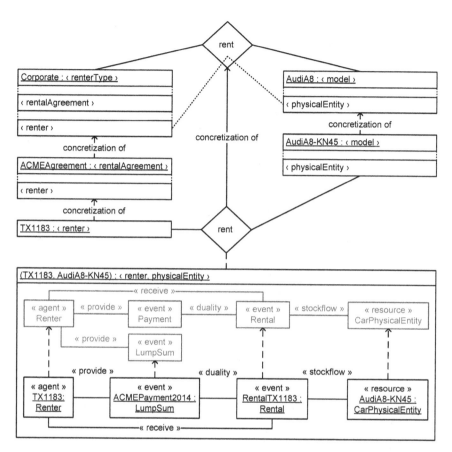

Figure 3.8: An m-relationship representing an individual rental transaction

a client enterprise may have several negotiated rental rates as the clauses of the contract. A corresponding RentalRate term represents an amount of money. For rentals under such a contract, renters may then choose among a set of pre-negotiated rental rates.

The m-relationship between m-objects ACMEAgreement and AudiA8 in Figure 3.10 describes a rental agreement between EU-Rent and the ACME company concerning the AudiA8 car model. This m-relationship associates with the ‹ rentalAgreement, model › level instances of the REA model elements defined by the m-relationship between Corporate and Car in Figure 3.9 for the ‹ rentalAgreement, model › level. This rental agreement contains as clause a negotiated rental rate of 120 (monetary units). Thus, the amount of 120 is one of the negotiated rental rates for future car rentals of the AudiA8 car model that EU-Rent and ACME have agreed upon. There may be additional rental rates as contract clauses which are not shown in the example.

An m-relationship's top level, just like the top level of an m-object, must be second level of a possibly existing abstraction. Therefore, the m-relationship between m-objects Rental and Car in Figure 3.9 introduces the ⟨ renterType, vehicleType ⟩ level in order to allow for a descendant at this level. On the one hand, this requirement forces modelers to carefully consider where changes in the multilevel model are allowed while restricting unwanted (and possibly unnecessary) changes. On the other hand, for some applications using m-objects, this requirement may prove too strict. For example, in data warehousing [80], enforcing this rule would deprive the modeler of much needed flexibility. In data warehouse applications, m-relationships associate measure definitions and measure values with their relationship levels. Unlike the general modeling case, which puts an emphasis on the top-down definition of data models, data warehousing places the focus on the bottom-up aggregation of data. Formally, one may consider the implicit existence of all combinations of the coordinate m-objects' levels as relationship levels of an m-relationship.

Figure 3.11 extends the core metamodel for m-objects (Figure 3.5) with elements for the representation of m-relationships. An m-relationship (metaclass MultilevelRelationship) is a kind of m-object, that is, the MultilevelRelationship metaclass is a specialization of MultilevelObject. An m-relationship has a sequence, that is, an ordered list, of coordinates (association end coordinate to metaclass MultilevelObject), the m-objects that are connected by the m-relationship; the m-relationship represents a connection between its coordinate m-objects. These connections may exist on several relationship levels (redefines association end level to metaclass RelationshipLevel). With each relationship level, the m-relationship may associate a number of arbitrary model elements, just like an individual m-object with atomic levels.

A relationship level is a kind of level that references several other levels (association end level to metaclass Level) in a sequence. Thereby, the associated levels mirror the coordinates of the relationship level's m-relationship: Each level stems from the respective coordinate's level hierarchy. The order of the relationship level's sequence of referenced levels corresponds to the order of the m-relationship's sequence of coordinates. For each position in a relationship level's sequence of referenced levels, the level at the respective position belongs to the m-object at the same position in the m-relationship's

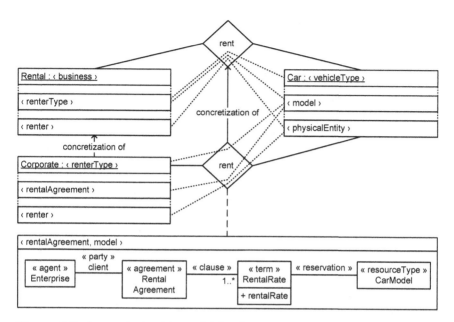

Figure 3.9: An m-relationship model for the representation of rental agreements and its terms

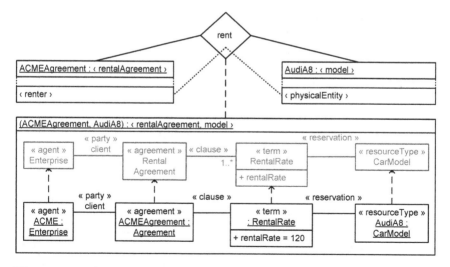

Figure 3.10: An m-relationship representing an individual rental agreement

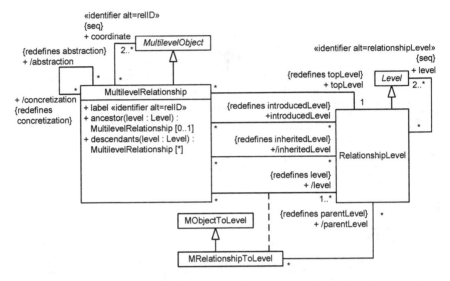

Figure 3.11: The core metamodel for multilevel relationships. Note that marking multiple attributes or association ends with the «identifier» stereotype amounts to the definition of a compound key. When using the same alt name, the thus marked components are part of the same alternative compound key.

sequence of coordinates (Rule 3.24). Conversely, for each position in an m-relationship's sequence of coordinates, a relationship level references some level from the coordinate m-object at the same position in the relationship level's sequence of levels (Rule 3.25). The sequence of referenced levels constitutes a relationship level's identifier.

Each level of an m-relationship indicates some kind of relationship between the referenced levels which belong to the m-relationship's coordinate m-objects. The exact semantics of the relationships between the referenced levels depends on the specific application domain, for example, in data warehousing [80], a relationship level represents a fact class at some level of granularity whereas in domain modeling a relationship level represents a relationship between the classes at the respective levels of the connected m-objects. In business process modeling, a relationship level may represent interaction of processes. At the same time, an m-relationship is a link, that is, a relationship occurrence, between its coordinate m-objects. The top relationship level of an m-relationship, therefore, must correspond to the list of top levels of all the m-relationship's coordinate m-objects (Rule 3.27).

Much like individual m-objects, concretization relationships organize m-relationships into abstraction hierarchies. Unlike m-objects, however, a concretization relationship between m-relationships is not explicitly modeled but rather derives from the hierarchical order of the connected m-objects. The coordinates of m-relationships determine the relative order between the m-relationships. Given some m-relationship, in order for another m-relationship with the same label to be considered an ancestor of the former, the two m-relationships must have the same number of coordinates and at each position in the respective sequence of coordinates, the former (descendant) m-relationship's coordinate must be a descendant of or equal to the latter (ancestor) m-relationship's coordinate (Rule 3.28); an m-relationship's descendants derive vice versa (Rule 3.29). An abstraction of an m-relationship is a most concrete ancestor of the m-relationship (Rule 3.30), a concretization of an m-relationship is a most abstract descendant (Rule 3.31).

Unlike individual m-objects, the unique introduction rule for levels does not concern m-relationships. Relationship levels are composed of other levels from the level hierarchies of the m-relationship's coordinate m-objects. The semantics of a relationship level's individual component levels determines the semantics of the relationship level itself. Thus, when two m-relationships that are not in a concretization relationship introduce the same relationship level, there is no ambiguity with respect to the semantics of these levels. The relationship level represents a relationship of some kind between objects at the component levels.

Much like the order of m-relationships, which derives from the coordinate m-objects, the order of relationship levels derives from the level hierarchies of the m-relationship's coordinate m-objects. Given some relationship level, in order for another relationship level to be considered an ancestor of the former within a particular m-relationship's level hierarchy, the two relationship levels must reference the same number of levels and at each position in the respective sequence of levels, the former (descendant) relationship level's referenced level must be a descendant of or equal to the latter (ancestor) relationship level's referenced level (Rule 3.32). A relationship level's parent level is an immediate ancestor level (Rule 3.26). Any two m-relationships with the same label must be in a direct or indirect concretization relationship with each other or have a common ancestor m-relationship (Rule 3.33). This requirement ensures compliance with the hetero-homogeneous modeling approach, allowing for the controlled introduction of heterogeneities while prohibiting the arbitrary introduction of heterogeneities under the same relationship label.

Rule 3.24: An m-relationship level references only levels from the coordinates

```
1 context MRelationshipToLevel inv:
2  Set{1..self.level.level->size()}->forAll(i |
3    self.MultilevelRelationship
4        .coordinate->at(i).level->includes(
5      self.level.level->at(i)
6    )
7  )
```

Rule 3.25: An m-relationship level references a level from every coordinate

```
1 context MRelationshipToLevel inv:
2  Set{1..self.MultilevelRelationship
3              .coordinate->size()}->forAll(i |
4    self.level.level->at(i)->exists(l |
5      self.MultilevelRelationship
6        .coordinate->at(i)->includes(l)
7    )
8  )
```

Rule 3.26: A relationship level's parent level is an immediate ancestor level

```
1 context MRelationshipToLevel::parentLevel :
2  Set(RelationshipLevel) derive:
3    self.ancestorLevel->select(a |
4      not self.ancestorLevel->exists(l |
5        l.ancestorLevel->includes(a)
6    )
7  )
```

Rule 3.27: An m-relationship's top level corresponds to the sequence of the coordinate top levels

```
1 context MultilevelRelationship inv:
2  Set{1..self.topLevel.level->size()}->forAll(i |
3    self.topLevel.level->at(i) =
4    self.coordinate->at(i).topLevel
5  )
```

Rule 3.28: An m-relationship's ancestors derive from the coordinates

```
1  context MultilevelRelationship def:
2   ancestors : Set(MultilevelRelationship) =
3   MultilevelRelationship.allInstances()
4    ->excluding(self)->select(
5    r | r.label = self.label and
6    r.coordinate->size() = self.coordinate->size()
7    and Set{1..r.coordinate->size()}->forAll(i |
8     let selfCoord = self.coordinate->at(i) in
9      selfCoord.ancestors->including(selfCoord)
10      ->includes(r.coordinate->at(i))
11    )
12   )
```

Rule 3.29: An m-relationship's descendants derive from the coordinates

```
1  context MultilevelRelationship def:
2   descendants : Set(MultilevelRelationship) =
3   MultilevelRelationship.allInstances()
4    ->excluding(self)->select(
5    r | r.label = self.label and
6    r.coordinate->size() = self.coordinate->size()
7    and Set{1..r.coordinate->size()}->forAll(i |
8     let selfCoord = self.coordinate->at(i) in
9      selfCoord.descendants->including(selfCoord)
10      ->includes(rCoord = r.coordinate->at(i))
11    )
12   )
```

Rule 3.30: An m-relationship's abstraction is a most concrete ancestor

```
1  context MultilevelRelationship::abstraction :
2   Set(MultilevelRelationship) derive:
3   self.ancestors->select(a |
4    not self.ancestors->exists(r |
5     r.ancestors->includes(a))
6   )
```

Rule 3.31: An m-relationship's concretization is a most abstract descendant

```
1 context MultilevelRelationship::concretization :
2  Set(MultilevelRelationship) derive:
3    self.descendants->select(d |
4      not self.descendants->exists(r |
5        r.descendants->includes(d)
6      )
7  )
```

Rule 3.32: A relationship level's ancestors derive from the coordinates

```
1 context MRelationshipToLevel def:
2  ancestorLevel : Set(RelationshipLevel) =
3    self.MultilevelRelationship.level
4    ->excluding(self)->select(l |
5    Set{1..l.level->size()}->forAll(i |
6      self.level.level->at(i) = l.level->at(i) or
7      self.MultilevelRelationship.coordinate->at(i)
8        .MObjectToLevel->exists(m |
9      m.level = self.level.level->at(i) and
10     m.ancestorLevel->includes(l.level->at(i))
11     )
12   )
13 )
```

Rule 3.33: Any two m-relationships with the same label are in a concretization relationship or have a common ancestor

```
1 context MultilevelRelationship inv:
2  MultilevelRelationship.allInstances()
3  ->excluding(self)->select(label = self.label)
4  ->forAll(r | r.ancestors->includes(self) or
5  self.ancestors->includes(r) or
6  MultilevelRelationship.allInstances()->exists(a |
7    self.ancestors->includes(a) and
8    r.ancestors->includes(a)
9  )
10 )
```

Note that we interpret the «identifier» stereotype as taking into account the sequential order of links to objects at an association end declared a sequence ({seq}), that is, two sequences shall only be considered equal if they have the same elements in the same order. For m-relationship coordinates, however, regardless the interpretation of the «identifier» stereotype, two m-relationships with the same label and equal sets of coordinates are always going to yield an inconsistent model. Consider two m-relationships r and r' with the same label and equal sets of coordinates. If both m-relationships reference the coordinates in the same sequential order then there is no ambiguity with respect to the equality of r and r'. On the other hand, if both m-relationships reference the coordinates in a different sequential order, the two m-relationships cannot be in a concretization relationship – a definition which considers the sequential order of coordinates – or have a common ancestor. In this case, the model violates an invariant, whether or not the coordinates are considered equal.

Since an m-relationship's coordinates are arbitrary m-objects, an m-relationship may also connect other m-relationships. Such an m-relationship would constitute a higher-order m-relationship in the spirit of higher-order relationships in the higher-order entity-relationship model (HERM [127]). Although the core metamodel permits higher-order m-relationships – indeed, the consistency criteria apply to such m-relationships as well – we leave their further examination to future work. In the following, we further restrict considerations to binary m-relationships although the generic metamodel allows for the definition of n-ary m-relationships.

3.4 The Finer Points of Multilevel Objects

The core metamodel imposes no restrictions on the specific nature of the model elements attached to the levels of an m-object. The generic Element metaclass represents the most elementary kind of model elements which subsumes all other model elements. Specific applications may restrict the set of allowed model elements to specializations of the Element class. The restriction to specific kinds of model elements, along with the definition of additional constraints on these model elements, reduces flexibility of modelers while increasing the amount of information that the m-object itself embodies. Business model intelligence [113], for example, associates RDF resources and properties with the levels of m-relationships that represent facts in an OLAP cube. With RDF being a very generic representation format, such

business model intelligence applications grant to modelers a great deal of
flexibility. In this case, modelers may more or less freely choose what kind
of information to attach with these levels, what specific ontology to use. At
the same time, the m-relationships become little more than hierarchically
ordered context boxes for the information represented by the attached RDF
triples, which describe the semantics of the application. Business analysts
interpret these RDF triples, using m-relationships merely as a framework
for aggregation of knowledge. In multilevel domain modeling [77], on the
other hand, m-objects and m-relationships attach classes and relationships,
objects and links with the different abstraction levels. A set of very specific
consistency criteria imposes on the modeler additional rules concerning the
expected relationship between inherited and introduced model elements. For
example, concretizations must define specializations of the inherited classes
and associations at each level. In that case, m-objects and m-relationships
have very specific meanings – an m-object presents characteristics of class
and object, an m-relationship presents characteristics of association and link
– for a clearly defined application scenario, namely the flexible representation
of multilevel hierarchies of data objects.

The model elements that are attached to the level of an m-object propagate downwards in a concretization hierarchy. Depending on the employed
modeling formalism, changes to model elements at one level of abstraction
may influence the model elements at another level. For example, an m-object
may associate a UML class and related model elements with some abstraction
level. In UML, every class refers to other model elements, namely attributes
and operations, among others. A concretization of said m-object inherits
for that level all the model elements related to the class, that is, the class
itself, the attributes and operations, and so on. The concretization may
then introduce an additional model element for that level, representing an
attribute of the inherited class. The element propagation from more abstract
to more concrete m-object preserves the identity of the model elements.
Thus, when considering a global model context, the additional element is
part of that class. In applications that employ UML models with m-objects,
modelers should rather resort to the UML specialization mechanism (see
Chapter 4) for adding attributes to inherited classes. On the other hand,
each m-object may be considered a local context. In this case, when working with a given m-object, only those model elements are considered that
the particular m-object associates with its levels. For example, only the
attributes and operations present in the local context are made available.
Similarly, when working with an m-object that attaches RDF triples to levels,

the m-object constitutes the knowledge base on which queries are executed, the m-object being a named RDF graph.

The Telos language [75] was among the first approaches towards the representation of domain knowledge at multiple instantiation levels. In modeling environments with multiple instantiation levels, an object is instance of another object at the next-higher level and, at the same time, acts as class for the objects at the next-lower level. This class/object duality is often referred to as "clabject" [9]. An m-object is a kind of clabject which instantiates its top level while acting as class for concretizations at lower levels.

Atkinson and Kühne [12] distinguish between linguistic instantiation and ontological instantiation, presenting the *orthogonal classification architecture* which "acknowledges the existence of multiple ontological domain levels and supports them directly with a uniform notation for all the levels" [13, p. 357]. The m-object approach [77] extends the orthogonal classification architecture with the possibility to specify different numbers and names of ontological domain levels depending on the kinds of modeled objects.

Deep instantiation [11] associates with an attribute a potency number that indicates the depth of characterization of the attribute, that is, the number of instantiation steps after which the attribute has a value assigned. M-objects associate attributes with named levels to indicate their depth of characterization. Named levels in place of potency numbers enables the introduction of new levels for sub-hierarchies

Dual deep instantiation (DDI [78]) builds on m-objects and deep instantiation. DDI associates a property with a source potency and a target potency in order to separately indicate the depth of characterization for a property's source and target, extending the principle of objects associated with singleton classes and properties with an object enumeration as range. In DDI, everything is an object, and objects are related by specialization and instantiation relationships as well as potency-based associations. The instantiation relationships collect objects into different strata, or levels of abstraction, with instantiation hierarchies of arbitrary depth. An object at a higher level of abstraction may specify the type of attributes and associations for its instances at a lower level of abstraction. Other instances may subsequently specialize the type of these attributes and associations for specific groups of objects.

4 Multilevel Business Artifacts

The representation of many real-world scenarios in conceptual models benefits from the use of multilevel abstraction hierarchies. Product models, for example, are typically grouped into product categories which, in turn, constitute the company's range of products. Multilevel abstraction hierarchies often reflect the organizational structure of a company and the different information needs of the various departments. Current modeling techniques, however, lack extensive support for the representation of multilevel abstraction hierarchies in business process models. The explicit consideration of multilevel abstraction hierarchies in business process models may improve the alignment of processes across different organizational units.

In this chapter we present, in an extended and revised form with respect to previous work [111, 114], the concept of multilevel business artifact (MBA) for the joint representation of data and process models in multilevel abstraction hierarchies. We set off from the core metamodel for multilevel objects in order to obtain an MBA metamodel. An MBA encapsulates, in a single object, the data and process models of various levels, thereby expanding consequently the idea of business artifacts to the realm of multilevel abstraction hierarchies. Multilevel predicates then allow for the synchronization of process models at different abstraction levels. Furthermore, multilevel relationships connect MBAs on different relationship levels.

4.1 Multilevel Objects with Life Cycle Models

The MBA modeling approach is the application of the core metamodel for multilevel objects to artifact-centric business process modeling. An MBA is a multilevel object (m-object) with data and life cycle models as the model elements attached to the different abstraction levels of the hierarchy. The attached data and life cycle models must satisfy well-defined additional consistency rules regarding type and relationship to each other. Throughout this section we focus on homogeneous MBA models with a single data and life cycle model per level.

4.1.1 Simple Level Hierarchies

An MBA encapsulates, in a single object, data and life cycle models at various levels of abstraction. With each abstraction level an MBA associates a class as the data model along with the corresponding state machine which defines a number of states that the instances of the class enter during their life cycle. Furthermore, the state machine specifies the legal execution order of the methods of the respective class which cause state changes when invoked on individual objects. At the same time, an MBA associates an object with its top level, that is, an instance of the top-level class, having an active state (or several) from the top-level state machine.

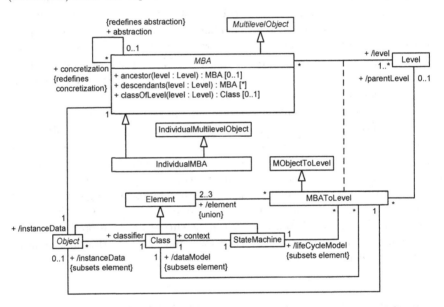

Figure 4.1: The metamodel for MBAs with simple hierarchies as a specialization of the core metamodel for m-objects (revised and extended from [111, 114])

Figure 4.1 defines, using UML, the MBA metamodel for homogeneous artifact-centric multilevel business process models with simple abstraction level hierarchies as a specialization of the core m-object metamodel (see Chapter 3). An MBA (metaclass MBA) is a kind of m-object with additional constraints for the model elements attached to the different levels. With each level, an MBA associates, represented by association class MBAToLevel, a class as data model (association end dataModel to metaclass Class) and a

Rule 4.1: An MBA must associate an object with its top level

```
1 context MBA inv:
2   self.MBAToLevel->forAll(l |
3     l = self.topLevel implies
4     not l.instanceData.oclIsUndefined()
5   )
```

Rule 4.2: Only with its top level an MBA may associate an object

```
1 context MBA inv:
2   self.MBAToLevel->forAll(l |
3     not l.instanceData.oclIsUndefined() implies
4     l = self.topLevel
5   )
```

Rule 4.3: An MBA's instance data object is the top-level instance data object

```
1 context MBA::instanceData : Object derive:
2   self.MBAToLevel->select(l |
3     l.level = self.topLevel
4   ).instanceData
```

state machine as life cycle model (association end lifeCycleModel to metaclass StateMachine). Metaclasses Class and StateMachine are specializations of the more general Element and basically correspond to their UML equivalents, although we make simplifications for demonstration purposes when needed in order to focus on the main aspects of multilevel business process models.

An MBA bears a certain class/object duality similar to the notion of *clabject* [9]. Conceptually, an MBA *is* a data object at the top level of the MBA's own level hierarchy – indeed, previous formalizations of the MBA metamodel represent MBA as a specialization of InstanceSpecification or ClassInstance [111, 114] – while describing the data and life cycle models for the non-top levels in the hierarchy. Formally, an MBA associates with its top level, besides the class and state machine, through association class MBAToLevel, an object as instance data (association end instanceData to metaclass Object). Note that an MBA must associate instance data with the top level in the hierarchy (Rule 4.1), and only with the top level (Rule 4.2). The instanceData association end from the MBA metaclass to Object reflects the object facet of the class/object duality, and corresponds to the MBA's top-level instanceData element (Rule 4.3).

Notice that MBA is an abstract metaclass just like MultilevelObject from the core m-object metamodel. The IndividualMBA metaclass (Figure 4.1) specializes MBA as well as the IndividualMultilevelObject metaclass from the core metamodel, thus inheriting the identifying name and the redefined association ends to the AtomicLevel metaclass as well as the *unique introduction rule* for levels. The MBA metaclass then defines the common features of individual MBAs and multilevel relationships between MBAs (see Section 4.2). The examples in this section focus on individual MBAs, that is, non-relationship MBAs, although the definitions apply to individual and general MBAs alike.

For the representation of life cycle models, we adopt the standard metamodel for UML state machines. More specifically, we use protocol state machines [88, p. 535 et seq.] for the representation of life cycle models. We stress, though, that the employed process modeling language is substitutable but variants of finite state machines are a popular choice for modeling object life cycles [47]. Besides variants of finite state machines, modelers may also resort to more declarative modeling approaches, for example, the guard-stage-milestone approach [48]. We use the UML state machine formalism since it is a widely-accepted standard and allows for the use of OCL [92] as a powerful constraint language. A state machine is defined in the context of a class and consists of states and transitions between theses states. A transition has a source state and a target state and is linked to a call event for a method of the context class. In general, a method may be called for a particular object if in the object's life cycle model there exists a transition that is linked to the called method and this transition originates in an active state of the object. Furthermore, possibly specified pre- and postconditions must be satisfied. A valid method call triggers the transition of the object from source state to target state. Methods that are not referred to by any transition may be called in any state and do not cause a state change [88, p. 549]. A state may have several substates which are also linked by transitions. When an object is in a substate it is also in the corresponding superstate. Furthermore, forks and parallel regions allow for an object to be in multiple states simultaneously.

In some way, an MBA bears similarities to the case folder in the *case management* paradigm [1]. The case folder "holds a collection of business

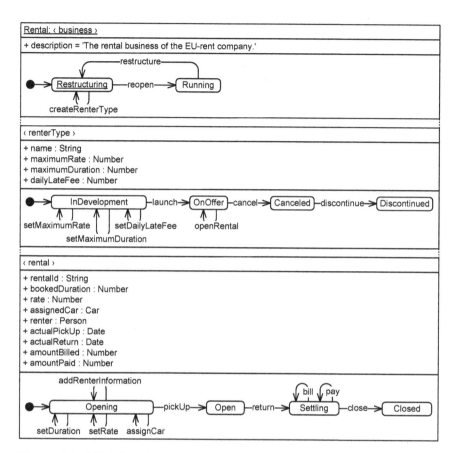

Figure 4.2: MBA Rental for the management of a company's car rental business (revised from [114])

documents and other information" [71] around which knowledge-intensive processes are organized. For case management, more declarative life cycle models are advantageous (cf. [71]). The MBA approach, in general, is compatible with the use of more declarative life cycle models.

The graphical representation of MBAs (Figure 4.2) borrows from UML class diagrams. Each level of an MBA is a box with several compartments. The top compartment of each box contains the name of the respective level between angle brackets (‹ *level* ›). The other compartments contain the definitions of attributes and the life cycle model; a fourth compartment could contain method definitions which may be omitted for presentation purposes, just like any other compartment, as in UML class diagrams. The boxes of an MBA are arranged according to the hierarchical order of the levels that these boxes represent. Dotted lines join the left and right corners of boxes that represent levels of the same MBA. The graphical representation of the data and life cycle models corresponds to the standard notations for UML class and state machine diagrams. The graphical representation of the instance data in the top-level box corresponds to the notation for UML object diagrams. Therefore, the top compartment in the top-level box contains, underlined, the name of the MBA followed by the level name separated by colon, signifying instantiation of the top-level models.

In the graphical representation of UML state machines, rounded boxes denote states, with the name of the state inside the box, a filled black circle denotes the initial state, a filled black circle surrounded by another circle denotes a final state, arrows between states denote transitions which are labeled with the triggering operation's call event name and possibly pre- and postconditions in square brackets before/above and after/below the event name, respectively. Pre- and postconditions also describe synchro- nization dependencies between the life cycle models of the different levels (see Section 4.3). The presented example models may omit final states when the representation of object destruction is not important or undesired – in some circumstances, an archival state may be more appropriate than termination/deletion of the object. Furthermore, in UML state machine diagrams associated with an MBA's top level, an underlined name denotes an active state of the MBA's instance data object.

Figure 4.2 illustrates an MBA model for the management of a company's car rental business; the example is based on the EU-Rent use case [90] and previous work [114]. In this example, EU-Rent is a multinational company which operates in the car rental business. Therefore, individual car rentals constitute the main focus of the company's business activities. The company's rental business is organized by renter types, each individual rental falling under such a type, for example, private or corporate, with different teams managing the different renter types. The operative business process for handling an individual rental differs considerably from the management process for renter types, though both levels are ultimately connected. At the highest level, top management steers the course of the company, deciding which renter types to serve.

MBA Rental with levels business, renterType, and rental represents the many abstraction levels of the car rental business. The business level represents the company's car rental business as a whole, consisting of several renter types (renterType), each having several individual rentals (rental) associated. The business has a description (attribute description). A renter type has a name, a maximum rate (maximumRate), a maximum rental duration (maximum-Duration), and a daily fee charged for late returns (dailyLateFee). A rental has an identifier (rentalId), an actual pickup date (actualPickUp), a booked rental duration (bookedDuration), a rental rate which determines the total rental fee, an assigned car (assignedCar), renter information (renter), an actual return date (actualReturn), the billed amount (amountBilled) and the paid amount (amountPaid) of money.

The rental business alternates between states Restructuring and Running. In the Restructuring state, new renter types are added to the business by calling the createRenterType method; calling the reopen method puts the business into the Running state. While in the Running state, new renter types cannot be added to the business, but calling the restructure method puts the rental business back into the Restructuring state. Note that a postcondition for the createRenterType method/transition could model the creation of a new renter type under the car rental business, thereby constituting a synchronization dependency (see Section 4.3). Since business is the top level, MBA Rental associates with this level an object as instance data which, in the example, is in the Restructuring state. Furthermore, the instance data assigns a value to the description attribute.

A renter type moves from being in development (state InDevelopment) to being on offer (OnOffer), Canceled, and eventually Discontinued. While in development, the maximum rental rate, the maximum rental duration, and the fee charged for late returns are set by methods setMaximumRate, setMaximumDuration, and setDailyLateFee, respectively. Calling the launch method puts a renter type into the OnOffer state. While on offer, the open-Rental method may be called; calling the cancel method puts a renter type into the Canceled state. Finally, in the Canceled state, calling the discontinue method puts a renter type into the Discontinued state. The Discontinued state, in this example, may be considered an archival state, similar to a final state. Rather than deleting the object after completion of its life cycle, the database may retain the object for documentation purposes and ex-post analysis in case the object stores a history.

A rental starts in the Opening state and then moves from being Open to the Settling state and eventually being Closed. While in the Opening state, the rental duration and rate are determined by calling methods setDuration and setRate, respectively. Furthermore, a car is assigned to the rental by calling the assignCar method, and personal information about the renter is captured by calling the addRenterInformation method. Calling the pickUp method signals the collecting of the car by the renter, sets the actual pickup date (attribute actualPickUp), and puts the rental into the Open state. In the Open state, calling the return method signals the return of the car to the station, sets the actual return data (actualReturn), and puts the rental into the Settling state. While in the Settling state, an amount of money is billed and finally paid by calling methods bill and pay, respectively. Finally calling the close method puts the rental into the Closed state. Note that a precondition for the pickUp transition could require the attribute values for duration, rental rate, assigned car, and renter information to be set before allowing the pickup of a car; postconditions to the methods could model the assignment of values to variables. Since such pre- and postconditions are not specific to multilevel business process models, the example model does not include these kinds of conditions. The model also omits method parameters when not used for expressing conditions.

Even though a protocol state machine actually represents, according to the UML standard [88, p. 545], only methods that cause state changes, we include in the examples also transitions that cause no state change. First, non state-changing transitions are a convenient possibility to model as precondition of a method that an object must be in a particular state in order for the method to be called. Furthermore, in hetero-homogeneous models (see Chapter 5), a behavior-consistent specialization of a state machine may refine an atomic state that has a non state-changing transition such that a previously non state-changing method call then causes, according to the refined state machine, a change in substates of the original atomic state. In this case, the inclusion of non state-changing transitions in the more general state machine allows for the stepwise refinement of business rules that the preconditions represent.

The data models that an MBA associates with the various abstraction levels are specializations of the Object metaclass (Rule 4.4), similar to the Object class in Java that all classes implicitly extend [120, p. 49]. Each Object instance is referenced by exactly one MBA as instanceData. Thus, when considering the association bidirectional, an Object instance has run-time access to the MBA it is associated with, thereby granting the object access to data from ancestor and descendant MBAs. An Object instance has a reference to its classifier, and the type of the instance always corresponds to this classifier (Rule 4.5). The Object metaclass could be defined as a specialization of InstanceSpecification from the UML standard or Class-

Instance from the MOF Instances Model [91, p. 48], but for the purposes of the MBA metamodel, such a clarification is not really necessary.

The classOfLevel method retrieves the most specific class that the instance data of an MBA's descendants at a particular level comply with. In a homogeneous model with a single class per level, the classOfLevel method's result corresponds to the data model that the MBA associates with the particular argument level (Rule 4.6). In a hetero-homogeneous model, where an MBA possibly associates many classes with each level, the class-OfLevel method has a different derivation rule (see Chapter 5). In any case, homogeneous or hetero-homogeneous, the classifier associated with an MBA's top-level object must conform to the class returned by the classOfLevel method for the top level (Rule 4.7). In a homogeneous model, the classifier of the object associated with the top level (top-level object) corresponds to the class returned by classOfLevel for the top level. In a hetero-homogeneous model, the top-level object's classifier is a subclass of or equal to that class.

Concretization relationships determine the hierarchical order of MBAs, just as with m-objects in the core metamodel. A concretizing MBA's top level corresponds to the second level of the abstraction (the parent MBA). In an MBA model with simple hierarchies, each MBA has at most one abstraction, or conversely, each MBA is the concretization of at most one MBA. The hierarchical order of the MBAs determines the inheritance of levels and model elements. Just as in the core m-object metamodel, the model elements that an MBA associates with the individual levels derive from the model elements associated with the introduced and inherited levels (Figure 4.3). The association classes MBAToIntroducedLevel and MBATo-InheritedLevel specialize MObjectToIntroducedLevel and MObjectToInherited-Level, respectively, from the core metamodel. In a homogeneous model, only the most abstract MBA of a particular hierarchy introduces levels (Rule 4.8) and, consequently, classes and state machines. Other MBAs, at more concrete levels, inherit levels and model elements according to the rules laid out in the core metamodel for m-objects (see Chapter 3). These MBAs at more concrete levels may only introduce instance data for their respective top level, which is always an inherited level. Furthermore, in a homogeneous model, an MBA inherits for each level exactly two model elements, namely the data model and the life cycle model. The elements associated with the inherited levels then correspond to the inherited model elements. A homogeneous model is thus very inflexible, yet easy to understand and well-structured; the hetero-homogeneous modeling approach increases the flexibility of modelers in multilevel business process modeling (see Chapter 5).

Rule 4.4: All classes that an MBA associates with a level are specializations of the Object metaclass

```
1 context MBA inv:
2  self.MBAToLevel->forAll(l |
3   l.dataModel.conformsTo(Object)
4  )
```

Rule 4.5: The classifier association end of Object represents the type of the object

```
1 context Object inv:
2  self.oclIsTypeOf(self.classifier)
```

Rule 4.6: A level's class is the data model that the MBA attaches to that level

```
1 context MBA::classOfLevel(level : Level) : Class
2  body: self.MBAToLevel->select(l |
3   l.level = level
4  ).dataModel
```

Rule 4.7: An object must be an instance of the MBA's class at that level

```
1 context MBA inv:
2  self.MBAToLevel->forAll(l |
3   l.instanceData.classifier.conformsTo(
4    self.classOfLevel(l)
5   )
6  )
```

Rule 4.8: In a homogeneous model, only a hierarchy's most abstract MBA introduces levels

```
1 context MBA inv:
2  not self.abstraction->isEmpty() implies
3  self.introducedLevel->isEmpty()
```

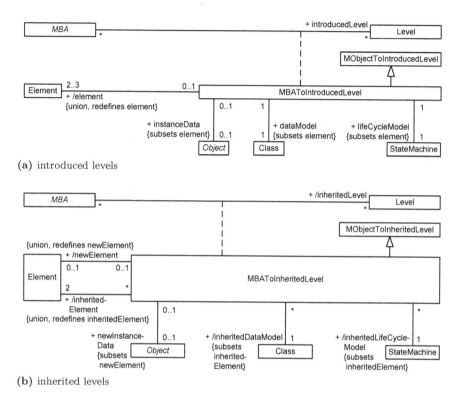

(a) introduced levels

(b) inherited levels

Figure 4.3: The data attached to a homogeneous MBA's introduced and inherited levels as a specialization of the core metamodel for m-objects

4.1.2 Parallel Level Hierarchies

In many practical situations, abstraction level hierarchies may provide alternative groupings of individual data objects. For example, a particular renter type provides a grouping of individual rentals and, at the same time, the country in which the rental occurs provides an alternative grouping. Each alternative path is then considered a separate hierarchy, although these hierarchies may share levels. Malinowski and Zimányi, in their comprehensive classification of hierarchies in multidimensional models [68], refer to such hierarchies as *parallel dependent* hierarchies. Previous work on m-objects [80] introduced parallel hierarchies for data warehouse modeling. The advantage of parallel hierarchies for business process modeling is twofold. On the one hand, a lower-level data object may fall into the constituency of several higher-level authorities. For example, both the regional management of the company's local branch and the management team responsible for the renter type may be concerned by the company's economic performance with respect to individual rentals. On the other hand, parallel hierarchies allow for a more finely-grained classification of lower-level data objects which facilitates the assignment of tasks to employees. For example, individual rentals must be managed and reviewed by accountants that work for the local branch from the rental's country.

When considering solely homogeneous MBA models, the introduction of parallel hierarchies necessitates only a few minor changes in the MBA metamodel. First, each level may have several parent levels, instead of a single parent level. Then, since for all ancestor levels of an MBA's top level there must be an ancestor MBA at this ancestor level, the MBA metamodel must allow multiple concretization. Thus, an MBA with parallel hierarchies possibly has several abstractions (or parent MBAs). The restriction to at most one ancestor MBA per abstraction level remains.

In the case of homogeneous multilevel business process models, that is, concretizations only instantiate the inherited top-level class while leaving other levels unchanged, the introduction of parallel hierarchies is straightforward. Since in a homogeneous model only the root MBA introduces schema information, which the more concrete MBAs at lower levels of abstraction then inherit, parallel hierarchies bear no potential for conflict with respect to multiple inheritance. In the case of hetero-homogeneous models (see Chapter 5), however, issues may arise with respect to multiple inheritance of both the data and the life cycle models.

THE MBA METAMODEL IN O-TELOS

Even though UML serves as the language for the definition of the MBA metamodel, MBAs are outside of traditional object-oriented thinking. Using UML for the representation of the MBA metamodel allows for the definition of business rules using OCL which is a convenient, easy-to-understand, yet formal expression language. Still, other modeling languages, for example, O-Telos [53], are also well-suited for defining the MBA metamodel. O-Telos has a simple and thus very flexible data model: Everything in O-Telos is an object and objects may be related with each other. An object may specialize and/or instantiate any object, including itself. Constraints and queries are formulated using expressions in first-order predicate logic. The implementation of O-Telos, ConceptBase, has already been successfully employed for (business) process modeling [51, 52]. Other work [78] has successfully employed ConceptBase for multilevel modeling.

Using a common notation for O-Telos, the following figure illustrates the MBA metamodel in O-Telos. The boxes represent objects. The arrows between these boxes represent directed relationships between objects. An arrow labeled "in" represents an instantiation relationship. Note that each relationship is also an object and may therefore be related to other objects as, for example, the level relationship between MBA and Level which itself has a parent relationship with Level.

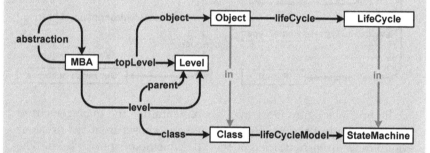

Each MBA is an instance of the MBA object. When instantiating MBA, each relationship from MBA to another object is also instantiated. The source object of such a relationship must be an instance of MBA, the target object must be an instance of the object that is targeted by the instantiated relationship.

Each level is an instance of the Level object. Levels have an identity independent from MBAs. Therefore, different MBAs may reference the same Level objects. MBAs establish the hierarchical order of the levels and associate class definitions with these levels. Therefore, rather than attaching the parent level to an instance of Level directly, the parent level is associated with the relationship between the corresponding Level object and the MBA. Similarly, the class definition for a level is associated with this relationship.

Each MBA has a single, designated top level. The topLevel relationship between the MBA object and the Level object may only be instantiated

once per MBA. Furthermore, the topLevel relationship has a relationship
with Object. An instance of the topLevel relationship has a relationship
to an instance of Object. Every class that an MBA references must be a
specialization of the Object class.

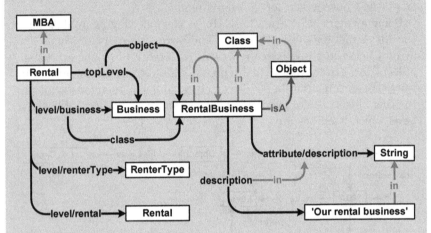

The previous figure illustrates MBA Rental for the management of
car rental data of the EU-Rent company as known from the previous
examples as an instantiation of the MBA metamodel in O-Telos. The
objects Business, RenterType, and Rental are instances of Level and
thus represent the levels of the MBA's level hierarchy. The Rental-
Business object is an instance of Class and a specialization of Object.
An arrow labeled "isA" represents a specialization relationships between
objects. Notice that the level relationship from the MBA metamodel is
instantiated multiple times. MBA Rental associates a clabject with its
top level, that is, an object presenting characteristics of both class and
object. This is possible since in O-Telos an object can be an instance of
itself, that is, an object may define its own class schema.

The object associated with an MBA's top level could also be the MBA
itself. This approach to class/object duality has one major advantage:
Even without knowledge of the MBA metamodel, a program may use
an MBA just like any other instance of a given class. If other levels are
not important for a particular program, there is no need to rewrite this
program in order to cope with MBAs.

4.2 Multilevel Business Artifact Relationships

In the core metamodel for m-objects, a multilevel relationship (m-relationship) connects m-objects at various levels of abstractions. Adapting the concept of m-relationship for multilevel business process modeling, an MBA relationship connects MBAs at various levels of abstraction. MBA relationships allow for a more accurate representation of many complex business situations. The presented metamodel for MBA relationships extends both the core m-object metamodel and the MBA metamodel as defined in the previous section. Throughout this section, we focus on homogeneous MBA relationships. We first propose MBA relationships with multilevel coherence and then discuss MBA relationships with arbitrary relationship levels.

4.2.1 Multilevel Coherence

An MBA relationship is a m-relationship between MBAs. Figure 4.4 defines the metamodel for MBA relationships as an extension of the MBA metamodel (Figure 4.1) and the core metamodel for m-relationships (see Chapter 3). An MBA relationship (metaclass MBARelationship) has both MBA and m-relationship properties. An MBA relationship associates with its levels the same model elements as ordinary MBAs. As opposed to ordinary m-relationships, an MBA relationship's set of potential coordinates is restricted to individual MBAs (association end coordinate to metaclass IndividualMBA); an MBA relationship cannot serve as coordinate. Furthermore, an MBA relationship always has two coordinates. Consequently, an MBA relationship level (metaclass MBARelationshipLevel) always references exactly two atomic levels (association end level to metaclass AtomicLevel). The restriction of an MBA relationship's coordinates to exactly two individual MBAs allows for a more concise examination of the particularities of m-relationships with respect to business process modeling.

We adopt a relaxed definition of multilevel coherence for MBA relationships with a focus on prohibiting multiple concretization. The original definition of multilevel coherence [77, p. 113] forbids the crossing of an m-relationship's relationship (or connection) levels. As opposed to this original definition, multilevel coherence for MBA relationships forbids the definition of crossing relationship levels only when their introduction leads to multiple parents of a relationship level within an m-relationship. The MBA relationship metamodel (Figure 4.4), therefore, restricts the maximum

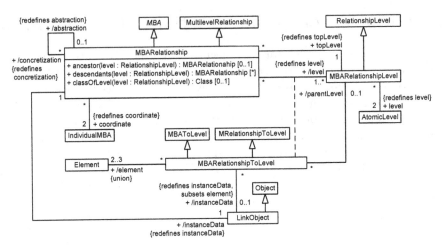

Figure 4.4: The metamodel for MBA relationships with multilevel coherence

number of a relationship level's parent levels to one. Thus, multilevel coherence is essentially the relationship equivalent to simple hierarchies in MBAs, although parallel relationship levels are allowed as long as they do not lead to multiple parent levels.

MBA relationships connect MBAs in different hierarchies, that is, MBAs that are not in a concretization relationship with each other and do not have a common ancestor (Rule 4.9). The core metamodel does not explicitly rule out the possibility of m-relationships between m-objects that are in a concretization relationships. The implications of such relationships, however, have not been investigated yet, neither by work on m-objects [76] nor by previous work on MBAs. The main question, in this respect, concerns the meaningfulness of MBA relationships between MBAs in a concretization relationship. The notion of MBA relationship may well be regarded as the counterpart of the concretization relationship, connecting MBAs in different hierarchies whereas the concretization relationship establishes membership in the same hierarchy of the thus connected MBAs.

An MBA relationship, being a kind of MBA, may associate data and life cycle models with the various relationship levels. With the top relationship level, an MBA relationship associates instance data, represented by metaclass LinkObject which is a specialization of Object. The classes that the MBA relationship associates with its levels are specializations of the LinkObject

Rule 4.9: The coordinates of an MBA relationship must not be in same concretization hierarchy

```
1 context MBARelationship inv:
2 let c1 = self.coordinate->at(1) in
3 let c2 = self.coordinate->at(2) in
4   not c1 = c2 and
5   not c1.descendants->includes(c2) and
6   not c2.descendants->includes(c1) and
7   not MBA.allInstances()->exists(o |
8    o.descendants->includesAll(Set{c1, c2})
9   )
```

Rule 4.10: All classes that an MBA relationship associates with a level are specializations of the LinkObject metaclass

```
1 context MBARelationship inv:
2 self.MBARelationshipToLevel->forAll(l |
3   l.dataModel.conformsTo(LinkObject)
4   )
```

class (Rule 4.10), which allows for references in OCL constraints to the information represented by the MBA itself.

Figure 4.5 illustrates an alternative representation of the EU-Rent use case (Figure 4.2) using an MBA relationship. The MBA relationship labeled rent links Rental at the business level with Car at the vehicleType level, signifying that the rental business deals with the car vehicle type. The MBA relationship further associates the renterType level with the model level, the renter level with the physicalEntity level. Notice that MBA Rental, as opposed to the previous example, features renter as the most specific level. The rental process itself is represented by the MBA relationship.

The MBA relationship between Rental and Car in Figure 4.5, at its top level, ⟨ business, vehicleType ⟩, describes the life cycle model of the Rental business division's involvement in the car rental sector. This involvement in the car rental sector is either Active or Terminated, the current state being Active. The Rental business division, under its involvement in the car rental sector, applies different business schemes, renting certain car models to specific renter types. The ⟨ renterType, model ⟩ level represents the life cycle

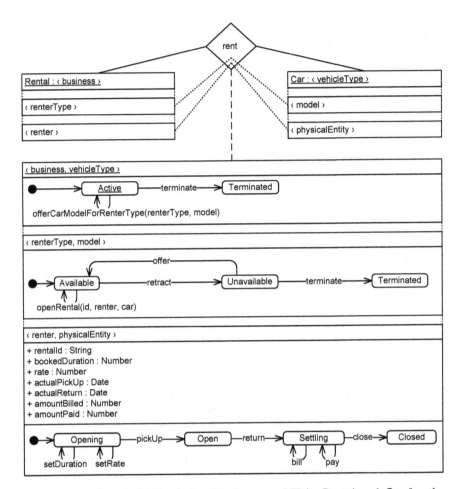

Figure 4.5: A multilevel relationship between MBAs Rental and Car for the management of car rentals

model of such business schemes, going from Available to Unavailable and, eventually, Terminated. An example MBA relationship that instantiates the association between the renterType level and the model level might connect MBA Corporate with AudiA8, or MBA Private with FiatPunto. Finally, the ⟨ renter, physicalEntity ⟩ level represents individual rentals of specific, physical car entities to individual renters with a life cycle going from Opening to Open, Settling and Closed. An example MBA relationship (not shown) that

instantiates the association between the renter level and the physicalEntity
level might connect some MBA named D12 at the renter level under Private
with FiatPuntoXS209 at the physicalEntity level under FiatPunto.

4.2.2 Arbitrary Relationship Levels

Multilevel coherence facilitates implementation, but many applications require the increased expressivity of parallel relationship levels. For example, in
data warehouse modeling, the representation of multilevel cubes [80] employs
arbitrary relationship levels for multilevel relationships, dropping the requirement of multilevel coherence. Similarly, the representation of multilevel
business process models may benefit from allowing arbitrary relationship
levels in MBA relationships.

In the previous section, we restrict a relationship level's number of parent
levels within the level hierarchy of a particular MBA relationship to at most
one. This means that the parentLevel end of the association between the MBA-
RelationshipToLevel association class and the MBARelationshipLevel metaclass
has a 0..1-multiplicity (Figure 4.4). Dropping the requirement of multilevel
coherence means replacing the 0..1-multiplicity of the parentLevel association
end with a *-multiplicity. As a consequence of multilevel coherence, an
MBA relationship can only (directly) concretize at most one other MBA
relationship. This means that the abstraction end of the reflexive association
of the MBARelationship metaclass has a 0..1-multiplicity. Dropping the
requirement of multilevel coherence means replacing the 0..1-multiplicity of
the abstraction association end with a *-multiplicity.

Assume, for example, the EU-Rent company offers a range of travel tours in
conjunction with car rentals. The range of tours consists of several categories,
each category consists of several tour packages, each tour package consists
of several trips. Along with each rental, a renter may book specific tour
packages. From this package, the renter may then select specific trips. Each
trip under a tour package is offered only to certain renter types. Consider
a relationship between an MBA Tour and an MBA Rental. MBA Tour
represents EU-Rent's range of tours, having levels range, category, package,
and trip. MBA Rental represents EU-Rent's car rental business, having levels
business, renterType, and rental. The MBA relationship has relationship levels
⟨ package, rental ⟩, ⟨ trip, renterType ⟩, and ⟨ trip, rental ⟩. The relationship
levels ⟨ package, rental ⟩ and ⟨ trip, renterType ⟩ are crossing and would
violate multilevel coherence, as ⟨ trip, rental ⟩ is a child level of both of these
relationship levels.

Assume now the existence of an MBA CityTripsPack at the package level, being a descendant of MBA Tour. Assume further the existence of MBAs ViennaBusinessTrip and SalzburgTrip at the trip level, being concretizations of CityTripsPack. An MBA relationship between ViennaBusinessTrip and an MBA Corporate at the renterType level defines that the business trip to the city of Vienna is available to corporate renters. An MBA relationship between SalzburgTrip and Corporate defines that the trip to the city of Salzburg is available to corporate renters. Likewise, an MBA relationship between SalzburgTrip and an MBA Private at the renterType level defines that the trip to the city of Salzburg is available to private renters. In order for a rental-level MBA to participate in an MBA relationship with ViennaBusinessTrip, the rental-level MBA must be a descendant of Corporate. In an MBA relationship with SalzburgTrip, rental-level MBAs under both Corporate and Private may participate.

4.3 Multilevel Predicates for Synchronization

Rather than existing in isolation, the objects at the different abstraction levels are interdependent and interact with each other. Multilevel predicates allow for a life cycle model at one level to refer to a life cycle model at another level, thereby establishing synchronization dependencies between object life cycles. Vertical synchronization refers to a synchronization dependency between object life cycles at one level and object life cycles at another level further up or down the same level hierarchy. Horizontal synchronization refers to a synchronization dependency between object life cycles at one level and object life cycles at a different, parallel, abstraction level of the same hierarchy, or an object life cycle of a different hierarchy altogether. In this section, we present revised and extended versions of multilevel predicates for vertical synchronization from previous work [114], and introduce multilevel predicates for horizontal synchronization.

4.3.1 Vertical Synchronization

We consider as *synchronization dependencies* those pre- and postconditions of transitions in a life cycle model that refer to attributes of another class or states in another life cycle model. Depending on whether a pre- or postcondition constitutes the synchronization dependency, the implications for the transition differ. In case of a postcondition, a transition in one object entails attribute or state changes in other objects as well. This consideration is consistent with other work on artifact-centric business process modeling, which considers pre- and postconditions as business rules and business rules that trigger state changes of multiple artifacts as synchronization rules [141, p. 288]. In case of a precondition, on the other hand, in order for a transition in one object to be taken, other objects must satisfy specified conditions; unlike a synchronization dependency in a postcondition, the transition itself has no side effects on other data objects.

We propose a set of *multilevel predicates* for various synchronization patterns across different abstraction levels. These multilevel predicates act as pre- or postconditions of transitions, and divide into the general categories of attribute, state, and concretization predicates. Predicates for attribute synchronization express conditions over attributes of an MBA's ancestors and descendants. The predicates for state synchronization derive from the attribute predicates and express conditions over the active states of an MBA's ancestors and descendants. Concretization predicates model the creation of objects at lower levels of abstraction by other objects at more abstract levels.

We define multilevel predicates as syntax macros [60] for OCL. A syntax macro consists of *structure* and *definition*. The macro structure constitutes the macro as such, that is, the syntax that the modeler writes in order to express a specific synchronization dependency. For the description of a macro structure, we use EBNF notation [140] and adopt existing production rules from the definition of the concrete OCL syntax in the standard [92, p. 69 et seqq.]. The macro definition consists of the expressions in the target language, that is, in this case, the standard OCL expressions which define the semantics of a synchronization dependency.

Consider, for example, the following production rules in EBNF notation as the structures of syntax macros that allow for the referencing of individual levels of MBAs and MBA relationships; terminal symbols are in single quotes:

LevelExpCS ::= AtomicLevelExpCS | RelationshipLevelExpCS

AtomicLevelExpCS ::= '⟨' simpleNameCS '⟩'

RelationshipLevelExpCS ::= '⟨' simpleNameCS, simpleNameCS '⟩'

The production rules for referencing levels describe what we refer to as *level expressions*, hence the "Exp" in the production rule names. The production rules also follow the convention in the OCL standard that each element of the concrete syntax has a "CS" suffix. A level expression (LevelExpCS)

references either an atomic level (AtomicLevelExpCS) or a relationship level
(RelationshipLevelExpCS). The simpleNameCS production rule from the OCL
standard denotes special strings used for names in OCL expressions which
we reuse without going into detail here.

The non-terminal symbols in the structure of a syntax macro correspond
to metavariables in the definition of that same syntax macro. The names
of these metavariables start with "$" followed by the ordinal number of
the corresponding non-terminal symbol in the macro structure. A macro
preprocessor, upon translation of an occurrence of a macro structure, inserts
the actual string values of the metavariables at the position of the respective
metavariable in the macro definition. Consider, for example, the following
definition of AtomicLevelExpCS:

```
AtomicLevel.allInstances()->any(l |
  l.name = "$1"
)
```

A valid level expression under the AtomicLevelExpCS production rule would
be ‹ renterType ›. Metavariable $1 would then assume the string value
"renterType" and the translation of the level expression into standard OCL
would read the following:

```
AtomicLevel.allInstances()->any(l |
  l.name = "renterType"
)
```

Similarly, the following OCL expression constitutes the definition of the
RelationshipLevelExpCS syntax macro:

```
MBARelationshipLevel.allInstances()->any(l |
  l.level->at(1).name = "$1" and
  l.level->at(2).name = "$2"
)
```

A valid level expression under the RelationshipLevelExpCS production rule
would be ‹renterType, model›. Metavariable $1 would then assume the string
value "renterType", metavariable $2 the string value "model", and the
translation of the level expression into standard OCL would read:

```
MBARelationshipLevel.allInstances()->any(l |
  l.level->at(1).name = "renterType" and
  l.level->at(2).name = "model"
)
```

Table 4.1: Multilevel predicates over ancestry relationships

predicate	isDescendantAtLevel(MBA, MBA, Level)
macro	'mba' OclExpressionCS 'is' 'descendant' 'at' 'level' LevelExpCS
define	`self.MBA.descendants($2)->includes($1)`
predicate	isAncestorAtLevel(MBA, MBA, Level)
macro	'mba' OclExpressionCS 'is' 'ancestor' 'at' 'level' LevelExpCS
define	`self.MBA.ancestor($2) = $1`

The production rules LevelExpCS, AtomicLevelExpCS, and Relationship-LevelExpCS are not considered multilevel predicates but rather represent auxiliary macros. The descriptions of the syntax macro structures of the actual multilevel predicates refer to these production rules in places where the predicate expresses conditions involving levels, which all of the proposed multilevel predicates do.

In mathematical logical terms, a predicate is a function which takes a number of parameters as input and returns a boolean value as result. Multilevel predicates are predicates in that sense although their semantics are defined in terms of OCL syntax macros. Thus, for each multilevel predicate, we provide a definition of the predicate signature, that is, the input parameters. But, rather than defining the semantics of these predicates in mathematical logical terms, we provide a syntax macro structure and definition for each multilevel predicate. A macro preprocessor could then translate the syntax macro into standard OCL expressions.

We first present multilevel predicates for the definition of expressions over ancestry relationships between MBAs. Table 4.1 defines the ancestry predicates isDescendantAtLevel and isAncestorAtLevel which require some argument MBA to be a descendant or ancestor, respectively, of another MBA in order for the predicate to evaluate to true. The ancestry predicates each have three parameters. Since an ancestry predicate is always defined in the context of an MBA, the first parameter is the MBA that the predicate is associated with. Of course, the syntax macro itself is attached to a particular model element – just like any other OCL constraint – which then constitutes the context in the OCL sense that the self variable references. In the macro definitions of multilevel predicates, self always refers to a specialization of the Object class which allows for the navigation to the context MBA. This also holds for macros used in the life cycle models, since the context of an OCL constraint that is defined for a state machine is the context class [92, p. 192].

The ancestry predicates then take another MBA as second parameter, the potential descendant or ancestor, as well as a level as third parameter at which this potential descendant or ancestor is situated.

The ancestry predicates in Table 4.1 constitute the most general class of multilevel predicates; the ancestry predicates subsume the groups of attribute, state, and concretization predicates. By adding expressions over the potential descendant or ancestor, the modeler may express any synchronization dependency using ancestry predicates; in OCL constraints, this is achieved by nesting the syntax macros inside other OCL expressions. But, the ancestry predicates, due to their generality, carry only little semantics themselves, leaving the burden of expressing conditions largely to the modeler. Thus, we introduce additional multilevel predicates where each predicate represents a specific synchronization pattern, already abstracting, to some extent, from routine OCL conditions for frequently occurring situations.

Attribute predicates allow for the definition of expressions over the data models of an MBA's ancestors or descendants (Table 4.2). Each attribute predicate takes as first parameter the MBA that the predicate is defined for. Predicates everyDescendantAtLevelSatisfies and someDescendantAtLevel-Satisfies take as further parameters a level and some expression which formalizes the condition that every or some descendant, respectively, at the argument level must satisfy in order for the predicates to evaluate to true. If the context MBA has no descendant at the given level, every-DescendantAtLevelSatisfies evaluates to true, someDescendantAtLevelSatisfies evaluates to false. Predicate isDescendantAtLevelSatisfying is similar to every-DescendantAtLevelSatisfies and someDescendantAtLevelSatisfies, but takes as additional parameter another MBA which must be a descendant at the argument level and satisfy the given condition in order for the predicate to evaluate to true. Analogously, predicates ancestorAtLevelSatisfies and isAncestorAtLevelSatisfying allow for expressing conditions over an ancestor at a particular level. If the context MBA has no ancestor at the given level, ancestorAtLevelSatisfies evaluates to OclInvalid.

For the definitions of the syntax macros for multilevel predicates, we introduce meta-metavariable $$classOfLevel, which has no corresponding production rule in the macro structures and takes a metavariable as argument. The macro preprocessor determines at translation time the value of $$classOf-Level in the context of a constraint, using model information from the MBA. In order to determine the value of $$classOfLevel, the macro preprocessor evaluates the argument level expression and retrieves the corresponding class using the MBA's classOfLevel method. Importantly, the macro preprocessor

Table 4.2: Multilevel predicates for vertical synchronization over attributes

predicate	everyDescendantAtLevelSatisfies(MBA, Level, Expression)
macro	'every' 'descendant' simpleNameCS 'at' 'level' LevelExpCS 'satisfies' OclExpressionCS

define	`self.MBA.descendants($2)->forAll(mba : MBA |`
	`let $1 : $$classOfLevel($2) =`
	`    mba.instanceData.oclAsType($$classOfLevel($2))`
	`    in $3`
	`)`

predicate	someDescendantAtLevelSatisfies(MBA, Level, Expression)
macro	'some' 'descendant' simpleNameCS 'at' 'level' LevelExpCS 'satisfies' OclExpressionCS

define	`self.MBA.descendants($2)->exists(mba : MBA |`
	`let $1 : $$classOfLevel($2) =`
	`    mba.instanceData.oclAsType($$classOfLevel($2))`
	`    in $3`
	`)`

predicate	isDescendantAtLevelSatisfying(MBA, MBA, Level, Expression)
macro	'mba' simpleNameCS '=' OclExpressionCS 'is' 'descendant' 'at' 'level' LevelExpCS 'satisfying' OclExpressionCS

define	`mba $2 is descendant at level $3 and`
	`let $1 : $$classOfLevel($3) =`
	`$2.instanceData.oclAsType($$classOfLevel($3)) in $4`

predicate	ancestorAtLevelSatisfies(MBA, Level, Expression)
macro	'ancestor' simpleNameCS 'at' 'level' LevelExpCS 'satisfies' OclExpressionCS

define	`let $1 : $$classOfLevel($2) =`
	`    self.MBA.ancestor($2).instanceData`
	`    .oclAsType($$classOfLevel($2)) in $3`

predicate	isAncestorAtLevelSatisfying(MBA, MBA, Level, Expression)
macro	'mba' simpleNameCS '=' OclExpressionCS 'is' 'ancestor' 'at' 'level' LevelExpCS 'satisfying' OclExpressionCS

define	`mba $2 is ancestor at level $3 and`
	`let $1 : $$classOfLevel($3) =`
	`$2.instanceData.oclAsType($$classOfLevel($3)) in $4`

replaces occurrences of the $$classOfLevel meta-metavariable with a static
reference to a class since the class of a particular level is already known at
translation time, thereby allowing for type checking of the resulting OCL
expression at compile time.

Notice that the syntax macro definitions of predicates isDescendantAt-
LevelSatisfying and isAncestorAtLevelSatisfying make use of previously defined
syntax macros themselves. Theoretically, the syntax macros could be arbi-
trarily combined, nested, and interweaved in standard OCL. In such cases,
however, the macro preprocessor must determine the adequate processing
order for the macro occurrences before translating into standard OCL. Fur-
thermore, depending on the parsing method, the description of the macro
structures may need rewriting in order for LL(1) parsers to be able to parse
the provided macros. In this work, however, we will not dwell on the details
of the development of a macro preprocessor for multilevel predicates, but
rather assume the existence of such a preprocessor which we regard more as
a device of formal specification.

Deriving from the attribute predicates, state predicates allow for the
definition of expressions over the active states of an MBA's ancestors or
descendants (Table 4.3). Just like the attribute predicates, each state
predicate takes as first parameter the MBA that the predicate is defined for.
As further parameters, each state predicate takes a level and state, which
formalizes the condition that each MBA in a set of ancestors or descendants
at the given level, depending on the particular predicate, is in the given
state. The most basic state predicates are everyDescendantAtLevelIsInState,
someDescendantAtLevelIsInState, and ancestorAtLevelIsInState, which allow
for expressing of the condition that every/some descendant or the ancestor
at a particular level is in a given state. Predicates everyDescendantAtLevelIn-
StateSatisfies, someDescendantAtLevelInStateSatisfies, everyDescendantAtLevel-
SatisfyingIsInState, and ancestorAtLevelIsInStateAndSatisfies take an additional
expression as parameter which formalizes a condition to be satisfied. In
case of everyDescendantAtLevelInStateSatisfies, every descendant at the given
level, in case of someDescendantAtLevelInStateSatisfies, some descendant at
the given level must satisfy the expressed condition. In case of predicate
everyDescendantAtLevelSatisfyingIsInState, the expression reduces the set of
descendants which are considered for evaluation; every descendant that
satisfies the expressed condition must be in the given state. Predicate
ancestorAtLevelIsInStateAndSatisfies requires the ancestor at the given level
to be in the given state and satisfy the expressed condition in order for the
predicate to evaluate to true in the context of a given MBA.

Table 4.3: Multilevel predicates for vertical state synchronization

predicate	everyDescendantAtLevelIsInState(MBA, Level, State)
macro	'every' 'descendant' 'at' 'level' LevelExpCS 'is' 'in' 'state' StateExpCS
define	every descendant o at level $1 satisfies o.oclIsInState($2)
predicate	everyDescendantAtLevelInStateSatisfies (MBA, Level, State, Expression)
macro	'every' 'descendant' simpleNameCS 'at' 'level' LevelExpCS 'in' 'state' StateExpCS 'satisfies' OclExpressionCS
define	every descendant $1 at level $2 satisfies $1.oclIsInState($3) implies $4
predicate	everyDescendantAtLevelSatisfyingIsInState (MBA, Level, Expression, State)
macro	'every' 'descendant' simpleNameCS 'at' 'level' LevelExpCS 'satisfying' OclExpressionCS 'is' 'in' 'state' StateExpCS
define	every descendant $1 at level $2 satisfies $3 implies $1.oclIsInState($4)
predicate	someDescendantAtLevelIsInState(MBA, Level, State)
macro	'some' 'descendant' 'at' 'level' LevelExpCS 'is' 'in' 'state' StateExpCS
define	some descendant o at level $1 satisfies o.oclIsInState($2)
predicate	someDescendantAtLevelInStateSatisfies (MBA, Level, State, Expression)
macro	'some' 'descendant' simpleNameCS 'at' 'level' LevelExpCS 'in' 'state' StateExpCS 'satisfies' OclExpressionCS
define	some descendant $1 at level $2 satisfies $1.oclIsInState($3) and $4
predicate	isDescendantAtLevelInState(MBA, MBA, Level, State)
macro	'mba' OclExpressionCS 'is' 'descendant' 'at' 'level' LevelExpCS 'in' 'state' StateExpCS
define	mba o = $1 is descendant at level $2 satisfying o.oclIsInState($3)

(continues on next page)

Table 4.3 (continued): Multilevel predicates for vertical state synchronization

predicate	isDescendantAtLevelInStateSatisfying (MBA, MBA, Level, State, Expression)
macro	'mba' simpleNameCS '=' OclExpressionCS 'is' 'descendant' 'at' 'level' LevelExpCS 'in' 'state' StateExpCS 'satisfying' OclExpressionCS
define	mba $1 = $2 is descendant at level $3 satisfying o.oclIsInState($4) and $5

predicate	ancestorAtLevelIsInState(MBA, Level, State)
macro	'ancestor' 'at' 'level' LevelExpCS 'is' 'in' 'state' StateExpCS
define	ancestor o at level $1 satisfies o.oclIsInState($2)

predicate	ancestorAtLevelIsInStateAndSatisfies (MBA, Level, State, Expression)
macro	'ancestor' simpleNameCS 'at' 'level' LevelExpCS 'is' 'in' 'state' StateExpCS 'and' 'satisfies' OclExpressionCS
define	ancestor $1 at level $2 satisfies o.oclIsInState($3) and $4

predicate	isAncestorAtLevelInState(MBA, MBA, Level, State)
macro	'mba' OclExpressionCS 'is' 'ancestor' 'at' 'level' LevelExpCS 'in' 'state' StateExpCS
define	mba o = $1 is ancestor at level $2 satisfying o.oclIsInState($3)

predicate	isAncestorAtLevelInStateSatisfying (MBA, MBA, Level, State, Expression)
macro	'mba' simpleNameCS '=' OclExpressionCS 'is' 'ancestor' 'at' 'level' LevelExpCS 'in' 'state' StateExpCS 'satisfying' OclExpressionCS
define	mba $1 = $2 is ancestor at level $3 satisfying o.oclIsInState($4) and $5

Unlike the other predicates for synchronization over states, predicates isDescendantAtLevelInState, isDescendantAtLevelInStateSatisfying, isAncestorAtLevelInState, and isAncestorAtLevelInStateSatisfying take a second MBA as additional parameter. These additional state predicates allow to formalize the condition that a particular, given MBA is a descendant or ancestor, respectively, at a given level in a given state, optionally satisfying an additional condition; they derive from the predicates isDescendantAtLevelSatisfying and isAncestorAtLevelSatisfying, respectively.

Attribute and state synchronization predicates may occur as pre- and postconditions alike. In both cases, the concrete syntax macro that a modeler employs in order to represent a synchronization dependency remains the same, which holds for both structure and definition of the syntax macro.

Figures 4.6 and 4.7 define a graphical notation for state synchronization predicates, which will be used in the examples. Note that predicates isDescendantAtLevelInState, isDescendantAtLevelInStateSatisfying, isAncestorAtLevelInState, and isAncestorAtLevelInStateSatisfying have no graphical representation. Dashed arrows between states and transitions of different levels visualize synchronization dependencies between object life cycles at the respective levels. The direction of the arrow determines whether the predicate occurs in a precondition or in a postcondition. An arrow from a state to a transition denotes a predicate in a precondition of the transition; an arrow from a transition to a state denotes a predicate in a postcondition. For example, Figures 4.6a and 4.7a both graphically represent the everyDescendantAtLevelIsInState predicate. The former figure denotes a precondition, the latter a postcondition. Similarly, Figures 4.6f and 4.7f both graphically represent the ancestorAtLevelIsInState predicate. Each graphical notation is equivalent to attaching the macro expression in the caption of the respective figure to the transition, with **pre** denoting the use as a precondition, **post** denoting the use as a postcondition, as in the OCL standard.

Annotations to the arrows in the graphical representation of multilevel predicates distinguish different kinds of multilevel predicates from each other and bind additional arguments for these predicates where required. For example, the mathematical symbol for universal quantification ($\forall$) marks predicates everyDescendantAtLevelInStateSatisfies (Figures 4.6b and 4.7b) and everyDescendantAtLevelSatisfyingIsInState (Figures 4.6c and 4.7c), the symbol for existential quantification ($\exists$) marks predicates someDescendantAtLevelIsInState (Figures 4.6d and 4.7d) and someDescendantAtLevelInStateSatisfies (Figures 4.6e and 4.7e). In addition, some predicates, including ancestorAtLevelIsInStateAndSatisfies (Figures 4.6g and 4.7g), take an OCL expression

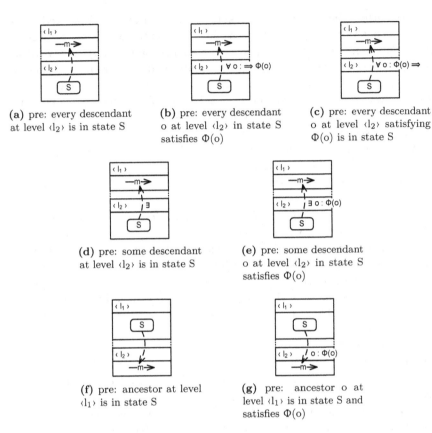

Figure 4.6: Graphical notation for the state synchronization predicates in Table 4.3 as preconditions (revised and extended from [114]). Note that predicates over a second MBA have no graphical representation.

over a quantified variable, represented by $\Phi(o)$ in Figures 4.6 and 4.7, denoting a generic predicate. The position of the implication arrow ($\Rightarrow$) before or after the generic predicate distinguishes everyDescendantAtLevelIn-StateSatisfies from everyDescendantAtLevelSatisfyingIsInState.

Figure 4.8 extends the EU-Rent example (Figure 4.2) with vertical synchronization dependencies, illustrating both attribute and state synchronization predicates. At the rental level, attribute synchronization predicates constrain the possible input values of methods setRate and setDuration, limiting these

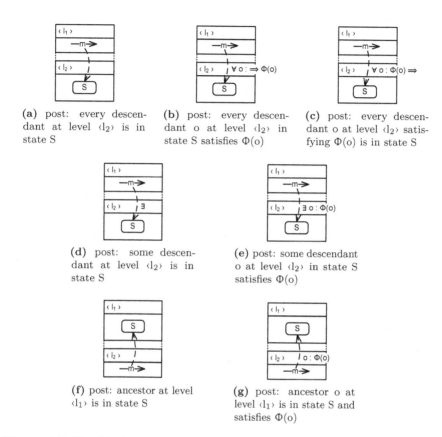

(a) post: every descendant at level ⟨l₂⟩ is in state S

(b) post: every descendant o at level ⟨l₂⟩ in state S satisfies Φ(o)

(c) post: every descendant o at level ⟨l₂⟩ satisfying Φ(o) is in state S

(d) post: some descendant at level ⟨l₂⟩ is in state S

(e) post: some descendant o at level ⟨l₂⟩ in state S satisfies Φ(o)

(f) post: ancestor at level ⟨l₁⟩ is in state S

(g) post: ancestor o at level ⟨l₁⟩ is in state S and satisfies Φ(o)

Figure 4.7: Graphical notation for the state synchronization predicates in Table 4.3 as postconditions (revised and extended from [114]). Note that predicates over a second MBA have no graphical representation.

input values to the maximumRate and maximumDuration, respectively, as defined by the ancestor at the renterType level. At the renterType level, the launch method has as precondition a state synchronization predicate which requires the ancestor at the business level to be in the Running state. The discontinue method has as precondition a state synchronization predicate which requires that every descendant at the rental level to be in the Closed state. At the business level, the restructure method has as postcondition a state synchronization predicate which requires every descendant that is not

in the Discontinued state to be in the Canceled state after the execution of
the method. Note that in each of the previous cases, the terms "ancestor"
and "descendant" refer to an ancestor or descendant, respectively, relative
to the object of which the particular method is called at run time. Moreover,
the example in Figure 4.8 features concretization predicates.

Concretization predicates constitute a class of synchronization predicates
which model the creation of new objects at lower levels of abstraction
(Table 4.4). Concretization predicates are permissible only in postconditions
of transitions. For example, the most elementary concretization predicate
(existsNewDescendantAtLevel) demands that a new descendant at a given level
exists after the execution of the method for which the predicate constitutes
a postcondition. Other concretization predicates allow for the definition of
additional conditions which a newly created descendant must satisfy. The
existsNewDescendantAtLevelSatisfying predicate takes an arbitrary expression
as parameter; this expression typically represents a condition over the
attributes of the newly created descendant. The existsNewDescendantAt-
LevelUnder demands that a new descendant at a given level exists after
the execution of the method and that this new descendant is, at the same
time, a descendant of another given MBA as well. The latter predicate
bears importance for MBAs with parallel hierarchies as well as in hetero-
homogeneous models (see Chapter 5). The existsNewDescendantAtLevelUnder-
Satisfying predicate is a combination of the former concretization predicates.

Figure 4.9 defines a graphical notation for the concretization predicates
as also employed by the extended EU-Rent example in Figure 4.8. Dashed
arrows between a transition at one level and the initial state of another
life cycle model further down the level hierarchy represent concretization
dependencies, the arrows being annotated with the new keyword. The
graphical notation for the existsNewDescendantAtLevelSatisfying predicate
(Figure 4.9b) takes an OCL expression over a variable standing in for the
newly created object, the expression being denoted by $\Phi(n)$ in the figure.
The graphical notation for the existsNewDescendantAtLevelUnder predicate
(Figure 4.9c) has an OCL expression, following the under keyword, which
refers to another MBA. The graphical notation for the existsNewDescendant-
AtLevelUnderSatisfying predicate (Figure 4.9d) is a combination of the former
notation variants.

In the extended EU-Rent example (Figure 4.8) each level assumes responsibility for the creation of the data objects at the child level. For example,
at the business level, the createRenterType method causes the creation of a
new descendant at the renterType level with the argument name. At the

Table 4.4: Multilevel predicates for concretization

predicate	existsNewDescendantAtLevel(MBA, Level)
macro	'exists' 'new' 'descendant' 'at' 'level' LevelExpCS

define	`self.MBA.descendants($1)->exists(mba : MBA |`
	`mba.oclIsNew()`
	`)`

predicate	existsNewDescendantAtLevelSatisfying(MBA, Level, Expression)
macro	'exists' 'new' 'descendant' simpleNameCS 'at' 'level' LevelExpCS 'satisfying' OclExpressionCS

define	`self.MBA.descendants($2)->exists(mba : MBA |`
	`mba.oclIsNew() and`
	`let $1 : $$classOfLevel($2) =`
	`mba.instanceData.oclAsType($$classOfLevel($2))`
	`in $3`
	`)`

predicate	existsNewDescendantAtLevelUnder(MBA, Level, MBA)
macro	'exists' 'new' 'descendant' 'at' 'level' LevelExpCS 'under' OclExpressionCS

define	`self.MBA.descendants($1)->exists(mba : MBA |`
	`mba.oclIsNew() and`
	`$2.descendants($1)->includes(mba)`
	`)`

predicate	existsNewDescendantAtLevelUnderSatisfying (MBA, Level, MBA, Expression)
macro	'exists' 'new' 'descendant' simpleNameCS 'at' 'level' LevelExpCS 'under' OclExpressionCS 'satisfying' OclExpressionCS

define	`self.MBA.descendants($2)->exists(mba : MBA |`
	`mba.oclIsNew() and`
	`$3.descendants($2)->includes(mba) and`
	`let $1 : $$classOfLevel($2) =`
	`mba.instanceData.oclAsType($$classOfLevel($2))`
	`in $4`
	`)`

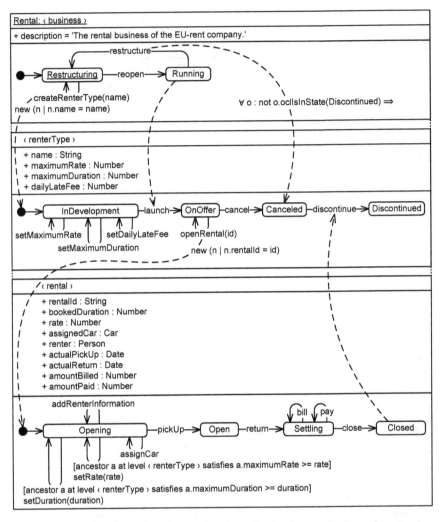

Figure 4.8: MBA Rental with multilevel predicates for vertical synchronization (revised from [114])

renterType level, the openRental method causes the creation of a new descendant at the rental level with the specified argument identifier as rentalId. Note that in this case, again, the term "descendant" refers to a descendant relative to the object that the particular method is called of at run time.

(a) post: exists new descendant at level ⟨l₂⟩

(b) post: exists new descendant n at level ⟨l₂⟩ satisfying Φ(n)

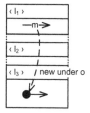

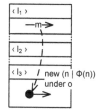

(c) post: exists new descendant n at level ⟨l₂⟩ under o

(d) post: exists new descendant n at level ⟨l₂⟩ under o satisfying Φ(n)

Figure 4.9: Graphical notation for the concretization predicates in Table 4.4 (revised from [114])

Figure 4.10 illustrates a variant with parallel hierarchies of MBA Rental from the previous examples; the example omits most details from the previous examples, such as the data model as well as the majority of the life cycle models, in order to focus on the distinct aspects of parallel hierarchies. Since every MBA at the rental level must have an ancestor at both the renterType and the country level, the openRental method which causes the creation of a new descendant at the rental level takes an MBA at the country level as additional parameter. A newly created MBA at the rental level must have the argument MBA at the country level as ancestor. An explicit constraint as a precondition demanding an argument MBA to be at the country level could be added for increased expressiveness of the model but is not necessary in order to guarantee a consistent model due to the consistency criteria defined in the core m-object and MBA metamodel. In the EU-Rent example, passing an MBA that is not at the country level as argument would result in a violation of the constraint that requires any MBA at the rental level to have exactly one single ancestor at the country level.

The attribute and state synchronization predicates apply to MBAs and, without adaptations, MBA relationships alike. The descriptions of the

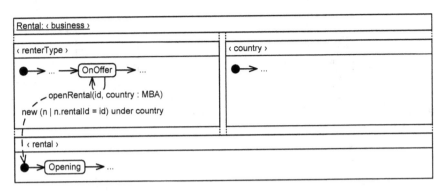

Figure 4.10: MBA Rental with parallel hierarchies and vertical synchronization dependency

macro structures of attribute and state synchronization predicates refer to the generic LevelExpCS production rule, thus applying to both atomic and relationship levels. Depending on the context, the modeler must employ the appropriate kind of level; the model becomes invalid otherwise.

We provide adapted concretization predicates for MBA relationships (Table 4.5). Even though the existing concretization predicates are applicable to MBA relationships as well, the existing predicates might be too unspecific for certain modeling situations. An MBA relationship always has coordinates, which the modeler might wish to include explicitly in the life cycle model. Thus, the adapted concretization predicates take as additional parameters the newly created relationship's coordinate MBAs. These adapted concretization predicates come in two variants: The basic variant taking only the coordinate MBAs (existsNewDescendantAtLevelBetween) and a variant with an additional condition which must be satisfied by the newly created relationship (exists-NewDescendantAtLevelBetweenSatisfying). The graphical representation of the adapted predicates derives from the basic concretization predicates, adding to the annotation expressions that refer to the coordinate MBAs, separated by and, following the between keyword.

Figure 4.11 extends the EU-Rent example as modeled using MBA relationships (Figure 4.5) with vertical synchronization dependencies, illustrating state synchronization as well as concretization predicates in MBA relationships. Each relationship level triggers the creation of links at the respective child level as expressed through the concretization predicates attached to the transitions triggered by the offerCarModelForRenterType and openRental

Table 4.5: Multilevel predicates for concretization of MBA relationships

predicate	existsNewDescendantAtLevelBetween
	(MBARelationship, RelationshipLevel, MBA, MBA)
macro	'exists' 'new' 'descendant' 'at' 'level' RelationshipLevelExpCS
	'between' OclExpressionCS 'and' OclExpressionCS
define	`self.MBARelationship.descendants($1)->exists(`
	`r	r.oclIsNew() and`
	`r.coordinate->at(1) = $2 and`
	`r.coordinate->at(2) = $3`
	`)`
predicate	existsNewDescendantAtLevelBetweenSatisfying
	(MBARelationship, RelationshipLevel, MBA, MBA, Expression)
macro	'exists' 'new' 'descendant' simpleNameCS
	'at' 'level' RelationshipLevelExpCS
	'between' OclExpressionCS 'and' OclExpressionCS
	'satisfying' OclExpressionCS
define	`self.MBARelationship.descendants($2)->exists(`
	`r	r.oclIsNew() and`
	`r.coordinate->at(1) = $3 and`
	`r.coordinate->at(2) = $4 and`
	`let $1 : $$classOfLevel($2) =`
	`r.instanceData.oclAsType($$classOfLevel($2))`
	`in $5`
	`)`

method, respectively. At the ⟨ business, vehicleType ⟩ level, the transition with the terminate method as trigger has as postcondition that every descendant at the ⟨ renterType, model ⟩ level that is not in the Terminated state must be in the Unavailable state. At the ⟨ renterType, model ⟩ level, the transition with the offer method as trigger has as precondition that the ancestor at the ⟨ business, vehicleType ⟩ level must be in the Active state. Likewise, at the ⟨ renterType, model ⟩ level, the transition with the terminate method as trigger has as precondition that every descendant at the ⟨ renter, physicalEntity ⟩ level must be in the Closed state.

The precise semantics of postconditions in life cycle models possesses a certain ambiguity. Referring to the declarative nature of OCL, Cabot [18] and Wazlawick [137, p. 205] point out that the assignment of some value,

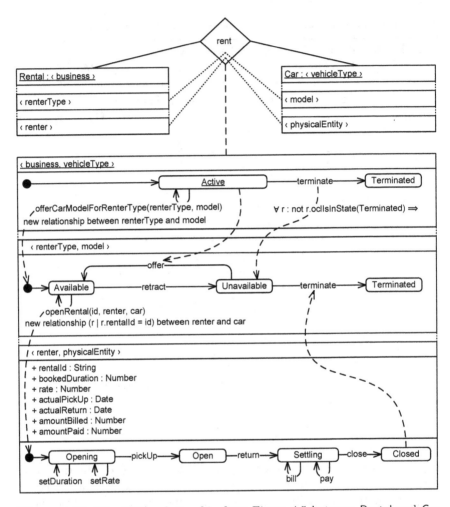

Figure 4.11: The MBA relationship from Figure 4.5 between Rental and Car extended with vertical synchronization dependencies

stored in some variable x, to another variable y has ambiguous interpretations with respect to the actual value both variables hold after the assignment. As a solution [18, p. 202], input parameters as employed in the life cycle models of the EU-Rent examples could and, in the case of MBAs, should be considered constants. An alternative solution [137, p. 205] employs

OCL message expressions [92, p. 32 et seqq.]. Using the caret (^) operator, preceded by an expression that evaluates to an object, followed by the name of the message sent to the object, a modeler may express the condition that a certain message was sent to a particular object. Assuming the existence of predefined *setter* methods, the representation of value assignment to variables then employs a message expression using call events for setter methods. For example, in Figure 4.11, the assignment `r.rentalId = id` that is part of the concretization predicate at the ⟨ renterType, model ⟩ level then becomes the message expression `r^setRentalId(id)`.

Practical considerations require a clarification of the execution semantics of state synchronization predicates in postconditions prior to the implementation of the multilevel business process model. A state synchronization predicate stating as a postcondition for a transition that every descendant or an ancestor at a particular level must be in a certain state after taking the transition makes no allusion as to the precise execution due to the declarative nature of OCL. More specifically, such a state synchronization predicate does not state whether the transition annotated with the synchronization predicate causes a transition of the respective descendants or ancestor to the specified state, or the transition annotated with the synchronization predicate waits for the descendants or ancestor to end up in the specified state before completing the transition. In the first step, the conceptual modeler might abstract from the specific execution semantics. In the second step, however, prior to the implementation of the conceptual model for a specific application, the modeler may wish to clarify the execution semantics of state synchronization predicates.

Two possibilities exist for the clarification of the precise execution semantics of state synchronization predicates (Figure 4.12). Using message expressions (Figure 4.12a), the modeler may specify the invocation of methods along with the state synchronization predicate, clarifying that the execution of a method at one level triggers the execution of methods at other levels as well. For example, the invocation of the restructure method at the business level of MBA Rental in the Running state has as postcondition that every descendant at the renterType level is in the Canceled state, provided the descendant is not already in the Discontinued state. As an additional condition, the synchronization predicate specifies that every descendant in the InDevelopment state, before the execution of the restructure method, must have received a message calling for the execution of the descendant's abort method, in case the descendant was in the InDevelopment state before the method call, or the cancel method, in case the descendant was in the OnOffer

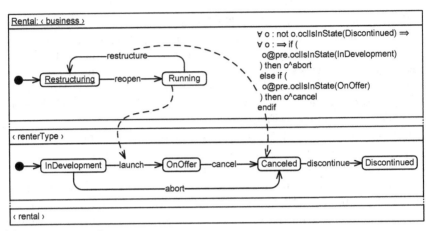

(a) message expressions

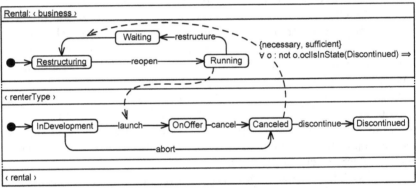

(b) intermediate state, necessary and sufficient precondition

Figure 4.12: Options for the specification of the execution semantics of synchronization dependencies

state. The second possibility for the clarification of the execution semantics (Figure 4.12b) splits the original transition into two other transitions and an intermediate Waiting state, thereby eliminating the postcondition. The restructure method, in this case, drops its postcondition and puts the MBA into the Waiting state. A new outgoing transition from the Waiting state, leading to the original target state of the transition triggered by the restructure method, has no event attached but rather has a precondition annotated *necessary* and *sufficient*. Thus, as soon as every descendant not in the Discontinued state is in the Canceled state, this necessary and sufficient transition is triggered.

4.3.2 Horizontal Synchronization

Horizontal synchronization dependencies occur between MBAs that are not in a concretization relationship. On the one hand, horizontal synchronization involves individual MBAs. On the other hand, though, in many cases, horizontal synchronization also involves an MBA relationship. In this section, we introduce multilevel predicates for the representation of horizontal synchronization dependencies.

The first class of horizontal synchronization dependencies consists of conditions expressed over states and attributes of MBAs at parallel levels; Table 4.6 defines multilevel predicates for this kind of synchronization dependencies. The isAtLevelSatisfies predicate is attached to a model element of an MBA and allows for expressing a condition over the instance data of an argument MBA at some argument level. From the isAtLevelSatisfies predicate derive predicates isAtLevelInState and isAtLevelInStateAndSatisfies. All of the just mentioned multilevel predicates require the argument level to be in the level hierarchy of the MBA that the predicate is attached to, or in the level hierarchy of another MBA that is connected with the MBA that the predicate is attached to, in order to allow the macro preprocessor to determine the class of the instance data ($\$\$classOfLevel$) at translation time, which is important for type checking of the resulting OCL constraint. Multilevel predicates isAtLevelSatisfies, isAtLevelInState, and isAtLevelInStateAndSatisfies, however, are not exclusively reserved for horizontal synchronization but also allow for expressing conditions over ancestor and descendant MBAs, although multilevel predicates explicitly dedicated to vertical synchronization better suit this purpose.

Figure 4.13 illustrates on the EU-Rent use case the application of horizontal synchronization dependencies over parallel hierarchies. Assume an individual rental in a country may only be opened if that particular country is currently a target market of the EU-Rent company. MBA Rental, which represents the rental business of the EU-Rent company, has parallel levels renterType and country. The renterType level handles the creation of new MBAs at the rental level, the openRental method triggering concretization. This openRental method takes an MBA at the country level as argument. A precondition of

Table 4.6: Multilevel predicates for synchronization over states and attributes of parallel MBAs

predicate	isAtLevelSatisfies(MBA, MBA, Level, Expression)
macro	'mba' simpleNameCS '=' OclExpressionCS
	'is' 'at' 'level' LevelExpCS 'and' 'satisfies' OclExpressionCS
define	`let $1 : $$classOfLevel($3) =`
	`    $2.instanceData.oclAsType($$classOfLevel($3))`
	`in $4`
predicate	isAtLevelInState(MBA, MBA, Level, State)
macro	'mba' OclExpressionCS 'is' 'at' 'level' LevelExpCS
	'in' 'state' StateExpCS
define	`mba o = $1 at level $2 satisfies`
	`    o.oclIsInState($3)`
predicate	isAtLevelInStateAndSatisfies
	(MBA, MBA, Level, State, Expression)
macro	'mba' simpleNameCS '=' OclExpressionCS
	'is' 'at' 'level' LevelExpCS 'in' 'state' StateExpCS
	'and' 'satisfies' OclExpressionCS
define	`mba $1 = $2 at level $3 satisfies`
	`    $1.oclIsInState($4) and $5`

the transition triggered by the **openRental** method requires the argument MBA to be at the country level and in the **TargetMarket** state.

Another class of horizontal synchronization dependencies concerns the outgoing links of one MBA to another MBA over MBA relationships; Table 4.8 defines multilevel predicates for this kind of synchronization dependencies. Predicates everyLinkEndAtLevelSatisfies and someLinkEndAtLevelSatisfies, which are attached to model elements of MBAs, require the instance data of all or some MBA, respectively, at a given level connected with the context MBA over an MBA relationship with a given label to satisfy a given condition in order to evaluate to true. Predicates everyLinkAtLevelSatisfies and someLinkAtLevelSatisfies, on the other hand, require the instance data of all or some MBA relationships, respectively, with a given label at a given relationship level connected with the context MBA to satisfy a given condition in order to evaluate to true.

The last class of horizontal synchronization dependencies concerns MBA relationships and consists of conditions expressed over states and attributes

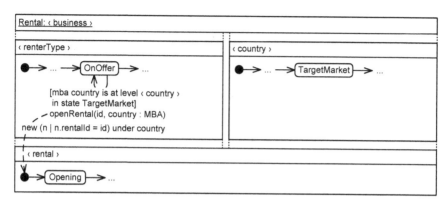

Figure 4.13: MBA Rental with parallel hierarchies and horizontal synchronization dependency

of the instance data of an MBA relationship's coordinates. For this kind of synchronization dependencies, Table 4.7 defines multilevel predicates coordinateSatisfies, coordinateIsInState, and coordinateIsInStateAndSatisfies, which are attached to model elements of MBA relationships. All of these predicates take as additional parameter a level which identifies the coordinate that the condition applies to. Therefore, valid argument levels are only those levels that compose the relationship level attached to the predicate; predicates coordinateSatisfies, coordinateIsInState, and coordinateIsInStateAndSatisfies are for horizontal synchronization only. The coordinateSatisfies predicate takes as additional parameter some condition over a coordinate of the MBA relationship that the predicate is attached to. Predicates coordinateIsIn-State and coordinateIsInStateAndSatisfies derive from the coordinateSatisfies predicate. The coordinateIsInState predicate requires a specific coordinate to be in a given state in order for the predicate to evaluate to true. The coordinateIsInStateAndSatisfies predicate requires a specific coordinate to be in a given state and satisfy some condition.

Figure 4.14 illustrates the use of multilevel predicates for the representation of horizontal synchronization over the coordinates of an MBA relationship. More specifically, the example illustrates the coordinateIsInState predicate, using a graphical representation analogous to the graphical representation of vertical state synchronization predicates (Figures 4.6 and 4.7). Assume a renter may only pick up an assigned car if it is not occupied. Picking up the car makes it unavailable for other customer whereas returning the car makes

Table 4.7: Multilevel predicates for expressing conditions over the coordinates of an MBA relationship

predicate	coordinateSatisfies(MBARelationship, Level, Expression)
macro	'coordinate' simpleNameCS 'at' 'level' LevelExpCS 'satisfies' OclExpressionCS
define	`let $1 : $$classOfLevel($2) =` `self.MBARelationship.coordiante->select(c |` `c.topLevel = $2` `).instanceData.oclAsType($$classOfLevel($2)) in $3`
predicate	coordinateIsInState(MBARelationship, Level, State)
macro	'coordinate' 'at' 'level' LevelExpCS 'is' 'in' 'state' StateExpCS
define	`coordinate o at level $1 satisfies` `o.oclIsInState($2)`
predicate	coordinateIsInStateAndSatisfies (MBARelationship, Level, State, Expression)
macro	'coordinate' simpleNameCS 'at' 'level' LevelExpCS 'is' 'in' 'state' StateExpCS 'and' 'satisfies' OclExpressionCS
define	`coordinate $1 at level $2 satisfies` `$1.oclIsInState($3) and $4`

it available. In the life cycle model at the ⟨ renter, physicalEntity ⟩ level of the MBA relationship between Rental and Car, the pickUp method triggers a transition from the Opening to the Open state, having as precondition that the coordinate at the physicalEntity level must be in the Free state. As a postcondition, the transition triggered by the pickUp method requires the coordinate at the physicalEntity level to be in the Occupied state. Similarly, as a postcondition, the transition triggered by the return method requires the coordinate at the physicalEntity level to be in the Free state.

In addition to horizontal synchronization over coordinates, Figure 4.14 illustrates the use of the isAtLevelInState predicate for expressing a condition over the state of the instance data of an input MBA for the openRental method at the ⟨ renterType, model ⟩ level of the MBA relationship between Rental and Car. Unlike in the previous example that employs the isAtLevelIn-State predicate (Figure 4.13), the context of the use of this predicate is an MBA relationship rather than an individual MBA. Though not a level of the MBA relationship, the physicalEntity level is known to the MBA relationship and the macro preprocessor is able to determine the class of this level from

Table 4.8: Multilevel predicates for expressing conditions over links

predicate	everyLinkEndAtLevelSatisfies(MBA, Label, Level, Expression)
macro	'every' 'end' simpleNameCS 'at' 'level' LevelExpCS
	'of' 'link' simpleNameCS 'satisfies' OclExpressionCS
define	`self.MBA.MBARelationship->select(r |`
	`    r.label = "$3"`
	`).coordinate->select(c |`
	`    c.topLevel = $2`
	`)->forAll(c |`
	`    let $1 : $$classOfLevel($2) =`
	`        c.instanceData.oclAsType($$classOfLevel($2))`
	`    in $4`
	`)`

predicate	someLinkEndAtLevelSatisfies(MBA, Label, Level, Expression)
macro	'some' 'end' simpleNameCS 'at' 'level' LevelExpCS
	'of' 'link' simpleNameCS 'satisfies' OclExpressionCS
define	`self.MBA.MBARelationship->select(r |`
	`    r.label = "$3"`
	`).coordinate->select(c |`
	`    c.topLevel = $2`
	`)->exists(c |`
	`    let $1 : $$classOfLevel($2) =`
	`        c.instanceData.oclAsType($$classOfLevel($2))`
	`    in $4`
	`)`

predicate	everyLinkAtLevelSatisfies
	(MBA, Label, RelationshipLevel, Expression)
macro	'every' 'link' simpleNameCS 'labeled' simpleNameCS
	'at' 'level' RelationshipLevelExpCS 'satisfies' OclExpressionCS
define	`self.MBA.MBARelationship->select(r |`
	`    r.label = "$2" and r.topLevel = $3`
	`)->forAll(r |`
	`    let $1 : $$classOfLevel($3) =`
	`        r.instanceData.oclAsType($$classOfLevel($3))`
	`    in $4`
	`)`

(continues on next page)

Table **4.8** (continued): Multilevel predicates for conditions over links

---

predicate someLinkAtLevelSatisfies
            (MBA, Label, RelationshipLevel, Expression)
macro   'some' 'link' simpleNameCS 'labeled' simpleNameCS
            'at' 'level' RelationshipLevelExpCS 'satisfies' OclExpressionCS
define `self.MBA.MBARelationship->select(r |`
            `r.label = "$2" and r.topLevel = $3`
            `)->exists(r |`
            `let $1 : $$classOfLevel($3) =`
            `    r.instanceData.oclAsType($$classOfLevel($3))`
            `in $4`
            `)`

---

the associated coordinate MBA. In this example, however, the classification of this particular use of the isAtLevelInState predicate purely as horizontal synchronization is disputable.

4.3.3 Hybrid Synchronization

We refer as hybrid synchronization to those dependencies that bear characteristics of both vertical and horizontal synchronization. The vertical synchronization dependencies in the previous section were limited to expressing conditions over the top-level data of the connected MBAs and MBA relationships. For example, the MBA relationship in Figure 4.14 between MBAs Rental and Car employs at the ⟨ renter, phyisicalEntity ⟩ level the coordinatesInState predicate for expressing a condition over the physical-Entity-level life cycle model of MBA Car as the pre-condition for the pickUp method. An instance of the ⟨ renter, phyisicalEntity ⟩ level of this MBA relationship evaluates the predicate over the top-level instance data of the connected MBA, requiring this MBA to be in the Free state in order to evaluate to true. In practical situations, modelers may also be interested in expressing conditions over the instance data of ancestors or descendants of connected MBAs and MBA relationships. For example, instead of requiring the physicalEntity coordinate to be in the Free state, the pre-condition might require the model-level ancestor of the physicalEntity coordinate to be in a particular state. The same scenario applies analogously to synchronization dependencies over the link ends of MBAs.

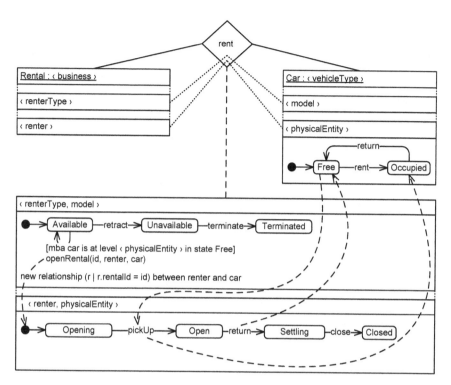

Figure 4.14: The MBA relationship from Figure 4.5 extended with horizontal synchronization dependencies over coordinates

In this book, we will not delve into the details of hybrid synchronization dependencies since the principles for the definition of corresponding multilevel predicates have already been discussed at great lengths in the previous sections. Although of practical importance for many business cases, the definition of such predicates does not present any particular challenges worth investigating here. The definition of multilevel predicates for hybrid synchronization does not differ qualitatively from the definition of multilevel predicates for vertical and horizontal synchronization. Rather, multilevel predicates for hybrid synchronization may be seen as a combination of the concepts for vertical and horizontal synchronization. The definition of predicates for hybrid synchronization is thus left as an exercise to the interested reader.

MULTILEVEL PREDICATES IN O-TELOS
With an O-Telos formalization of MBAs, managed in the ConceptBase, multilevel predicates may be realized using query classes which return all instances of a specific class that satisfy a given membership condition [54, p.32 et seq.]. Generic query classes take additional parameters which are instantiated at query time. Consider, for example, the following generic query class which retrieves all MBAs that have every descendant at the argument level in the argument state.

```
GenericQueryClass EveryDescendantAtLevelIsInState
  isA MBA with
parameter
  level: Level;
  state: State
constraint
  everyDescendantAtLevelIsInStateRule: $
    forall descendant/MBA t/MBA!topLevel obj/Object
    (descendant descendantOf ~this) and
    From(t,descendant) and To(t,~level) and
    (t object obj)
    ==> (obj isInState ~state)
  $
end
```

5 Hetero-Homogeneous Business Process Models

Today's dynamic business environment demands from companies variable and flexible processes. Rather than imposing a single fixed process, process models must account for the variability of real-world business problems. For example, in the car rental business, a company might handle rentals of private renters differently from rentals of corporate renters. At the same time, the company might impose a common process model which applies to rentals of private and corporate renters alike. Then, the process models for private and corporate renters are variants of the common process model. Furthermore, a process model should cater for the possibility of process owners deviating from the standard process under specific circumstances.

In this chapter, we propose a hetero-homogeneous approach to modeling business process variability and flexibility, revised and extended from previous work [111, 114]. We employ the multilevel business artifact (MBA) in order to represent within a single object the homogeneous schema of an abstraction hierarchy of business processes. We employ multilevel concretization for the introduction of heterogeneities into well-defined sub-hierarchies which, although basically compliant with the homogeneous global schema, offer to a certain degree much needed flexibility in situations that necessitate a deviation from standard processes. In order to allow for hetero-homogeneous business process modeling, we adapt the MBA metamodel as introduced in Chapter 4 by allowing the introduction of additional model elements in concretizations. We further investigate the possibility of different variants within the same level, yielding to the association of an entire specialization hierarchy of classes (and life cycle models) with a single level.

5.1 Multilevel Business Artifact Hierarchies

A single MBA is a hierarchically-ordered collection of artifact-centric business process models, a multilevel business process model. Using concretization, MBAs are themselves hierarchically organized, yielding a hierarchy of multilevel business process models. In such a hierarchy, a more concrete MBA, with respect to its abstraction, describes a specialized multilevel business process model applicable to a sub-domain.

5.1.1 Concretization with Simple Hierarchies

In homogeneous multilevel business process models (see Chapter 4), multi-level concretization merely serves as an indication of aggregate membership, with the more concrete MBAs reduced to their object facet; the introduction of model elements or abstraction levels is prohibited in the course concretiza-tion. In hetero-homogeneous multilevel business process models, however, a more concrete MBA – the concretization – may introduce additional model elements and abstraction levels with respect to the more abstract, concretized MBA – the abstraction. The introduction of additional model elements follows well-defined rules: Newly introduced classes and state machines must specialize the inherited model elements at the respective level.

Figure 5.1 illustrates the use of multilevel concretization for the introduc-tion of heterogeneities in a particular sub-hierarchy; the example derives from the EU-Rent use case [90] and previous work [114]. The EU-Rent company is active in the car rental business. The company manages business related to different renter types as well as individual rentals under a specific renter type. MBA Rental represents the company's rental business as a whole and describes the business process models related to managing renter types and individual rentals. For the management of the private renter type and its associated rentals, the company captures additional data and follows a specialized business process model. As a concretization of Rental, MBA Private at the renterType level represents the private renter type as well as a sub-hierarchy within the multilevel business process model. MBA Private inherits from its abstraction the classes and state machines attached to the different levels. At the same time, MBA Private specializes the inherited classes and state machines, capturing additional data as well as having additional states, transitions, and synchronization dependencies.

MBA Rental has levels business, renterType, and rental. The business level describes the life cycle model of the rental business as a whole, going from Establishing over Running to Abandoned. The renterType level describes the life cycle model of each renter type, going from InDevelopment over OnOffer to Canceled and Discontinued. The rental level describes the life cycle model of each individual rental, going from Opening over Open to Closed. At the business level, in the Establishing state, invocation of the createRenterType method creates a new descendant at the renterType level. In the Running state, invocation of the abandon method puts the business into the Abandoned state and all descendant MBAs at the renterType level that are not in the Discontinued state into the Canceled state. At the renterType level, in the InDevelopment state, invocation of the launch method puts a renter type into the OnOffer state, provided the business-level ancestor is in the Running state. While OnOffer, invocation of the openRental method creates a new new individual rental underneath the respective renter type. Invocation of the cancel method puts a renter type into the Canceled state and all descendant MBAs at the rental level previously not in the Opening state into the Closed state. In the Canceled state, invocation of the discontinue method puts a renter type into the Discontinued state, provided all descendant MBAs at the rental level are in the Closed state. At the rental level, in the Opening state, invocation of the pickUp method puts the individual rental into the Open state, provided the renterType-level ancestor is in the OnOffer state. Invocation of the close method allows for the closing of the rental before the actual pick-up of the car.

   MBA Private inherits from Rental the levels renterType and rental as well as the associated model elements. In the graphical representation (Figure 5.1), inherited attributes are not shown; inherited states, transitions, and synchronization dependencies are shown in gray color. With respect to Rental, MBA Private describes a more detailed multilevel business process model, the state machines associated with the individual levels of MBA Private being observation-consistent specializations [125, 108] of the state machines associated with the respective levels of MBA Rental. At the renterType level of MBA Private, the state machine has a refined OnOffer state with sub-states Active and PhasingOut. At the rental level, the class additionally captures bad experiences (attribute badExperiences), the state machine has a refined Opening state, with sub-states RateFixing, CarChoosing, and Ready, a refined Open state, with sub-states Moving and Returning, as well as a refined Closed state with sub-states Returned, Settled, Canceled, and Archived. Furthermore, at the rental level, the state machine introduces the Evaluating state parallel to the Open state. Also, there are specialized synchronization dependencies in the state machines of MBA Private, meaning that the inherited pre- and postconditions are strengthened. At the renterType level of MBA Private, the post-condition of the cancel method in the OnOffer state requires all descendants at the rental level previously not in the Opening state to be in the Canceled state after invocation of the method. This postcondition is a refinement of the post-condition in MBA Rental

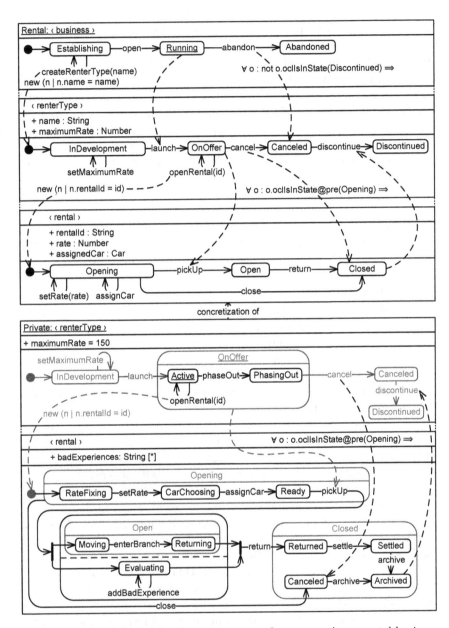

Figure 5.1: MBA Rental for the management of a company's car rental business and a concretization for the management of private rentals

that requires all descendants at the rental level to be in the Closed state after invocation of the cancel method since MBA Private, at the rental level, introduces Canceled as a sub-state of Closed. Similarly, at the renterType level, the pre-condition of the discontinue method in the Canceled state requires all descendants at the rental level to be in the Archived state and, thus, is a refinement of the corresponding pre-condition in MBA Rental which requires all descendants to be in the Closed state; the Canceled state is introduced as a sub-state of Closed.

Besides specializing data and life cycle models of inherited levels, a concretization may introduce a whole new level altogether, provided this level does not become the concretization's top level (see the core m-object metamodel in Chapter 3). Figure 5.2 illustrates MBA Corporate at the renterType level as a concretization of MBA Rental (Figure 5.1). Inherited attributes, states, transitions, and synchronization dependencies are shown in gray color. MBA Corporate represents the corporate renter type itself as well as describing data and life cycle model of individual rentals under the corporate renter type. These corporate rentals, unlike private rentals, are part of a corporate rental agreement, represented by the newly introduced agreement level of MBA Corporate between renterType and rental. A rental agreement has an agreement identifier (attribute agreementId), a set of negotiated rental rates (negotiatedRates), and during its life cycle, an agreement goes from being UnderNegotiation over InEffect to Dissolved.

The introduction of a new abstraction level in MBA Corporate entails at the inherited abstraction levels an introduction of new transitions and the modification of inherited transitions as well as a redefinition of inherited pre- and postconditions. At the renterType level, the OnOffer state has an additional transition triggered by the negotiateAgreement method, the invocation of which creates a new descendant at the agreement level. As in MBA Rental, the OnOffer state has a transition triggered by the openRental method, the invocation of which creates a new descendant at the rental level. In MBA Corporate, at the renterType level, the transition triggered by the openRental method has a refined post-condition and an additional parameter with respect to the life cycle model defined by MBA Rental. Although still applicable, satisfying the original post-condition alone will not suffice in order to obtain a valid concretization at the rental level. Since all individual rentals under the corporate renter type must belong to a rental agreement, a descendant of MBA Corporate at the rental level must be a descendant of some MBA under MBA Corporate at the agreement level as well. Thus, the refined post-condition requires the new MBA to be a descendant under

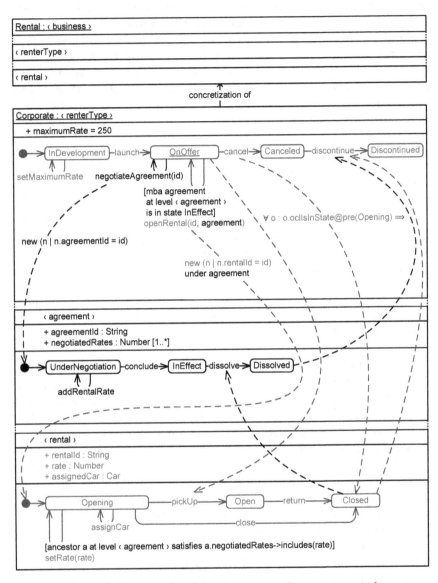

Figure 5.2: MBA Corporate for the management of corporate rentals as a concretization of MBA Rental

the argument MBA passed for the agreement parameter. Furthermore, the newly introduced pre-condition of the transition triggered by the openRental method restricts the value of the agreement parameter to MBAs at the agreement level that are in InEffect.

Notice that the MBA Corporate inherits a synchronization dependency between renterType and rental level, stating at the renterType level that in the Canceled state, the invocation of the discontinue method requires all descendants at the rental level to be in the Closed state. Furthermore, MBA Corporate introduces two synchronization dependencies which together represent a refinement of the former synchronization dependency. First, at the renterType level, the invocation of the discontinue method requires all descendants at the agreement level to be in the Dissolved state. Second, at the agreement level, while InEffect, the invocation of the dissolve method, which puts the agreement into the Dissolved state, requires all descendants at the rental level to be in the Closed state. Thus, when an agreement is in the Dissolved state, all its descendants at the rental level already are in the Closed state. Then, at the renterType level, the requirement that all descendants at the agreement level be in the Dissolved state subsumes the requirement that all descendants at the rental level be in the Closed state. In practice, however, deducing subsumption between synchronization dependencies may be costly. Therefore, replacing inherited synchronization dependencies with their refinements may be impracticable. Rather, inherited synchronization dependencies are kept in the specialized state machine. The specialization of a state machine may only strengthen pre- and postconditions [125, p. 538], which is equivalent to appending to the original constraint an additional condition using logic conjunction; the Eiffel language [73, p. 578 et seq.] employs a similar solution for checking subsumption between logic expressions. In the graphical representation, of course, modelers may wish to omit inherited synchronization dependencies that are subsumed by newly introduced synchronization dependencies.

Formally, as opposed to the MBA metamodel for homogeneous business process models (see Chapter 4), the MBA metamodel for hetero-homogeneous models (Figure 5.3), while leaving other elements unchanged, allows for an MBA to possibly associate multiple classes and state machines with each level. An MBA may introduce a single class and life cycle model per level and may inherit multiple classes and life cycle models from its ancestors (Figure 5.4). The introduction of classes and life cycle models, however, is not arbitrary but follows well-defined rules. First, the classes that an MBA associates with a particular level must be organized in a specialization hierarchy with

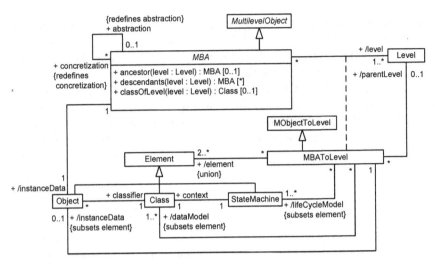

Figure 5.3: Adaptation for hetero-homogeneous modeling of the MBA metamodel in Figure 4.1 (Metaclass IndividualMBA omitted)

a single root (Rule 5.1); a new class may then only be introduced as a leaf node in this specialization hierarchy (Rule 5.2). Second, the corresponding state machines of two classes that are in a specialization relationship must be in a specialization relationship as well (Rule 5.3). Thus, the data and life cycle models associated with the different levels are guaranteed to specialize along a particular path in the concretization hierarchy.

The class hierarchy within a level follows the *abstract superclass rule* [50] which requires that only leaf nodes of the hierarchy are instantiable classes. For a non-top level of an MBA, all associated classes must be abstract (Rule 5.4). At the top level, however, there exists a single non-abstract class (Rule 5.5). This non-abstract class must be a leaf node. This follows from the metamodel, which allows the introduction of only a single class at each level, and Rule 5.2, which permits the introduction of new classes only as leaf nodes, as well as Rule 5.4, which implies that all inherited classes are abstract. The classOfLevel method returns the leaf node of the specialization hierarchy (Rule 5.6).

Figure 5.5 illustrates a simplified and slightly adapted metamodel for UML state machines. According to this metamodel, a state machine (metaclass StateMachine) consists of a region (metaclass Region). A region consists of transitions and vertices. A Transition instance refers to a source and a target

Rule 5.1: A level's data models are arranged in a specialization hierarchy with a single root

```
1 context MBAToLevel inv:
2  self.dataModel->select(r |
3   r.general->isEmpty() and
4   self.dataModel->excluding(r)->forAll(s |
5    s.general->closure(general)->includes(r)
6   )
7  )->size() = 1
```

Rule 5.2: A newly introduced class must be a leaf node in the class hierarchy

```
1 context MBAToInheritedLevel inv:
2  self.newDataModel.general->forAll(c |
3   not self.inheritedDataModel->exists(i |
4    i.general->includes(c)
5   )
6  )
```

Rule 5.3: A specialized class' life cycle model is the specialization of the general class' life cycle model

```
1 context MBAToLevel inv:
2  self.dataModel->forAll(c1, c2 |
3   let s1 : StateMachine =
4    self.lifeCycleModel->any(s |
5     s.context = c1
6    ) in
7   let s2 : StateMachine =
8    self.lifeCycleModel->any(s |
9     s.context = c2
10    ) in
11   c1.general->includes(c2) implies
12   s1.extendedStateMachine = s2
13  )
```

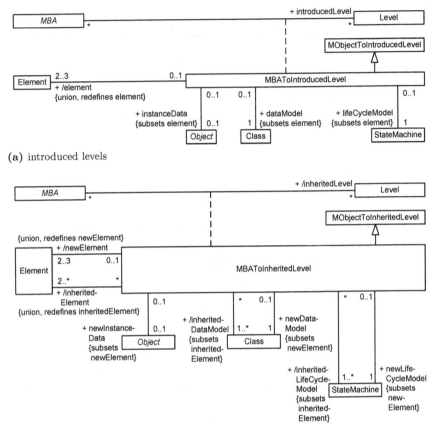

(a) introduced levels

(b) inherited levels

Figure 5.4: The data attached to a hetero-homogeneous MBA's introduced and inherited levels as a specialization of the core metamodel for m-objects

vertex. A transition references an Operation as instance, the operation must be a method of the state machine's context class. A transition may also refer to multiple constraints (metaclass Constraint) as pre- and post-conditions. The constraint language may be chosen arbitrarily; we use OCL as the constraint language. The Vertex metaclass subsumes states in the proper sense (metaclass State) and pseudo states (metaclass Pseudostate), that is, forks, joins, and so on. An instance of State may have multiple subregions which consist again of vertices. When referring to the states of a state machine, we mean the states of the state machine's main region as well as all states in the transitive closure of the sub-states of the states in the main region. Similarly, when referring to the transitions of a state machine, we mean the transitions of the state machine's main region as well as the transitions in the regions of states in the transitive closure of the sub-states of the states in the main region. When using the term "state", we usually mean the non-pseudo states of a state machine.

The UML standard provides for a mechanism for state machine specialization. The extendedStateMachine association end of the StateMachine metaclass represents the specialization relationship between state machines. An outgoing extendedStateMachine association end of a StateMachine instance links to the more general state machine of which the former state machine is a specialization. The metaclasses Region, State, Transition, and Operation are specializations of RedefinableElement. The redefinition relationships extendedRegion, redefinedState, redefinedTransition and redefinedOperation define mappings between specialized elements and their corresponding elements in the more general state machine. For multilevel concretization of MBAs with simple hierarchies, multiple specialization of state machines is no possibility. Thus, for simplicity, we do not allow multiple specialization in the state machine metamodel.

The employed semantics for behavior-consistent specialization determines the possibilities for extension and refinement of an MBA's life cycle models in the course of multilevel concretization. Various notions for behavior consistency exist in the literature [125, 108, 3], differing in the degree of freedom offered to the modeler with respect to the possibilities for extension and refinement. In general, invocation-consistent specialization denotes a specialization mechanism which results in the specialized life cycle model being executable in the same fashion as the more general life cycle model, imposing a rather strict specialization regime. Compared to invocation consistency, observation consistency is less strict with a higher degree of freedom offered to the modeler, possibly at the cost of incompatibility with applications relying on invocation consistency. Observation-consistent specialization denotes a specialization mechanism which results in the specialized life cycle model, with all refined states and transitions considered unrefined and all extensions disregarded, being observable in the same fashion as the more general life cycle model. In this book, we employ a specific notion of observation consistency, although we stress that the employed notion of behavior consistency may vary between applications, depending on the desired degree of freedom for concretization.

Rule 5.4: A non-top level's data models are abstract classes

```
1 context MBA inv:
2  self.MBAToLevel->reject(m |
3    m.level = self.topLevel
4  ).dataModel->forAll(c |
5    c.isAbstract
6  )
```

Rule 5.5: The top level has a single non-abstract class

```
1 context MBA inv:
2  self.MBAToLevel->select(m |
3    m.level = self.topLevel
4  ).dataModel->select(c |
5    not c.isAbstract
6  )->size() = 1
```

Rule 5.6: The class of a level is the most specific data model in that level's class hierarchy

```
1 context MBA::classOfLevel(level : Level) : Class
2  derive:
3  let mbaToLevel : MBAToLevel =
4    self.MBAToLevel->select(l |
5      l.level = level
6    ) in
7 mbaToLevel.dataModel->select(c : Class |
8    not mbaToLevel.dataModel->exists(s : Class |
9      s.general = c
10   )
11 )
```

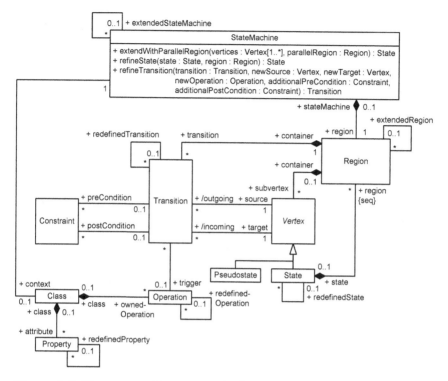

Figure 5.5: The state machine metamodel (adapted and extended from the UML standard [88, p. 536]) with reflection pattern methods

In the previous examples, the state machines associated with the levels of concretizing MBAs are observation-consistent specializations with respect to the abstractions. The employed notion of observation consistency allows for the refinement of states through addition of sub-states. Transitions may have source and/or target state refined, replacing either state by a sub-state of the original. Furthermore, parallel regions may be added, splitting the life cycle at some point using a fork. Note that according to the UML standard, redefinition of transitions allows refinement only for the source state. Unlike the UML standard, we allow for the refinement of a transition's source state.

We define a notion of observation consistency adapted from the definition of Stumptner and Schrefl [125]. Let $sc = (S, T)$ and $sc' = (S', T')$ be UML state machines with S, S' sets of their non-pseudo states, T, T' sets of their transitions, and sc'.extendedStateMachine = sc. The function

$h : S' \cup T' \to S \cup T \cup \{\varepsilon\}$ maps the states and transitions of sc' to states and transitions of sc according to object identity and redefinition relationships. For every element $e' \in S' \cup T'$ without correspondence in $S \cup T$ holds $h(e') = \varepsilon$, the empty set. The function $g : \mathcal{P}(S') \cup \mathcal{P}(T') \to \mathcal{P}(S \cup \{\varepsilon\}) \cup \mathcal{P}(T \cup \{\varepsilon\})$ returns for any set $\{e_1', \ldots, e_n'\} \in \mathcal{P}(S') \cup \mathcal{P}(T')$ the corresponding set $\{h(e_1'), \ldots, h(e_n')\}$. Let $tr' = \tau_1', \sigma_1', \ldots, \tau_n', \sigma_n'$ be an arbitrary life cycle trace of the state machine sc', where $\tau_i' \subseteq T'$ and $\sigma_i' \subseteq S'$ for $i = 1 \ldots n$. Let $tr'/sc = [g(\tau_1'), g(\sigma_1'), \ldots, g(\tau_n'), g(\sigma_n')]$ be the restriction of tr' to the state machine sc. The state machine sc' is an observation-consistent specialization of sc if, and only if, for every life cycle trace tr' the restriction tr'/sc is a valid life cycle trace of sc, disregarding any $g(\tau_i') = \{\varepsilon\}$ where $g(\sigma_{i-1}') = g(\sigma_{i+1}')$.

Consider, for example, the rental-level state machines of MBAs Rental (sc) and Private (sc') in Figure 5.1. The life cycle trace $tr' = [\{t_{init}\}, \{RateFixing\}, \{t_{setRate}\}, \{CarChoosing\}, \{t_{assignCar}\},$ $\{Ready\}, \{t_{pickUp}, t_{fork1}, t_{fork2}\}, \{Moving, Evaluating\}, \{t_{enterBranch}\},$ $\{Returning, Evaluating\}, \{t_{addBadExperience}\}, \{Returning, Evaluating\},$ $\{t_{join1}, t_{join2}, t_{return}\}, \{Returned\}, \{t_{settle}\}, \{Settled\}, \{t_{archive}\},$ $\{Archived\}]$ is a valid life cycle trace of sc'. The RateFixing, CarChoosing, and Ready states map to the Opening state. The Moving and Returning states map to the Open state. The Evaluating state maps to the empty set ε. The Returned, Settled, and Artchived states map to the Closed state. The $t_{enterBranch}$, $t_{addBadExperience}$, t_{settle}, and $t_{archive}$ transitions map to the empty set ε. In the restriction $tr'/sc = [\{t_{init}\}, \{Opening\}, \{t_{setRate}\},$ $\{Opening\}, \{t_{assignCar}\}, \{Opening\}), \{t_{pickUp}\}, \{Open\}, \{\varepsilon\}, \{Open\},$ $\{\varepsilon\}, \{Open\}, \{t_{return}\}, \{Closed\}, \{\varepsilon\}, \{Closed\}, \{\varepsilon\}, \{Closed\}]$ are four empty-set entries but since in all of these cases the previous and the following set of states are equal, the restriction tr'/sc is nevertheless a valid life cycle trace of the state machine sc'.

We hold a data-centric view on state machines: The transitions of a state machine represent manipulation operations on the corresponding data object. We further adopt the zero-time assumption for these manipulation operations. Manual tasks with non-zero execution time carried out by humans or time-consuming data processing tasks must be modeled as separate states. The MBA modeling approach, however, supports the zero-time and non-zero time assumption alike. The abandoning of the zero-time assumption has implications on the employed definition of observation consistency.

We stress that the employed life cycle modeling formalism, the time model, and the notion of behavior consistency are orthogonal concerns to the MBA modeling approach. Specific applications may opt for another modeling language, for example, Petri nets, adopt a non-zero time model for the execution of transitions, and define stricter or looser notions of behavior consistency. The decision for a particular notion of behavior consistency, for example, depends on the specific purpose of a particular MBA model. A focus on the enforcement of top-down compliance with business policies requires adherence to the rules of (at least) observation-consistent specialization. Likewise, for analysis purposes, observation consistency is a sufficiently strong notion of behavior consistency. From a software engineering perspective, however, with a focus on code reusability, invocation consistency may seem more appropriate.

Since MBA relationships are a special kind of MBAs, the statements in this section equally apply to the concretization of MBA relationships. An MBA relationship may specialize data and life cycle models of inherited levels or introduce an additional relationship level altogether. For the specialization of life cycle models, concretizations of MBA relationships must also adhere to the employed notion of behavior consistency.

5.1.2 Concretization with Parallel Hierarchies

The possibility of parallel hierarchies in hetero-homogeneous business process models introduces the issue of multiple inheritance. Different MBAs at parallel levels may specialize independently from each other an inherited life cycle model for a given level. Through multiple concretization, an MBA may then concretize these parallel MBAs and inherit all the life cycle models from each abstraction, including the adaptations made by these abstractions. These adaptations, however, may be incompatible with each other, defining contradicting specializations which must be resolved explicitly by the concretization. For an in-depth analysis on multiple inheritance we refer to related work on object behavior diagrams [108, p. 124 et seq.].

In order to avoid potential conflicts in connection with multiple inheritance, in the case of parallel paths in a level hierarchy, only MBAs in one of the parallel paths may be allowed to specialize the inherited life cycle model for a particular level. Consider, for example, an MBA Rental with business as the top level. The child levels of business are renterType and country. The rental level has both renterType and country as parent levels. An MBA Private at the renterType level may concretize Rental and specialize the rental-level life cycle model. A rental-level MBA that concretizes Private must then concretize a country-level MBA that does not specialize the rental-level life cycle model with respect to MBA Rental. Conversely, a rental-level MBA that concretizes a country-level MBA specializing the rental-level life cycle model must not concretize MBA Private.

As an alternative, in the case of parallel paths in a level hierarchy, MBAs in different paths may be allowed to specialize only orthogonal regions of an inherited life cycle model for a particular level. Consider again an MBA Rental with levels business, renterType, country, and rental, where renterType and country are both child levels of renterType. An MBA Private at the renterType level may then refine the Opening state of the inherited rental-level life cycle model whereas an MBA Austria at the country level may refine the Closed state of the same inherited life cycle model. These changes are orthogonal, a rental-level MBA may safely concretize both MBA Private and MBA Austria.

5.1.3 Incremental Evolution through Reflection

Concretization is not a one-shot activity. Rather, concretization itself is an incremental process. Consider, for example, MBA Corporate in Figure 5.6a and assume this MBA inherits its levels as well as the data and life cycle models from another, more abstract MBA. Initially, right after its creation, MBA Corporate has only the inherited data and life cycle models, is in the InDevelopment state, and has NULL values assigned to the top-level attributes, as shown in Figure 5.6a. While InDevelopment, a value is assigned to the maximumRate attribute. Furthermore, the inherited data and life cycle models are specialized, and an additional level is introduced. The invocation of the launch methode terminates the InDevelopment phase and puts MBA Corporate into the OnOffer state (Figure 5.6b). In this state, the maximumRate attribute at the top level has a value assigned. The data and life cycle models differ from the inherited models. In particular, the rental-level data model contains an additional businessAddOns attribute and the Opening state at the rental level was refined during the InDevelopment phase. The agreement level was introduced between renterType and rental.

By modeling transitions with reflective methods as trigger, modelers may explicitly define the amount of flexibility for the adaptation of business process models at run time. Reflective methods represent modifications at run time of the data and life cycle model. In this sense, the MBA metaprocess activities capture the requirements engineering process in the spirit of evolutionary objects [100], albeit in a more prescriptive way. When directly implemented, the inclusion of reflective methods also presents characteristics of the models@run.time paradigm [15, 14], which champions a causal connec-

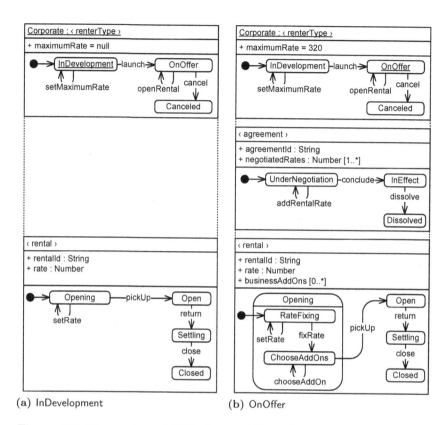

(a) InDevelopment   (b) OnOffer

Figure 5.6: Changes in an MBA's data and life cycle models from one state to another (adapted from previous work [111])

tion between model and implementation, allowing for changes on the model to directly propagate to the implementation. The MBA modeling approach in conjunction with reflective methods generalizes for multiple levels of abstraction the two-tier framework for handling flexibility in artifact-centric business process models [65], which consists of the business process model itself and a process design entity.

For state machines, there exist two kinds of reflective methods, namely reflective CRUD and redefinition methods. Reflective CRUD (= **C**reate, **R**ead, **U**pdate, **D**elete) methods allow for the dynamic creation, querying, and manipulation at run time of instances of the state machine metamodel.

In other words, reflective CRUD methods are *getter* and *setter* methods of metaclasses. Redefinition methods, on the other hand, represent behavior-consistent specialization patterns. Each redefinition method is a combination of reflective CRUD methods which extends and refines a state machine with respect to its base state machine. The StateMachine class in Figure 5.5 has three redefinition methods. The extendWithParallelRegion function takes a number of vertices from the state machine as argument – the states must belong to the same region – as well as a new region that is to be inserted in parallel to the argument vertices using a fork. The refineState takes a state from the state machine as argument as well as a new region that is added to the argument state's set of regions. The refineTransition refines an argument transition from the state machine by defining new source and/or target states, associating a different operation, or adding pre- and post-conditions. An invocation of these reflective methods must not yield a behavior-inconsistent life cycle model.

Since concretization itself is a process, an MBA may also account for metaprocess activities in order to regulate local changes made to the imposed data and life cycle models. To this end, the Object metaclass must have specific methods which invoke the reflective methods of the corresponding MBA and associated model elements. By default, these methods are invocable in any state, the life cycle model may be specialized as long as the employed notion of behavior consistency is obeyed. The explicit inclusion of reflective methods in the life cycle model empowers a modeler to restrict the possibilities for specialization in sub-hierarchies and, consequently, deliberately limit flexibility.

Figure 5.7 illustrates MBA Rental for the management of car rentals with reflective methods in the life cycle models. For the renterType level, MBA Rental defines metaprocess activities in a region of the InDevelopment state. For each renterType descendant of Rental, while in the AddingAttributes state, modelers may add attributes to the rental-level data model of the descendant MBA. While in the RefiningRentalOpeningAndSettling state, modelers may refine states and transitions under the Opening and Settling state of the rental-level life cycle model of the descendant MBA. The add-AttributeAtLevel, refineTransitionAtLevel, and refineStateAtLevel are examples of the Object-metaclass methods which invoke reflective methods of the corresponding MBA. The macro expressions |<rental>::Opening| and |<rental>::Settling| retrieve the Opening level and the Settling level, respectively, from the rental-level life cycle model of the MBA in the context of which the expression is evaluated.

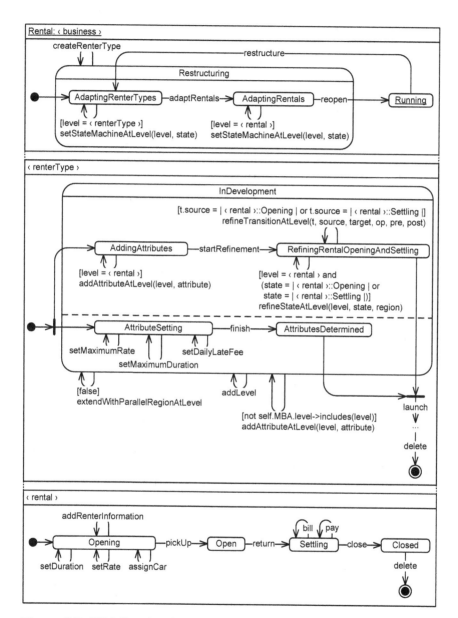

Figure 5.7: MBA Rental with meta-process model elements (adapted from previous work [111])

Issues may arise when an operation changes at run time the life cycle model of an MBA's level which already has instances. Specializations of life cycle models for already instantiated classes may be prohibited altogether. Already existing instantiations may also be deleted before modifying the life cycle model. Depending on the nature of the specialization, under specific circumstances, specializations of life cycle models for already instantiated classes may be possible. If the more abstract MBA specializes the life cycle model of a level for which there already exist descendants, then the specialization must occur at a point in the life cycle model that the already existing descendants have yet to traverse.

Consider, for example, MBA Rental in Figure 5.7 as an example for metaprocess activities at multiple levels of abstraction. At the business level, the MBA switches between the Running and Restructuring states. While in the Restructuring state, modelers may change the life cycle models associated with the renterType and rental levels. In such a case, however, prior to effecting the changes, descendants at the affected levels must be deleted. In order to preserve historical data, modelers may also opt for an MBA relationship between MBA Rental and a time dimension, and instead associate the life cycle models of MBA Rental with the relationship levels of this MBA relationship.

5.2 Process Model Hierarchies within Levels

By linking multiple classes and state machines to a particular abstraction level, an MBA may define different process variants for this level. The newly created MBA chooses a top-level variant for instantiation. The final instantiation decision may also be deferred to a specified point in the life cycle, the object being instance of a superclass until then. This section is a revised version of our previous work on variability [114].

5.2.1 Business Process Variants

A multilevel business artifact (MBA) may link an entire specialization hierarchy of classes with an abstraction level, which allows for the definition of process variants within a single level. In this case, instead of a single class, an MBA defines a set of classes for the abstraction level. A single most-general class serves as the superclass for an arbitrary number of specializations. The life cycle models of these classes follow rules for behavior-consistent specialization. Thus, each class in such a specialization hierarchy, together with the corresponding life cycle model, is a variant of an artifact-centric business process model.

For example, in Figure 5.8, MBA Corporate links an entire class hierarchy with the rental level. In this hierarchy, CorporateRental is the most general class, with CorporateAdvanceRental and CorporateCarsharingRental being specializations. The life cycle model of class CorporateAdvanceRental refines the Opening state. An advance rental has a scheduled pick-up date (scheduled-PickUp) and separates the recording of basic rental information (done in the Booking state) from the assignment of an actual car which is carried out at a later point when the rental is already Booked. The life cycle model of class CorporateCarsharingRental refines the Open state. A carsharing rental is billed by driven distance (drivenDistance) and may involve changes of the assigned car. The renter may pause an Active rental and choose another car from a car pool before resuming the rental.

After creation, an MBA's instance data, by default, has as classifier the single most-general class that is linked to the top level. An MBA may then change the classifier of the top-level instance data during the life cycle. The setClassifier method of the Object metaclass allows for the explicit consideration of classifier change in the life cycle model. This possibility of *incremental classification* defers the final instantiation decision, increasing the flexibility of the employees that are responsible for carrying out the process. Incremental classification allows for the dynamic specialization and generalization of the classifier of an MBA's top-level object. Instance specialization refers to a change of an object's classifier from more general to specialized. Instance generalization, in turn, refers to a change of an object's classifier from specialized to more general. Both types of incremental classification can be combined for *instance mutation* which allows for a change of an object's classifier to another classifier that is the subclass of a common superclass (cf. [100, p. 217]).

In order for instance specialization to be valid, certain conditions must be met by the object. The change of classifier of an MBA's top-level object from more general to specialized is valid if the previous processing steps of the object in the more general life cycle model also represent a valid execution of the specialized life cycle model. In this case, the object can resume execution in the specialized life cycle model. For example, consider an MBA which associates as instance data an object of CorporateRental that is in the Opening state. The change of this object's classifier to Corporate-AdvanceRental is possible and puts the object in the Booking state, a substate

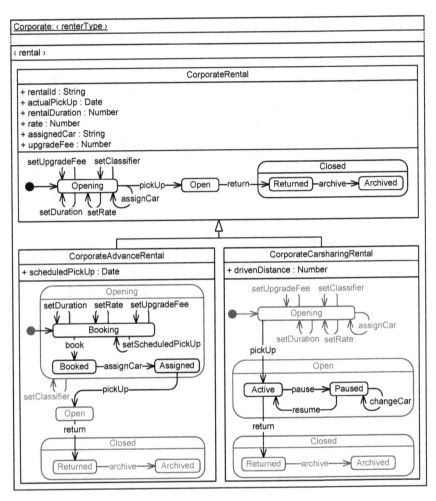

Figure 5.8: An MBA which associates an entire class hierarchy with one of its levels [114]

of Opening. Consider now an MBA which associates as instance data an object of CorporateRental that is in the Open state. The change of this object's classifier to CorporateAdvanceRental is not allowed. The change of classifier would put the object in the Open state. As an instance of Corporate-AdvanceRental the object would have had to run through the refined Opening state in order to present a valid life cycle. A change of classifier to Corporate-CarsharingRental, on the other hand, is possible and puts the object in the Active state, a substate of Open.

Instance generalization is always possible unless explicitly prohibited by the life cycle model. Values of attributes that are introduced by the specialized class are dropped. If in a refined state at first, after change of classifier the MBA's top-level instance data is in the unrefined state of the general life cycle model. For example, consider an MBA which associates as instance data an object of CorporateAdvanceRental in the Assigned state. A change of this object's classifier to CorporateRental puts the object in the Opening state, the unrefined superstate of Assigned. The value of scheduledPickUp is dropped since the more general class does not have this attribute.

Instance mutation refers to a change of an object's classifier to another subclass of the superclass of the object's current classifier; instance mutation is realized as a sequence of instance generalization and specialization. For example, consider an MBA which associates as instance data an object of CorporateAdvanceRental. A change of this object's classifier from Corporate-AdvanceRental to CorporateCarsharingRental is a two-step procedure. First, the classifier changes from CorporateAdvanceRental to the more general CorporateRental class which is the common superclass of both the Corporate-AdvanceRental class and the CorporateCarsharingRental class. Second, the classifier changes from CorporateRental to the CorporateCarsharingRental class.

5.2.2 Incremental Evolution through Mutation

For each inherited level, a concretization inherits all of the linked data and life cycle models. If an inherited level is linked to a class hierarchy, the concretization inherits the entire class hierarchy. This inherited class hierarchy may be specialized. On the one hand, the concretization may introduce additional subclasses. On the other hand, the concretization may specialize individual classes of the inherited class hierarchy.

With class hierarchies involved, multilevel concretization may lead to double specialization of classes and life cycle models. Each class of a concretization's inherited class hierarchy is a specialization of the abstraction's corresponding class. When the concretization adds additional features to one of the subclasses of the inherited class hierarchy, this subclass as well as its life cycle model must be consistent with both the abstraction's corresponding class and the superclass within the inherited class hierarchy. This superclass may also have additional features with respect to the abstrac-

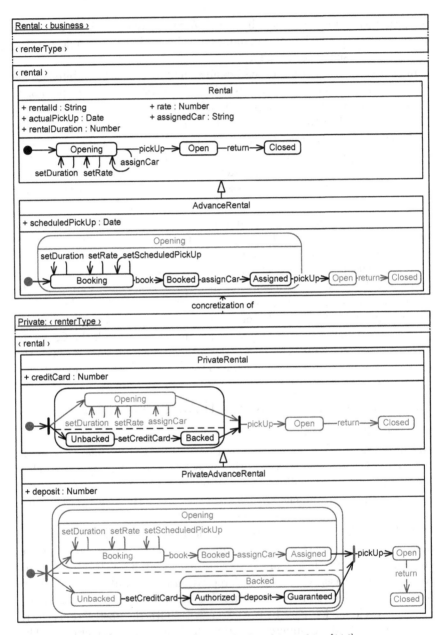

Figure 5.9: Multilevel concretization with class hierarchies [114]

tion's corresponding class. In this case, for the specialized subclass in the concretization's inherited class hierarchy, double specialization occurs.

For example, in Figure 5.9, MBA Private is a concretization of MBA Rental which links a class hierarchy with the rental level. At the rental level, MBA Rental defines classes Rental and AdvanceRental which are in a specialization/generalization relationship with each other. MBA Private, at the rental level, defines classes PrivateRental and PrivateAdvanceRental. Class PrivateRental is a specialization of class Rental which is defined by MBA Rental. A private rental must have credit card information and is either Unbacked or Backed, depending on the availability of credit card information. Class PrivateAdvanceRental is a specialization of class PrivateRental as well as class AdvanceRental which is defined by MBA Rental. A private advance rental requires the customer to deposit an amount of money in order to guarantee the reservation. Once deposited, a private advance rental turns from Authorized into Guaranteed, thereby refining the Backed state.

In this book, we do not focus on the details of behavior consistency with multiple inheritance. We provide, however, two modeling guidelines for the realization of observation-consistent multiple inheritance. These guidelines simplify consistency checking under multiple inheritance but restrict the freedom of the modeler.

In order to avoid multiple inheritance, a modeler may choose to specialize only the leaf nodes of a class hierarchy. In this case, behavior consistency must only be checked against the life cycle model of the superclass in the inherited class hierarchy. This simplification, however, limits the freedom of the modeler and reduces flexibility. Thus, it is desirable to allow multiple inheritance for life cycle models.

Multiple inheritance with life cycle model specialization is non-conflicting if the specializations occur in parallel regions or independent states of the life cycle model. For example, the life cycle model of the AdvanceRental class refines the Opening state of the life cycle model of the Rental class (Figure 5.9). The PrivateRental class extends the life cycle model of the Rental class with a region that is parallel to the Opening state. These specializations are independent from each other. A combination of the two life cycle models in the PrivateAdvanceRental class's life cycle model is without problems.

6 XML Representation

The multilevel business artifact (MBA) allows for the artifact-centric representation of business processes at multiple levels of abstraction. Relying on a UML formalization, Chapters 4 and 5 as well as previous work [111, 114] focus on the conceptual modeling aspects of MBAs. Yet, the (semi-)automated MBA-based execution of artifact-centric business processes requires a suitable logical representation of conceptual MBA models. Many business process modeling languages are represented in or have a standardized serialization format based upon XML, for example, BPMN [89], WS-BPEL [84], and ActiveXML [7]. Therefore, when using an XML-based representation format for MBAs, an XML database may store MBAs without the need for developing a separate logical representation format for life cycle models as would be the case when storing MBAs in a relational database, for example. Moreover, due to its semi-structured nature, XML allows for a flexible handling of heterogeneities in the data model and is thus well-suited for the representation of hetero-homogeneous models. In this chapter, as a prerequisite for the development of an MBA-based execution environment for artifact-centric business processes, we define a logical representation of MBAs which is based on State Chart XML (SCXML), a W3C proposed recommendation [136] for an XML-based state machine language.

6.1 Multilevel Business Artifacts in XML

The XML schema for the representation of MBAs derives from the MBA metamodel in UML (see Chapters 4 and 5) and depends on the employed flavor of MBAs. A concretization hierarchy of MBAs with simple level hierarchies naturally translates into a nested collection of MBA elements in the XML-based logical model, with advantages for the formulation of queries over the concretization hierarchy. The introduction of parallel hierarchies, however, renders such nested collections of MBAs inadequate and requires a sequential representation of the MBAs in the concretization hierarchy. In this section, we first examine the logical representation of MBAs with simple hierarchies before discussing the representation of parallel hierarchies.

6.1.1 Simple Hierarchies

Each MBA in the conceptual business process model translates into an mba element in the XML-based logical model. Figure 6.1 illustrates, using a UML-like notation, an XML schema for the representation of MBAs. In this graphical notation, boxes denote XML elements, with the element's name in the first compartment and the element's attributes in the second. An attribute's data type may be one of the standard XML data types. Next to an attribute, in square brackets, a multiplicity of "1" denotes a mandatory, "0..1" an optional attribute. An outgoing, directed line from one element leading to another element, going through an octagon with three squares inside, denotes a sequence of child elements, the child element being the element that has arrowhead and multiplicity attached to its end of the line[1]. An mba element has a mandatory name attribute, an optional isDefault attribute – which is a prerequisite for invocation-consistent implementations – contains a topLevel element and, optionally, a concretizations element which stores the children of the MBA.

The restriction to simple hierarchies allows for the nested storage of a concretization hierarchy of MBAs in an XML document. XML naturally represents simple hierarchies, each element containing a number of children and each child element belonging to exactly one parent. The children of an mba element's concretizations child are full-fledged mba elements themselves, each describing an MBA from the conceptual model. The most abstract MBA in a concretization hierarchy becomes the root mba element of the XML document. All concretizations of the most abstract MBA become mba elements under the concretizations child of the root mba element. The concretizations of these concretizations are again mba elements under the concretizations child of the respective mba element, and so forth. Thus, when selecting an mba element from a nested collection of MBAs, the selected mba element contains all data related to a particular sub-hierarchy, with the selected MBA being the root of this sub-hierarchy.

The value of an mba element's name attribute is unique within a concretization hierarchy; there must not exist another mba element with the same name in the same concretization hierarchy. The topLevel child element of an mba element describes the MBA's top level. The elements child element of the topLevel element contains the data and life cycle models associated with the top level. Each data and life cycle model of an MBA

---

[1]This notation for sequences is similar to the XML schema visualization employed by tools such as Altova XMLSpy, Oxygen XML Developer, and Oracle JDeveloper.

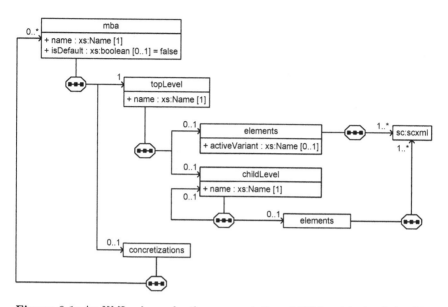

Figure 6.1: An XML schema for the representation of MBAs with simple level hierarchies. Note that the proposed elements are in the http://www.dke.jku.at/MBA namespace, except the imported sc:scxml element which belongs to the http://www.w3.org/2005/07/scxml namespace.

translates into an scxml element according to the SCXML standard. In the case of the existence of multiple variants, the optional activeVariant attribute of elements denotes the actually instantiated data and life cycle model. The value of the activeVariant attribute then refers to the value of the name attribute (not shown in Figure 6.1) of one of the scxml elements under the elements element.

The childLevel child of a topLevel element describes an MBA's second level. Just like the topLevel element, childLevel has an elements child containing data and and life cycle models for the particular level. Since an MBA instantiates only the data and life cycle models at the top level, the childLevel element lacks an activeVariant attribute. A childLevel element may again have a childLevel child which describes the child level of the respective level, and so forth.

Consider, for example, the mba element in Listing 6.1 with the value "Rental" for the name attribute which is the logical representation of an MBA Rental. This example follows the EU-Rent use case as described in

Listing 6.1: The logical representation of the level hierarchy of an MBA named Rental for the management of car rental data

```
1  ⊟<mba name="Rental"
2  │    xmlns="http://www.dke.jku.at/MBA"
3  │    xmlns:sc="http://www.w3.org/2005/07/scxml">
4  │  ⊟<topLevel name="business">
5  │  │  ⊞ <elements ...
6  │  │  ⊟<childLevel name="renterType">
7  │  │  │  ⊞ <elements ...
8  │  │  │  ⊟<childLevel name="rental">
9  │  │  │  │  ⊞ <elements ...
10 │  │  │  └ </childLevel>
11 │  │  └ </childLevel>
12 │  └ </topLevel>
13 │  ⊞ <concretizations ...
14 └ </mba>
```

previous chapters, although it adapts the running example for illustration purposes. Assume Rental is an MBA at the business level and the most abstract MBA in the concretization hierarchy. The top level of MBA Rental being business, the topLevel child of the mba element has value "business" for the name attribute (Line 4). As the child level of business, and thus second level in the hierarchy, assume MBA Rental defines the renterType level. The topLevel child in the logical representation of MBA Rental then has a childLevel element with the value "renterType" for the name attribute (Line 6). Furthermore, as child of renterType, assume MBA Rental defines the rental level. Consequently, the childLevel element with "renterType" as name has a childLevel child with value "rental" for the name attribute (Line 8). Under concretizations, the mba element with "Rental" as name stores representations of the direct concretizations of MBA Rental.

Assume MBAs Corporate and Private are at the renterType level and concretizations of MBA Rental. Assume further that MBA Corporate introduces the additional agreement level between renterType and rental. Then, MBA ACMEAgreement is at the agreement level and a concretization of MBA Corporate. Moreover, MBAs RentalTX1183 and RentalHX3006 are at the rental level and concretizations of MBA ACMEAgreement and thus indirect concretizations – or descendants – of MBA Corporate.

Listing 6.2: The logical representation of MBAs Corporate and Private as concretizations of Rental

```
1  ⊟ <mba name="Rental"
2       xmlns="http://www.dke.jku.at/MBA"
3       xmlns:sc="http://www.w3.org/2005/07/scxml">
4    ⊞ <topLevel name="business" ...
5    ⊟ <concretizations>
6      ⊟ <mba name="Corporate">
7        ⊟ <topLevel name="renterType">
8          ⊞ <elements ...
9          ⊟ <childLevel name="agreement">
10           ⊞ <elements ...
11           ⊟ <childLevel name="rental">
12             ⊞ <elements ...
13             └ </childLevel>
14           └ </childLevel>
15         └ </topLevel>
16       ⊞ <concretizations ...
17       └ </mba>
18     ⊟ <mba name="Private">
19       ⊟ <topLevel name="renterType">
20         ⊞ <elements ...
21         ⊟ <childLevel name="rental">
22           ⊞ <elements ...
23           └ </childLevel>
24         └ </topLevel>
25       ⊞ <concretizations ...
26       └ </mba>
27     └ </concretizations>
28   └ </mba>
```

Listing 6.2 shows the logical representation of the direct concretizations of MBA Rental. The mba element with "Rental" as name has a concretizations child (Line 5) which contains mba elements with values "Corporate" (Line 6) and "Private" (Line 18), respectively, for the name attribute. The topLevel child of the mba element with "Corporate" as name has a childLevel element with "agreement" as name (Line 9), the

Listing 6.3: The logical representation of a concretization hierarchy of MBAs for the management of car rental data with an MBA named Rental as root

```
 1 ⊟<mba name="Rental"
 2  |    xmlns="http://www.dke.jku.at/MBA"
 3  |    xmlns:sc="http://www.w3.org/2005/07/scxml">
 4  | ⊞ <topLevel name="business" ...
 5  | ⊟<concretizations>
 6  |   ⊟<mba name="Corporate">
 7  |   | ⊞ <topLevel name="renterType" ...
 8  |   | ⊟<concretizations>
 9  |   |   ⊟<mba name="ACMEAgreement">
10  |   |   | ⊟<topLevel name="agreement">
11  |   |   |   ⊞ <elements ...
12  |   |   |   ⊟<childLevel name="rental">
13  |   |   |   | ⊞ <elements ...
14  |   |   |   └</childLevel>
15  |   |   | └</topLevel>
16  |   |   | ⊟<concretizations>
17  |   |   |   ⊟<mba name="RentalTX1183">
18  |   |   |   | ⊟<topLevel name="rental">
19  |   |   |   |   ⊞ <elements ...
20  |   |   |   | └</topLevel>
21  |   |   |   └</mba>
22  |   |   | ⊞ <mba name="RentalHX3006" ...
23  |   |   └</concretizations>
24  |   | └</mba>
25  |   └</concretizations>
26  | └</mba>
27  | ⊟<mba name="Private">
28  |   ⊞ <topLevel name="renterType" ...
29  |   ⊞ <concretizations ...
30  | └</mba>
31  └</concretizations>
32 └</mba>
```

childLevel element of which has "rental" as name (Listing 6.2, Line 11).
On the other hand, the topLevel child of the mba element with "Private"
as name has a childLevel element with "rental" as name (Listing 6.2,
Line 21), just like the childLevel element with "renterType" as name
in the logical representation of MBA Rental in Listing 6.1. The logical
representation of an MBA's level hierarchy thus allows for the introduction
of a level through replacement of an inherited childLevel element with
the representation of the introduced level.

Listing 6.3 shows the logical representation of direct and transitive concretizations of MBA Corporate. The mba element with value "Corporate"
for the name attribute has a concretizations child that contains an
mba element with value "ACMEAgreement" for the name attribute (Line 9).
This mba element has a concretizations child (Line 16) that contains
mba elements with values "RentalTX1183" (Line 17) and "RentalHX3006"
(Line 22), respectively, for the name attribute. Possible concretizations of
MBA Private (Line 29) are omitted.

Assume now MBA Rental has a business-level life cycle model with two
states, namely Restructuring and Running, as well as methods reopen, restructure, and setMissionStatement. The invocation of the reopen method puts the
MBA into the Running state, the invocation of the restructure method puts
the MBA back into the Restructuring state. Furthermore, MBA Rental has a
missionStatement attribute at the business level. The setMissionStatement
method changes the value of the missionStatement attribute when invoked
in the Restructuring state.

Listing 6.4 shows the XML representation of the data and life cycle
model of the top level of MBA Rental. The topLevel child of the mba
element that represents MBA Rental in Listing 6.4 has an scxml element
which represents both data and life cycle model of this level. Under the
datamodel child (Listing 6.4, Line 7), a data element with the value
"missionStatement" for the id attribute (Listing 6.4, Line 8) represents
the missionStatement attribute, the existence of text contents for the data
element reflects the class/object duality at the MBA's top level. The state
elements with the values "Restructuring" (Listing 6.4, Line 17) and "Running"
(Listing 6.4, Line 27) for the id attribute represent the Restructuring and
Running state, respectively. The state element for the Restructuring state
has two transition children. The transition child with the value
"setMissionStatement" for the event attribute (Listing 6.4, Line 18) has no
target attribute, signifying that the transition triggers no state change.
The transition element, however, has an assign child (Listing 6.4,

Line 20) which is an SCXML action element that models assignment of
a value to an attribute as a consequence of a triggered transition. The
value "$missionStatement" of the assign element's location attribute
identifies as the target of the assignment the missionStatement attribute of
MBA Rental at the business level. The value of the expr attribute is an
XPath expression which identifies the value that is to be assigned to the
missionStatement attribute. For this expression to be evaluated properly, each
data element under the datamodel element becomes a variable with its
id as the name, for example, $missionStatement, and a system variable
$_event must hold the data that the user passed to the MBA along with
the latest event raised. The other transition child (Listing 6.4, Line 24)
with value "reopen" for the event attribute and the value "Running" for the
target attribute represents the transition between the states Restructuring
and Running triggered by the reopen method. The state element for the
Running state has a transition child (Listing 6.4, Line 28) with the value
"restructure" for the event attribute and the value "Restructuring" for the
target attribute which represents the transition between the states Running
and Restructuring triggered by the restructure method. The initial element
(Listing 6.4, Line 14) with its transition child establishes Restructuring
as the initial state.

The data elements that have an id starting with an underscore are
system variables used for SCXML interpretation [130, #SystemVariables[2]].
Only the top-level SCXML state machine of a particular MBA assigns values
to system variables. Consider, for example, the top-level SCXML state
machine in the logical representation of MBA Rental in Listing 6.5. The
data element with "_event" as id (Listing 6.5, Line 16) holds the name
and payload of the currently processed event. The data element with "_x"
as id holds platform-dependent system data which includes, in the case
of MBAs, the names of database and collection as well as the name of the
MBA itself. Each child element of this data element represents a platform-
dependent system variable, the children being in the empty namespace. The
db element (Listing 6.5, Line 10) holds the name of the XML database that
stores the MBA in the database management system. The collection
element (Listing 6.5, Line 11) holds the name of the collection that the
MBA belongs to, that is, the name of the MBA concretization hierarchy.
The mba element (Listing 6.5, Line 14) holds the name of the MBA itself.
The values of these system variables are accessible in the expressions used

---

[2]When citing W3C standards we refer to specific sections using named anchors from the
HTML documents, the names of which may be appended to the document URL.

Listing 6.4: The logical representation of the top-level data and life cycle model of MBA Rental

```
 1 <mba name="Rental"
 2       xmlns="http://www.dke.jku.at/MBA"
 3       xmlns:sc="http://www.w3.org/2005/07/scxml">
 4   <topLevel name="business">
 5     <elements>
 6       <sc:scxml>
 7         <sc:datamodel>
 8           <sc:data id="missionStatement">
 9             Renting cars
10           </sc:data>
11           <sc:data id="_x" ...
12           <sc:data id="_event" ...
13         </sc:datamodel>
14         <sc:initial>
15           <sc:transition target="Restructuring"/>
16         </sc:initial>
17         <sc:state id="Restructuring">
18           <sc:transition
19             event="setMissionStatement">
20             <sc:assign location="$missionStatement"
21               expr="$_event/data/missionStatement
22               /text()"/>
23           </sc:transition>
24           <sc:transition event="reopen"
25             target="Running"/>
26         </sc:state>
27         <sc:state id="Running">
28           <sc:transition event="restructure"
29             target="Restructuring"/>
30         </sc:state>
31       </sc:scxml>
32     </elements>
33     <childLevel ...
34   </topLevel>
35   <concretizations ...
36 </mba>
```

Listing 6.5: System variables in the logical representation of the top-level data model of MBA Rental

```
 1 ⊟<mba name="Rental"
 2        xmlns="http://www.dke.jku.at/MBA"
 3        xmlns:sc="http://www.w3.org/2005/07/scxml">
 4   ⊟<topLevel name="business">
 5     ⊟<elements>
 6       ⊟<sc:scxml>
 7         ⊟<sc:datamodel>
 8           ⊞<sc:data id="missionStatement" ...
 9           ⊟<sc:data id="_x">
10             ⊟<db xmlns="">myMBAse</db>
11             ⊟<collection xmlns="">
12                 CarRentals
13               └</collection>
14             ⊟<mba xmlns="">Rental</mba>
15             └</sc:data>
16           ⊟<sc:data id="_event">
17             ⊟<name xmlns="">
18                 setMissionStatement
19               └</name>
20             ⊟<data xmlns="">
21               ⊟<missionStatement>
22                   Moving people
23                 └</missionStatement>
24               └</data>
25             └</sc:data>
26           └</sc:datamodel>
27         ⊞<sc:initial ...
28         ⊞<sc:state id="Restructuring" ...
29         ⊞<sc:state id="Running" ...
30         └</sc:scxml>
31       └</elements>
32     ⊞<childLevel ...
33     └</topLevel>
34   ⊞<concretizations ...
35   └</mba>
```

as guard conditions and in the attributes of action elements; each `data` element becomes a variable with the `id` of the `data` element as variable name. The current event data are accessible under the `$_event` variable. The platform-dependent system variables are accessible as the children of the `$_x` variable.

A collection corresponds to a single concretization hierarchy. The collection is important for the unique identification of a concretization hierarchy in case that there are multiple concretization hierarchies having a root MBA with the same name. The attribution of a collection name to a concretization hierarchy should be managed by the MBA database and may be system-dependent. In case of simple hierarchies, the only requirement for the logical representation is the existence of a `collection` element under the `data` element for platform-dependent variables in the `datamodel` of the top-level SCXML state machine of an MBA. All MBAs that are in the same concretization hierarchy must assign the same value to this `collection` element; all MBAs that are in a different concretization hierarchy must have a different value.

The contents of the `data` element with value "_event" as `id` describe the event currently processed by the SCXML interpreter for that particular MBA. This description consists of the event's name and payload. The `name` child contains the name. The `data` child contains the payload, which can be an arbitrary sequence of XML elements. Note that in both cases, the child element is from the empty rather than the SCXML namespace. For example, the currently processed event for MBA Rental in Listing 6.5 has the name "setMissionStatement" (Line 17) and as payload a `missionStatement` element (Line 20) that contains the new value for the mission statement `data` element. When finished processing the event, the SCXML interpreter clears the contents of the `data` element with value "_event" as `id` and proceeds with the contents of the next event in the external event queue.

An `mba` element's optional `isDefault` attribute, with default value `false`, marks a possibly system-generated default MBA at a particular level which subsumes those MBAs that initially do not have an ancestor at the respective level. The existence of a default MBA at a particular level is important in order to allow for the introduction of additional levels in the course of concretization under the requirement of invocation consistency (see Section 6.3). Since the m-object metamodel does not allow skip levels, the introduction of a level requires the modification of concretization dependencies, unless there exists a default element for each level which the system may add newly created descendants to.

The XML schema in Figure 6.1 and the corresponding example XML documents assume full specification of MBAs and concretization hierarchies in the logical model, that is, each mba element contains both introduced and inherited data about an MBA's levels. The SCXML interpreter operates on the fully-specified mba elements. The full specification of MBAs in the logical model, however, redundantly stores inherited data, the first time in the MBA that introduces the data, and then again in the direct and indirect concretizations that inherit the data.

From a data management perspective, partial specification of MBAs and concretization hierarchies in the logical model may seem more convenient than full specification. In the spirit of database normalization, the partial specification of MBAs in the logical model avoids redundancies caused by the full specification of MBAs, which includes introduced and inherited data alike. The full specification then becomes a view over the partial specification. XML view maintenance is a separate topic [8] not covered in this book.

6.1.2 Parallel Hierarchies

The introduction of parallel hierarchies for the levels of MBAs renders inadequate the nested storage of MBAs in an XML document. Then, an MBA database consists of multiple collection documents, each collection document containing the MBAs of a single concretization hierarchy. Figure 6.2 illustrates an XML schema for the representation of MBAs with parallel hierarchies using the same UML-like notation as in the previous section. The root node of a collection document is the collection element which has a mandatory name attribute and contains a sequence of mba elements. A collection's name must be unique within a database, across the different collection documents. The value of the name attribute of an mba element must be unique within a collection document. All MBAs that are in the same concretization hierarchy must be in the same collection document. All MBAs that are in a different concretization hierarchy must be in a different collection document.

The levels child of an mba element contains an MBA's level definitions, referred to as level hierarchy and given as a sequence of level elements; an MBA must have at least one level. Each level has a unique name (attribute name) within the level hierarchy. The topLevel attribute of an mba element references the name attribute of a level element under the levels child of the mba element. A level element further consists of an elements child and a parentLevels child, both being optional. These child elements

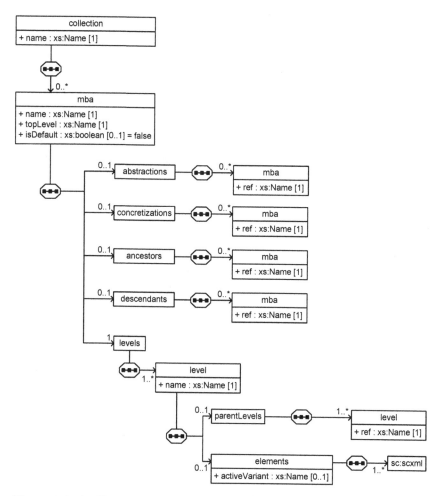

Figure 6.2: An XML schema for the representation of MBAs with parallel level hierarchies. Note that the proposed elements are in the http://www.dke.jku.at/MBA namespace, except the imported sc:scxml element which belongs to the http://www.w3.org/2005/07/scxml namespace.

form the level definition. The `elements` child consists of a number of `scxml` elements, which represent the data and life cycle models of the level. The `parentLevels` child establishes the hierarchical order of the levels and consists of a sequence of `level` elements with a `ref` attribute which refers to another level in the same hierarchy. The representation of an MBA's top level must not have a `parentLevels` child. Across MBAs of the same collection, levels with the same name are considered equal, possibly having different definitions, which must be consistent according to the rules of concretization for MBAs (see Chapter 4).

In the case of parallel hierarchies, the representation of concretization relationships between a collection's MBAs cannot follow the natural hierarchy of XML elements; two different forms of representation are conceivable. First, an MBA may keep an `abstractions` element with a sequence of `mba` elements having a `ref` attribute which refers to the `name` attribute of another MBA in the same collection. Each of these `mba` elements refers to an abstraction. Second, an MBA may keep a `concretizations` element with a sequence of `mba` elements having a `ref` attribute which refers to the `name` attribute of another MBA in the collection, just like the `abstractions` element, only that each of these `mba` elements refers to a concretization. Both solutions have their own drawback: Whereas the former performs well on upward navigation, the latter presents advantages for downward navigation. Large MBA collections should therefore employ both solutions simultaneously, with one being a view of the other, in order to speed up navigation along the concretization hierarchy. In such a case, using the `abstractions` element as the primary form of representation of concretization relationships and defining the `concretizations` element as a view over `abstractions` is advantageous. In the course of concretization, when using the `abstractions` element as the primary representation, the `mba` element that represents the more abstract MBA must not be altered. In addition, the logical representation of an MBA may also keep, for convenience and performance reasons, an `ancestors` and a `descendants` element as additional (materialized) views.

Modelers must handle the pitfalls of multiple concretization in the conceptual model. A direct translation of a correct conceptual model into a logical representation avoids problems at the logical level associated with multiple inheritance of life cycle models. Possible XQuery implementations of MBA reflective functions, on the other hand, will give rise to the same issues concerning multiple inheritance as encountered in conceptual modeling, and necessitates the implementation of consistency checks.

6.2 Multilevel Relationships in XML

The XML representation of MBA relationships derives from the representation of individual MBAs. MBA relationships are organized in a relationship space which defines the dimensionality of the contained relationships, that is, a set of MBA collections which contain the MBAs that are connected by the MBA relationships in the relationship space. The relationship space stores the MBA relationships, represented as mbaRelationship elements. Such an mbaRelationship element has a schema similar to the mba element's. Instead of a name attribute, an mbaRelationship has a label attribute and a coordinates child. The label attribute is a string that defines the label of the MBA relationship. The coordinates element has a child for each collection of the MBA relationship space, the node name of this child element corresponds to the name of the collection, the value corresponds to the name of an MBA from that collection. Assume the existence of collections named "renter" and "commodity", the former containing an MBA Rental, the latter containing an MBA Car. Assume further the existence of a corresponding relationship space. The following coordinates element then characterizes a relationship between MBAs Rental and Car:

```
<coordinates>
  <renter>Rental</renter>
  <commodity>Car</commodity>
<coordinates>
```

The levels of an MBA relationship are not atomic. Instead of a name attribute, relationship levels have a relationshipLevelId element. Such a relationship level identifier references an atomic level from each coordinate of the relationship. To this end, a relationshipLevelId element has a child for each collection of the relationship space, the node name of this child element corresponds to the name of the collection, the value corresponds to the name of a level from the connected MBA in the respective collection. Consider, for example, the following relationshipLevelId element for the logical representation of relationship level ⟨ renterType, model ⟩ of a relationship between MBAs Rental and Car:

```
<relationshipLevelId>
  <renter>renterType</renter>
  <commodity>model</commodity>
</relationshipLevelId>
```

From a semantics point of view, the use of collection names as the names of the child elements leads to more expressive data models compared to generic elements. Even though the node names of the children of coordinates and relationship level identifiers are application-dependent and not necessarily known at programming time, programmers may still write generic queries by using the standard `fn:local-name()` function for expressing select conditions in XPath expressions.

Since the hierarchical order of MBA relationships and relationship levels derives from the coordinate MBAs and atomic levels, the explicit storage of this information, in general, is not necessary. In order to avoid frequent, rather costly calculations of the hierarchical order of MBA relationships, the MBA database may store a pre-computed list of an MBA relationship's ancestors and descendants. These pre-computed lists of ancestor and descendant relationships may be stored in a fashion similar to the materialization of ancestors and descendants of an MBA with parallel hierarchies (see Section 6.1.2).

6.3 Multilevel Predicates in State Chart XML

In the conceptual artifact-centric business process model, multilevel predicates allow for expressing synchronization dependencies between different abstraction levels of an MBA. A multilevel predicate as part of the precondition of a transition in the conceptual model translates into an invocation of a corresponding boolean XQuery function as part of the transition's guard expression in the logical representation. A multilevel predicate as part of the post-condition of a transition in the conceptual model translates into the corresponding SCXML custom action element in the logical representation. The SCXML interpreter then conducts the operation that corresponds to a particular custom action element.

Dedicated XQuery functions allow for expressing transition guard conditions over ancestors and descendants of the MBA in the context of which the state machine is interpreted. Tables 6.1 and 6.2 define XQuery functions for vertical level synchronization over states and attributes, respectively. The SCXML interpreter must evaluate these functions in the context of the particular MBA that the state machine is interpreted for; the $mba variable in the definition of the functions represents this context MBA. Therefore, the value of the $mba variable is not passed to the functions as an argument but provided by the SCXML interpreter.

The cond attribute of a transition contains an XQuery expression which the SCXML interpreter evaluates at run-time in order to determine whether a transition shall be triggered. The XQuery functions in Tables 6.1 and 6.2 are available as *inline functions* for use in the cond attribute of transitions, hence the "$" in front of their name. The definition as inline function allows for the context-specific provision of the $mba variable by the SCXML interpreter, transparent to the designer. Consider, for example, the following transition with a guard condition that contains a function call for the vertical synchronization over the attribute value of an ancestor:

```
<sc:transition event="setRate"
  cond="$_ancestorAtLevelSatisfies(
   'renterType',
   '$maximumRate >= ' || $_event/data/rate/text()
  )"
/>
```

Conceptually, a setRate method call triggers the previously defined transition under the condition that the ancestor at the renterType level has an attribute value for maximumRate that is greater or equal to the argument rate passed to the setRate method. For the evaluation of the expression in the cond attribute of a transition, the contents of each data element in one of the available datamodel elements of the state machine execution are bound to a variable bearing the identifier of the respective data element. In the previously defined transition, the expression in the cond attribute refers to the data element with value "_event" as id in the data model of the MBA that the SCXML interpreter executes the state machine of. Note that $maximumRate refers to the value of an ancestor's data element as it is under single quotes and evaluated dynamically when executing the $_ancestorAtLevelSatisfies function.

The SCXML interpreter does not independently, without context, evaluate the expression in the cond attribute of a transition element. Rather, the SCXML interpreter evaluates a FLWOR expression with additional bindings, the result of the expression from the cond attribute being the final return value. The FLWOR expression provides context information for the evaluation of the expression in the cond attribute. Thus, in the course of the state machine execution for a particular MBA, when evaluating the expression in the cond attribute of the previously defined example transition element, the SCXML interpreter must execute XQuery code equivalent to the following:

```
let $mba :=
mba:getMBA($_x/db, $_x/collection, $_x/mba)
let $_ancestorAtLevelSatisfies :=
 function($level as xs:string, $cond as xs:string) {
  let $ancestor :=
   mba:getAncestorAtLevel($mba, $level)
  let $dataModels :=
   sc:selectDataModels(mba:getConfiguration($ancestor))
  return sc:eval($cond, $dataModels)
 }
return $_ancestorAtLevelSatisfies(
 'renterType',
 '$maximumRate >= ' || $_event/data/rate/text()
)
```

The definitions of the XQuery functions for vertical synchronization make use of auxiliary functions for the management of MBA databases. An XQuery module in the MBA namespace, prefixed "mba", organizes these management functions. In this module, the getMBA function retrieves an mba element from the database, using the name of the collection and the name of the MBA as identifier. The getAncestorAtLevel function returns an mba element that represents the ancestor at the argument level of the argument MBA, the argument level being referred to by name, the argument MBA being passed as the corresponding mba element from the database. Similarly, the getDescendantsAtLevel function returns a sequence of mba elements, each representing a descendant at the argument level of the argument MBA. The getConfiguration function retrieves the currently active states of the argument MBA, that is, the current status of the argument MBA's top-level SCXML state machine, the argument MBA passed as the mba element from the database.

Besides the MBA management functions, the definitions of the XQuery functions for vertical synchronization make use of (non-standard) functions for the interpretation of SCXML state machines. An XQuery module in the SCXML namespace, prefixed "sc", organizes the functions of the SCXML interpreter. In this module, the selectDataModels function retrieves the currently valid datamodel elements of an SCXML state machine given the state machine's current configuration, that is, the set of active states. The eval function dynamically evaluates an XQuery expression, passed as string, taking into account a set of argument datamodel elements.

Table 6.1: Functions for vertical synchronization over attributes

function	`$_everyDescendantAtLevelSatisfies`
param	`$level as xs:string, $cond as xs:string`

define	`let $descendants :=`
	`mba:getDescendantsAtLevel($mba, $level)`
	`return every $descendant in $descendants`
	`satisfies`
	`  let $dataModels :=`
	`   sc:selectDataModels(`
	`    mba:getConfiguration($descendant)`
	`   )`
	`  return sc:eval($cond, $dataModels)`

function	`$_someDescendantAtLevelSatisfies`
param	`$level as xs:string, $cond as xs:string`

define	`let $descendants :=`
	`mba:getDescendantsAtLevel($mba, $level)`
	`return some $descendant in $descendants`
	`satisfies`
	`  let $dataModels :=`
	`   sc:selectDataModels(`
	`    mba:getConfiguration($descendant)`
	`   )`
	`  return sc:eval($cond, $dataModels)`

function	`$_isDescendantAtLevelSatisfying`
param	`$obj as element(), $level as xs:string,` `$cond as xs:string`

define	`let $descendants :=`
	`mba:getDescendantsAtLevel($mba, $level)`
	`let $dataModels :=`
	`  sc:selectDataModels(`
	`   mba:getConfiguration($obj)`
	`  )`
	`return sc:eval($cond, $dataModels) and (`
	`  some $descendant in $descendants`
	`   satisfies $obj is $descendant`
	`)`

(continues on next page)

Table 6.1 (continued): Functions for vertical attribute synchronization

function	`$_ancestorAtLevelSatisfies`
param	`$level as xs:string, $cond as xs:string`
define	`let $ancestor :=`
	`  mba:getAncestorAtLevel($mba, $level)`
	`let $dataModels :=`
	`  sc:selectDataModels(`
	`    mba:getConfiguration($ancestor)`
	`  )`
	`return sc:eval($cond, $dataModels)`

function	`$_isAncestorAtLevelSatisfying`
param	`$obj as element(), $level as xs:string,`
	`$cond as xs:string`
define	`let $ancestor :=`
	`  mba:getAncestorAtLevel($mba, $level)`
	`let $dataModels :=`
	`  sc:selectDataModels(`
	`    mba:getConfiguration($obj)`
	`  )`
	`return sc:eval($cond, $dataModels) and`
	`  $ancestor is $obj`

Table 6.1 defines XQuery functions for expressing pre-conditions over attributes of an MBA's ancestors and descendants. Both the `$_every-DescendantAtLevelSatisfies` function and the `$_someDescendant-AtLevelSatisfies` function take a level name and an expression string as arguments, and dynamically evaluate the expression over currently valid top-level `datamodel` elements of each descendant at the argument level. The former function returns true if the argument expression evaluates to true for every descendant at given level, the latter returns true if the expression evaluates to true for at least one descendant. The `$_isDescendantAt-LevelSatisfying` function, in addition, takes an `mba` element as argument, and returns true if the argument `mba` element is descendant at given level and the argument expression evaluates to true for this descendant. The `$_ancestorAtLevelSatisfies` function evaluates an argument expression over an ancestor. The `$_isAncestorAtLevelSatisfying` function takes an `mba` element as argument which must be the ancestor at the given level and the argument expression must evaluate to true for this ancestor.

Table 6.2: Functions for vertical synchronization over states

function	`$_everyDescendantAtLevelIsInState`
param	`$level as xs:string, $stateId as xs:string`

define	`let $descendants :=`
	`  mba:getDescendantsAtLevel($mba, $level)`
	`return every $descendant in $descendants`
	`satisfies`
	`  mba:isInState($descendant, $stateId)`

function	`$_everyDescendantAtLevelInStateSatisfies`
param	`$level as xs:string, $stateId as xs:string,` `$cond as xs:string`

define	`let $descendants :=`
	`  mba:getDescendantsAtLevel($mba, $level)`
	`let $descendantsInState :=`
	`  $descendants[mba:isInState(., $stateId)]`
	`return every $desc in $descendantsInState`
	`satisfies`
	`  let $dataModels := sc:selectDataModels(`
	`   mba:getConfiguration($desc)`
	`  )`
	`  return sc:eval($cond, $dataModels)`

function	`$_everyDescendantAtLevelSatisfyingIsInState`
param	`$level as xs:string, $cond as xs:string,` `$stateId as xs:string`

define	`let $descendants :=`
	`  mba:getDescendantsAtLevel($mba, $level)`
	`let $descendantsSatisfying :=`
	`  $descendants[sc:eval(`
	`   $cond,`
	`   sc:selectDataModels(`
	`    mba:getConfiguration(.)`
	`   )`
	`  )]`
	`return every $desc in $descendantsSatisfying`
	`satisfies`
	`  mba:isInState($desc, $stateId)`

(continues on next page)

Table 6.2 (continued): Functions for vertical state synchronization

function	`$_someDescendantAtLevelIsInState`
param	`$level as xs:string, $stateId as xs:string`

define	`let $descendants :=`
	`  mba:getDescendantsAtLevel($mba, $level)`
	`return`
	` some $descendant in $descendants`
	` satisfies`
	`   mba:isInState($descendant, $stateId)`

function	`$_someDescendantAtLevelInStateSatisfies`
param	`$level as xs:string, $stateId as xs:string,` `$cond as xs:string`

define	`let $descendants :=`
	`  mba:getDescendantsAtLevel($mba, $level)`
	`let $descendantsInState :=`
	` $descendants[`
	`  mba:isInState(., $stateId)`
	` ]`
	`return`
	` some $desc in $descendantsInState`
	`  satisfies`
	`    let $dataModels :=`
	`     sc:selectDataModels(`
	`      mba:getConfiguration($desc)`
	`     )`
	`     return sc:eval($cond, $dataModels)`

function	`$_isDescendantAtLevelInState`
param	`$obj as element(), $level as xs:string,` `$stateId as xs:string`

define	`let $descendants :=`
	`  mba:getDescendantsAtLevel($mba, $level)`
	`return (`
	` some $desc in $descendants`
	` satisfies $desc is $obj`
	`) and`
	`mba:isInState($obj, $stateId)`

(continues on next page)

Table 6.2 (continued): Functions for vertical state synchronization

function	`$_isDescendantAtLevelInStateSatisfying`
param	`$obj as element(), $level as xs:string,`
	`$stateId as xs:string, $cond as xs:string`
define	`let $descendants :=`
	`mba:getDescendantsAtLevel($mba, $level)`
	`let $dataModels :=`
	`sc:selectDataModels(`
	`mba:getConfiguration($obj)`
	`)`
	`return (some $desc in $descendants`
	`satisfies $desc is $obj`
	`) and mba:isInState($obj, $stateId)`
	`and sc:eval($cond, $dataModels)`
function	`$_ancestorAtLevelIsInState`
param	`$level as xs:string, $stateId as xs:string`
define	`let $ancestor :=`
	`mba:getAncestorAtLevel($mba, $level)`
	`return mba:isInState($ancestor, $stateId)`
function	`$_ancestorAtLevelIsInStateAndSatisfies`
param	`$level as xs:string, $stateId as xs:string,`
	`$cond as xs:string`
define	`let $ancestor :=`
	`mba:getAncestorAtLevel($mba, $level)`
	`let $dataModels := sc:selectDataModels(`
	`mba:getConfiguration($ancestor)`
	`)`
	`return mba:isInState($ancestor, $stateId)`
	`and sc:eval($cond, $dataModels)`
function	`$_isAncestorAtLevelInState`
param	`$obj as element(), $level as xs:string,`
	`$stateId as xs:string`
define	`let $ancestor :=`
	`mba:getAncestorAtLevel($mba, $level)`
	`return $ancestor is $obj and`
	`mba:isInState($obj, $stateId)`

(continues on next page)

Table 6.2 (continued): Functions for vertical state synchronization

function	`$_isAncestorAtLevelInStateSatisfying`
param	`$obj as element(), $level as xs:string,`
	`$stateId as xs:string, $cond as xs:string`
define	`let $ancestor :=`
	`mba:getAncestorAtLevel($mba, $level)`
	`let $dataModels :=`
	`sc:selectDataModels(`
	`mba:getConfiguration($obj)`
	`)`
	`return $ancestor is $obj`
	`and mba:isInState($obj, $stateId)`
	`and sc:eval($cond, $dataModels)`

Note that the mba elements in the synchronization functions are compared based on *node identity* according to the XPath data model [135, #node-identity]. Each node in an XML document has an implicit identifier, similar to an object identifier in object-oriented systems. The getMBA, getDescendantsAtLevel, and getAncestorAtLevel functions retrieve mba elements from the database which preserve their node identity. Thus, when passing an mba element to the $_isDescendantAtLevel-Satisfying and the $_isAncestorAtLevelSatisfying functions for comparison, the argument mba element must have been retrieved from the database and not be a copy with a new identity.

Table 6.2 defines XQuery functions for expressing pre-conditions over the active states of ancestors and descendants of an MBA. The definitions of these functions make use of the isInState function from the MBA namespace which takes an mba element and a state identifier as arguments, and returns true if the argument MBA is in the given state. One group of functions allows for state synchronization with the ancestor, the other for state synchronization with the descendants at a particular level; there are several variants for each group of functions. The $_everyDescendant-AtLevelIsInState function takes a level name and a state identifier as arguments, and returns true if every descendant at the argument level is in the argument state. Similarly, the $_someDescendantAtLevelIsIn-State function returns true if some descendant at a specified argument level is in the specified argument state. The $_ancestorAtLevelIsIn-

State function, on the other hand, returns true if the ancestor at a specified argument level is in the specified argument state.

Other state synchronization functions in Table 6.2 allow for the specification of an additional condition that must be satisfied by the ancestors and descendants at the respective levels, similar to the attribute synchronization functions. The $_everyDescendantAtLevelInStateSatisfies function returns true if every descendant at the argument level that is in the argument state satisfies the given condition. The $_everyDescendantAt-LevelSatisfyingIsInState function, on the other hand, returns true if every descendant at the argument level that satisfies the given argument condition is in the given argument state. The $_someDescendantAt-LevelInStateSatisfies function returns true if some descendant at the argument level is in the argument state and satisfies the given condition. Similarly, the $_ancestorAtLevelIsInStateAndSatisfies function returns true if the ancestor at the argument level is in the argument state and satisfies the given condition.

Similar to the corresponding functions for attribute synchronization, Table 6.2 defines state synchronization functions which check whether a particular MBA is an ancestor or descendant at a particular level in a given state. The $_isDescendantAtLevelInState function takes an mba element as argument which must be a descendant at an argument level and currently be in an argument state in order for the function to return true; the $_isDescendantAtLevelInStateSatisfying function takes an additional condition which the descendant must satisfy in order for the function to return true. Similarly, the $_isAncestorAtLevelInState function takes an mba element as argument which must be ancestor at a given level and in an argument state in order for the function to return true; the $_isAncestorAtLevelInStateSatisfying function takes an additional condition which the ancestor must satisfy.

Assume the existence of an MBA Rental with the business level as the top level in the level hierarchy. Conceptually, at the rental level, MBA Rental defines a rate and a duration attribute; the life cycle model consists of the states Opening, Open, Settling, and Closed. At the renterType level, MBA Rental defines a maximumRate and a maximumDuration attribute; the life cycle model consists of the states InDevelopment, OnOffer, Canceled, and Discontinued. Between the life cycle models of these different abstraction levels there exist several synchronization dependencies; the logical representation of MBA Rental in Listings 6.6-6.8 emphasizes these multilevel synchronization dependencies.

Listing 6.6: The logical representation of the rental-level data and life cycle model of MBA Rental with an emphasis on multilevel synchronization

```
 1  ⊟<mba name="Rental" ⊞xmlns=...>
 2   ⊟<topLevel name="business">
 3    ⊞ <elements ...
 4    ⊟<childLevel name="renterType">
 5     ⊞ <elements ...
 6     ⊟<childLevel name="rental">
 7      ⊟<elements>
 8       ⊟<sc:scxml>
 9        ⊟<sc:datamodel>
10         ⊟<sc:data id="rate"/>
11         ⊟<sc:data id="duration"/>
12         └</sc:datamodel>
13        ⊞ <sc:initial ...
14        ⊟<sc:state id="Opening">
15         ⊟<sc:transition event="setRate"
16             cond="$_ancestorAtLevelSatisfies(
17              'renterType',
18              '$maximumRate >= ' ||
19              $_event/data/rate/text()
20             )"/>
21          ⊟<sc:assign location="$rate"
22              expr="$_event/data/rate/text()"/>
23          └</sc:transition>
24         ⊞ <sc:transition event="setDuration" ...
25         ⊞ <sc:transition event="pickUp" ...
26         └</sc:state>
27        ⊞ <sc:state id="Open" ...
28        ⊞ <sc:state id="Settling" ...
29        ⊟<sc:state id="Closed"/>
30        └</sc:scxml>
31       └</elements>
32      └</childLevel>
33     └</childLevel>
34    └</topLevel>
35   ⊞ <concretizations ...
36  └</mba>
```

The logical representation of MBA Rental contains, at the rental level (Listing 6.6), an `assign` element under a `transition` element with value "setRate" for the `event` attribute (Line 21) represents the assignment of a value to the rate attribute by event occurrences of setRate. The `transition` element with value "setRate" for the `event` attribute (Line 15) defines an additional guard condition in the `cond` attribute over an attribute value of the respective ancestor at the renterType level. This `transition` element makes use of the `$_ancestorAtLevelSatisfies` function, thereby expressing the condition that the transition requires the ancestor's maximum-Rate attribute to be greater or equal than the value passed as event payload. The SCXML interpreter dynamically evaluates the expression over the ancestor's `datamodel` elements, with the `$maximumRate` variable referring to a `data` element with value "maximumRate" as `id` in the ancestor's `datamodel` and the value in the event payload fixed in the argument string before calling the synchronization function. Analogously, the `transition` element with value "setDuration" for the `event` attribute (Line 24) may have a guard condition that expresses the condition that the ancestor MBA's maximumDuration attribute must be greater or equal to the value passed as argument to the setDuration method which triggers the transition.

The logical representation of MBA Rental contains, at the renterType level (Listing 6.7), an `assign` element under a `transition` element with value "setMaximumDuration" for the `event` attribute (Line 14) which represents the assignment of a value to the maximumDuration attribute by event occurrences of setMaximumDuration. The `transition` element makes use of the `$_everyDescendantAtLevelInStateSatisfies` function to express the condition that, in order for the transition to assign a new value to the maximumDuration attribute, the argument value passed as the new maximum duration must be greater or equal to the value of the duration attribute of every descendant at the rental level that is in the Open state. Consider, for example, an event occurrence of setMaximumDuration to assign the value "60" to maximumDuration, which according to the logical model causes an execution of the `$_everyDescendantAtLevelInStateSatisfies` function in the course of the evaluation of the guard condition. The XPath expression `$_event/data/maximumDuration/text()` evaluates to "60". Then, for every descendant MBA in the Open state, using the `datamodel` elements valid in the currently active states of each descendant, the SCXML interpreter dynamically evaluates the expression $60 >= \$duration$, with the `$duration` variable referring to the value of the `data` element with value "duration" as `id` from the descendant's top-level data models.

Listing 6.7: The logical representation of the renterType-level data and life cycle model of MBA Rental with an emphasis on multilevel synchronization – Part 1

```
 1 ⊟<mba name="Rental" ⊞xmlns=...>
 2   ⊟<topLevel name="business">
 3     ⊞<elements ...
 4     ⊟<childLevel name="renterType">
 5       ⊟<elements>
 6         ⊟<sc:scxml>
 7           ⊟<sc:datamodel>
 8             ⊟<sc:data id="maximumRate"/>
 9             ⊟<sc:data id="maximumDuration"/>
10           └</sc:datamodel>
11           ⊞<sc:initial ...
12           ⊟<sc:state id="InDevelopment">
13             ⊞<sc:transition event="setMaximumRate" ...
14             ⊟<sc:transition event="setMaximumDuration"
15                 cond="$_everyDescendantAtLevelIn-
16                 StateSatisfies('rental', 'Open',
17                 $_event/data/maximumDuration/text()
18                 || ' >= $duration'
19                 )">
20               ⊞<sc:assign location="$maximumDurat ...
21             └</sc:transition>
22             ⊟<sc:transition event="launch"
23                 target="OnOffer"
24                 cond="$_ancestorAtLevelIsInState(
25                 'business', 'Running'
26                 )"/>
27           └</sc:state>
28           ⊞<sc:state id="OnOffer" ...
29           ⊞...
30         └</sc:scxml>
31       └</elements>
32       ⊞<childLevel name="rental" ...
33     └</childLevel>
34   └</topLevel>
35   ⊞<concretizations ...
36 └</mba>
```

Listing 6.8: The logical representation of the renterType-level data and life cycle model of MBA Rental with an emphasis on multilevel synchronization – Part 2

```
1  ⊟<mba name="Rental" ⊞ xmlns=...>
2   ⊟<topLevel name="business">
3    ⊞<elements ...
4    ⊟<childLevel name="renterType">
5     ⊟<elements>
6      ⊟<sc:scxml>
7       ⊟<sc:datamodel>
8        ⊟<sc:data id="maximumRate"/>
9        ⊟<sc:data id="maximumDuration"/>
10       └</sc:datamodel>
11      ⊟<sc:initial>
12       ⊟<sc:transition target="InDevelopment"/>
13       └</sc:initial>
14      ⊞<sc:state id="InDevelopment" ...
15      ⊟<sc:state id="OnOffer">
16       ⊟<sc:transition event="cancel"
17          target="Canceled"/>
18       └</sc:state>
19      ⊟<sc:state id="Canceled">
20       ⊟<sc:transition event="discontinue"
21          target="Discontinued"
22          cond="$_everyDescendantAtLevel-
23           IsInState('rental', 'Closed')
24          "/>
25       └</sc:state>
26      ⊟<sc:state id="Discontinued"/>
27      └</sc:scxml>
28     └</elements>
29    ⊞<childLevel name="rental" ...
30    └</childLevel>
31   └</topLevel>
32  ⊞<concretizations ...
33 └</mba>
```

The logical representation of MBA Rental, at the renterType level (Listings 6.7 and 6.8), also contains transition elements with values "launch" and "discontinue" for the event attribute which represent transitions from the InDevelopment to the OnOffer state and from the Canceled to the Discontinued state, respectively. These transition elements make use of the $_ancestorAtLevelIsInState and $_everyDescendantAtLevelIsInState function, respectively, for multilevel synchronization over states. The guard condition of the transition element with value "launch" for the event attribute (Listing 6.7, Line 22) represents the pre-condition that the ancestor MBA at the business level must be in the Running state in order for the transition to be followed. The guard condition of the transition element with value "discontinue" for the event attribute (Listing 6.8, Line 20) represents the pre-condition that every descendant MBA at the rental level must be in the Closed state in order for the transition to be followed.

Custom action elements allow for the manipulation of ancestors and descendants in the course of a transition between states; they are the SCXML equivalent to multilevel predicates from the conceptual model used in transition post-conditions. Tables 6.3-6.8 define attributes and children of these custom action elements for multilevel synchronization. Several of these custom action elements derive from standard SCXML action elements for modeling executable content [130, #executable], namely those for the assignment of attribute values for and the sending of messages to ancestor and descendant MBAs at a particular level.

The assignAncestor action element signalizes the assignment of a given value to a particular attribute of an ancestor MBA at some abstraction level. Table 6.3 defines the attributes and children of the assignAncestor element. The mandatory level attribute contains the name of the level that the data manipulation concerns. The other features of the assignAncestor element derive from the SCXML assign element [130, #assign]. The mandatory location attribute contains an XPath expression that specifies the location in the SCXML datamodel that is to be manipulated. The optional expr attribute contains an XQuery expression that returns the value that is to be assigned to the specified location. As an alternative to the expr attribute, the children of the assignAncestor element may constitute the value that is to be assigned; either variant is permissible for the specification of the value, but not both. The type attribute determines the type of the manipulation operation to be performed (see [130, #assign_xpath]). If, and only if, the type of operation is "addattribute", the attr attribute contains the name of the attribute that is to be added.

Table 6.3: Action element for the manipulation of an ancestor's data model

<assignAncestor>

ATTRIBUTE	TYPE	DESCRIPTION
level	xs:Name	Defines the level of the ancestor that is to be manipulated.
location	Path expression	Specifies the location in the data model that is to be manipulated. See SCXML [130, #LocationExpressions].
expr	Value expression	Optionally determines the value that is to be assigned. See SCXML [130, #ValueExpressions].
type	enumeration	Optionally specifies the type of data manipulation to be performed. See SCXML [130, #xpath_assign].
attribute	xs:Name	Optionally specifies the name of the attribute that is to be inserted in case the type of assignment operation is "addattribute". See SCXML [130, #xpath_assign].

CHILDREN

A sequence of XML nodes to be assigned to the specified location in the data model of the newly created descendant. The assignAncestor element must not have any children when the expr attribute occurs. See SCXML [130, #assign].

The sendAncestor action element signalizes the sending of a given event to an ancestor at a particular level. Table 6.4 defines the attributes and children of the sendAncestor element. The mandatory level element contains the name of the level that the target ancestor MBA is defined at. The other features of the sendAncestor element derive from the SCXML send element [130, #send], though, in order to focus on the core aspects of multilevel business processes, the sendAncestor element as described here omits most attributes of the standard send element. Optionally, an event has a payload attached, which in the logical model is the equivalent to the parameters of a method in the conceptual model. Most directly,

Table 6.4: Action element for sending an external event to an ancestor

`<sendAncestor>`

ATTRIBUTE	TYPE	DESCRIPTION
level	xs:Name	Defines the level of the ancestor.
event	EventType.datatype	Specifies the name of the event that is to be sent to the ancestor.

CHILDREN	
`<sc:param>`	Allows for the definition of key/value pairs that are passed to the descendant as event payload. Occurs 0 or more times. See SCXML [130, #param].
`<sc:content>`	Alternatively, the event payload may be specified as a sequence of XML nodes. Must not occur together with `<sc:param>`. Occurs 0 or 1 times. See SCXML [130, #content].

this equivalence surfaces when a sequence of SCXML `param` elements as the children of a `sendAncestor` element describes the event payload. As an alternative, the `sendAncestor` element may have a single SCXML `content` child element which contains the event payload either as a sequence of arbitrary child elements or describes the event payload stating an XQuery expression in the `expr` attribute [130, #content].

The `assignDescendants` element (Table 6.5) as well as the `send-Descendants` element (Table 6.6) are similar to the `assignAncestor` and `sendAncestor` element, respectively. Rather than manipulating an ancestor's `datamodel` or sending an event to an ancestor, the `assign-Descendants` element and the `sendDescendants` element affect the descendants at a particular level. The optional `state` attribute contains a state identifer; value assignment applies to every descendant in this state. The optional `satisfying` attribute allows for a further restriction of the considered descendants by specifying a boolean XQuery expression that every descendant must satisfy in order to be affected by the action.

The `newDescendant` custom action element signalizes the creation of a new descendant at a given level. Table 6.7 defines the attributes and children of the `newDescendant` element. The mandatory `level` attribute contains the name of the level at which to create the descendant. A value expression

Table 6.5: Action element for the manipulation of descendants' data models

<assignDescendants>

ATTRIBUTE	TYPE	DESCRIPTION
level	xs:Name	Defines the level of the descendants that are to be manipulated.
state	xs:Name	Optionally defines a state that a descendant must be in for the manipulation to take place.
satisfying	Value expression	Optionally defines a condition that a descendant must satisfy for the manipulation to take place.
location	Path expression	Specifies the location in the data model that is to be manipulated. See SCXML [130, #LocationExpressions].
expr	Value expression	Optionally determines the value that is to be assigned. See SCXML [130, #ValueExpressions].
type	enumeration	Optionally specifies the type of data manipulation to be performed. See SCXML [130, #xpath_assign].
attribute	xs:Name	Optionally specifies the name of the attribute that is to be inserted in case the type of assignment operation is "addattribute". See SCXML [130, #xpath_assign].

CHILDREN

A sequence of XML nodes to be assigned to the specified location in the data model of the newly created descendant. The assignDescendants element must not have any children when the expr attribute occurs. See SCXML [130, #assign].

in the optional name attribute determines the name of the descendant that is to be created. There must not exist another MBA with the same name in the concretization hierarchy. The optional parents attribute determines the names of the new MBA's parents, which is important for level introduction.

Table 6.6: Action element for sending an external event to descendants

`<sendDescendants>`

ATTRIBUTE	TYPE	DESCRIPTION
level	xs:Name	Defines the level of the descendants.
state	xs:Name	Optionally defines the state that a descendant must be in for the event to be sent.
satisfying	Value expression	Optionally defines a condition that a descendant must satisfy for the event to be sent.
event	EventType.datatype	Specifies the name of the event that is to be sent to the descendants.

CHILDREN	
`<sc:param>`	Allows for the definition of key/value pairs that are passed to the descendant as event payload. Occurs 0 or more times. See SCXML [130, #param].
`<sc:content>`	Alternatively, the event payload may be specified as a sequence of XML nodes. Must not occur together with `<param>`. Occurs 0 or 1 times. See SCXML [130, #content].

The `assignNewDescendant` custom action element signalizes the assignment of a given value to a particular attribute of the newly created descendant in the course of concretization and occurs only as a child of the `newDescendant` element. Table 6.8 defines the attributes and children of the `assignNewDescendant` element. The features of the `assignNewDescendant` element derive from the SCXML `assign` element [130, #assign, #xpath_assign].

Listing 6.9 emphasizes multilevel synchronization dependencies in the logical representation of the **business** level of MBA **Rental**. The `transition` element with value "createRenterType" as `event` (Line 12) has a `newDescendant` child element which represents the creation of a new descendant MBA at the **renterType** level by invoking the **createRenterType** method at the **business** level. Under this `newDescendant` element, an `assignNewDescendant` element models the assignment of attribute values to

Table 6.7: Action element for concretization

<newDescendant>

ATTRIBUTE	TYPE	DESCRIPTION
level	xs:Name	Defines the level at which to create a new MBA.
name	Value expression	Optionally determines the name of the newly created MBA.
parents	Value expression	Optionally determines the names of the parents of the newly created MBA.

CHILDREN	
<assignNewDescendant>	Manipulates the data model of the newly created descendant. Occurs 0 or more times. See Table 6.8.

the newly created descendant MBA. The first assignNewDescendant element represents the assignment of value to the new descendant's data element with "maximumRate" as id, using the value of the maximumRate child element (from the empty namespace) of the event data element in the data model (Line 15). Analogously, the second assignNewDescendant element (Line 19, not shown in detail) represents the assignment of value to the new descendant's data element with "maximumDuration" as id, using the value of the maximumDuration child element of the event data element in the data model. Another transition element (Line 25), with value "restructure" as event, has a sendDescendant child element which represents the invocation of the cancel method of every descendant MBA at the renterType level that is in the OnOffer state.

For MBA relationships, the presented functions and custom action elements will have to be slightly adapted. First, when specifying the level that the multilevel predicate refers to, relationship levels instead of individual levels are referenced. To this end, a serialization format for relationship levels is required, which might be a dedicated XML element, or simply a sequence of strings. Second, for the concretization of MBA relationships, the new-Descendant must be extended with additional parameters for the names of the coordinates. Again, a serialization format for coordinates is required (see Section 6.2).

Table 6.8: Action element for the manipulation of a newly created descendant's data model

<assignNewDescendant>

ATTRIBUTE	TYPE	DESCRIPTION
location	Path expression	Specifies the location in the data model that is to be manipulated. See SCXML [130, #LocationExpressions].
expr	Value expression	Optionally determines the value that is to be assigned. See SCXML [130, #ValueExpressions].
type	enumeration	Optionally specifies the type of data manipulation to be performed. See SCXML [130, #xpath_assign].
attribute	xs:Name	Optionally determines the name of the attribute that is to be inserted in case the type of assignment operation is "addattribute". See SCXML [130, #xpath_assign].

CHILDREN
A sequence of XML nodes to be assigned to the specified location in the data model of the newly created descendant. The assignNewDescendant element must not have any children when the expr attribute occurs. See SCXML [130, #assign].

Multilevel predicates for the representation of horizontal and hybrid synchronization dependencies may be implemented according to the same principles as multilevel predicates for vertical synchronization dependencies. In that case, inline functions and custom action elements would express horizontal and hybrid synchronization dependencies. The OCL constraints defined in Chapter 4 may serve as blueprint for the implementation of the corresponding XQuery statements.

Moreover, custom action elements may also implement reflective functions (see Section 5.1.3). In the most basic case, such a custom action element may allow for the introduction of an additional scxml element at a particular level of an MBA. The newly introduced scxml element becomes the payload

Listing 6.9: The logical representation of the business-level data and life cycle model of MBA Rental with an emphasis on multilevel synchronization

```
 1  ⊟ <mba name="Rental"
 2       xmlns="http://www.dke.jku.at/MBA"
 3       xmlns:sync="http://www.dke.jku.at/MBA/Sync"
 4       xmlns:sc="http://www.w3.org/2005/07/scxml">
 5    ⊟ <topLevel name="business">
 6      ⊟ <elements>
 7        ⊟ <sc:scxml>
 8          ⊞ <sc:datamodel ...
 9          ⊞ <sc:initial ...
10          ⊟ <sc:state id="Restructuring">
11            ⊞ <sc:transition event="setMissionStatem ...
12            ⊟ <sc:transition event="createRenterType">
13              ⊟ <sync:newDescendant level="renterType"
14                  name="$_event/data/name/text()">
15                ⊟ <sync:assignNewDescendant
16                    location="$maximumRate"
17                    expr="$_event/data/
18                    maximumRate/text()"/>
19                ⊞ <sync:assignNewDescendant ...
20                └ </sync:newDescendant>
21            └ </sc:transition>
22            ⊞ <sc:transition event="reopen" ...
23          └ </sc:state>
24          ⊟ <sc:state id="Running">
25            ⊟ <sc:transition event="restructure"
26                target="Restructuring">
27              ⊟ <sync:sendDescendants level="renterType"
28                  state="OnOffer" event="cancel"/>
29            └ </sc:transition>
30          └ </sc:state>
31        └ </sc:scxml>
32      └ </elements>
33      ⊞ <childLevel name="renterType" ...
34    └ </topLevel>
35    ⊞ <concretizations ...
36  └ </mba>
```

of the event and eventually, given successful processing of the event, a child of the respective level's elements element. The system may check adherence to the selected notion of behavior consistency. Modelers may then specify additional pre-conditions over the argument scxml element to further constrain the possibility of introducing heterogeneities in sub-hierarchies. Another custom action element may then allow for changing an MBA's active scxml element.

Part II

Data Analysis

7 Multilevel Business Process Automation

In previous chapters, we have discussed the use of the multilevel business artifact (MBA) for multilevel business process modeling in order to better represent the interactions between the different hierarchy levels within a company. As the preparation for a proof-of-concept implementation, in Chapter 6, we have introduced an XML-based logical representation for MBAs. Relying on this XML representation, in this chapter, we present the implementation concept for a business process management system that enables the MBA-based (semi-)automated execution of multilevel business processes. A business process management system manages process-related data and allows for the event-driven execution of business processes; a business process management system also records event data. The recording of event data in event logs is a pre-requisite for business process intelligence which allows for performance analysis and the subsequent improvement of business processes based on the analysis results.

7.1 Multilevel Business Process Management System

The presented multilevel business process management system follows a generic architecture for business process management systems, the main components of which are the business process model repository, the business process environment, and the process engine [139, p. 120 et seqq.]; the modeling tool is another component, which may be built according to the rules defined in the modeling part of this thesis. The implementation concept relies heavily on XML technologies. An MBA database serves as the multilevel business process model repository and is realized using an XML database management system which stores an XML representation of the MBAs that conceptually model the automated business processes. The business process environment handles event occurrences which drive process execution. Basically, the business process environment is an event processor which retrieves from the MBA database the XML document representing the MBA that is affected by an event occurrence and passes this XML document to the process engine along with the event data. The process engine consists of a set of XQuery functions which manipulate the XML document according to the life cycle model.

7.1.1 Multilevel Business Artifact Database

The MBA database (also: MBAse, read: m-base) holds the logical representation of the MBAs that model the automated multilevel business process. This logical representation being in XML, an XML database management system handles the physical storage of the XML documents representing the MBAs, and an XQuery module provides a set of functions for the creation, manipulation, and retrieval of MBAs from the database. Table 7.1 describes the functions of the XQuery module for MBA data management. The createMBAse, createCollection, and insertMBA functions allow for the creation of an MBA database and collection as well as the subsequent insertion of mba elements. The getMBA function allows for the retrieval of an mba element by name from a collection in the MBA database. The other functions take an mba element as argument and allow for the retrieval and manipulation of data from this element.

The XQuery functions described in Table 7.1 provide the fundamental for the various components of the multilevel business process management system; these functions represent a basic requirement for multilevel business process automation. The implementation of multilevel predicates for synchronization between abstraction levels (see Chapter 6) requires the getAncestorAtLevel and getDescendantsAtLevel functions. The getSCXMLAtLevel function retrieves scxml elements that an MBA associates with a given abstraction level. the getSCXML function returns the single active scxml element that an MBA associates with its top level. The thus retrieved SCXML documents may serve as the input for an SCXML interpreter. The getAttribute function retrieves a data element by name from a given MBA's active top-level scxml element. The getConfiguration and isInState functions grant access to an argument mba element's current states. The getConfiguration function returns the given MBA's configuration, that is, the set of currently active state and parallel elements from the MBA's active top-level scxml element. The isInState function takes a string as additional argument and returns true if the given MBA's configuration contains a state or parallel ele-

Table 7.1: Main XQuery functions for MBA database management

FUNCTION	PARAMETERS	DESCRIPTION
createMBAse	$name xs:string	Creates a new MBA database.
createCollection	$db xs:string, $name xs:string	Creates a new collection within an MBA database.
insertMBA	$db xs:string, $collection xs:string, $mba element()	Inserts an mba element into a collection within an MBA database.
getMBA	$db xs:string, $collection xs:string, $name xs:string	Returns mba element with given name from a collection within an MBA database.
getAncestor-AtLevel	$mba element(), $level xs:string	Returns mba element that is ancestor at given level of given MBA.
getDescendants-AtLevel	$mba element(), $level xs:string	Returns mba elements that are descendants at given level of given MBA.
getSCXMLAtLevel	$mba element(), $level xs:string	Returns scxml elements that the given MBA defines for given level.
getSCXML	$mba element()	Returns given MBA's active top-level scxml element.
getAttribute	$mba element(), $name xs:string	Returns data element with given name from the MBA's active top-level scxml element.

(continues on next page)

Table 7.1 (continued): XQuery functions for MBA database management

FUNCTION	PARAMETERS	DESCRIPTION
`getConfiguration`	`$mba element()`	Returns currently active `state` elements from MBA's active top-level `scxml` element.
`isInState`	`$mba element()`, `$stateId xs:string`	Returns `true` if given MBA's configuration contains `state` element with given identifier.
`add-CurrentStates`	`$mba element()`, `$entrySet element()*`	Adds to MBA's set of current states a set of `state` elements from given MBA's active top-level `scxml` element.
`remove-CurrentStates`	`$mba element()`, `$exitSet element()*`	Removes from MBA's set of current states a set of `state` elements from given MBA's active top-level `scxml` element.

ment with the argument string value as `id`. The `addCurrentStates` and `removeCurrentStates` functions change a given MBA's configuration as recorded in the database. Both functions take a set of `state` and `parallel` elements from the MBA's active top-level `scxml` element.

The MBA data management functions rely on node identity [135, #node-identity], passing and manipulating `mba` elements, the changes made on these elements being effective on the database. The employed XML database management system must therefore support the retrieval of nodes from the database under preservation of node identity and allow for the subsequent manipulation of these nodes using the XQuery Update Facility (XQUF) [128]. Furthermore, the database management system should transparently persist the thus executed update operations.

An MBA has a set of currently active states; the MBA database must store the currently active states of each MBA. The SCXML standard makes no prescriptions concerning the persistence of active states – with the exception of `history` states [135, #history]. One possibility is the use of a custom

Listing 7.1: The logical representation of the top-level data model of MBA Rental with external event queue and current status

```
 1  <mba name="Rental" ⊞ xmlns=...>
 2   <topLevel name="business">
 3    <elements>
 4     <sc:scxml>
 5      <sc:datamodel>
 6       <sc:data id="mission">Renting</sc:data>
 7       <sc:data id="_x">
 8        <db xmlns="">myMBAse</db>
 9        <collection xmlns="">
10          CarRentals
11        </collection>
12        <mba xmlns="">Rental</mba>
13        <currentStatus xmlns="">
14         <state ref="Running"/>
15        </currentStatus>
16        <externalEventQueue xmlns="">
17         <event name="setMission">
18          <mission>Moving people</mission>
19         </event>
20         <event name="reopen"/>
21        </externalEventQueue>
22       </sc:data>
23       <sc:data id="_event">
24        <name xmlns="">restructure</name>
25        <data xmlns="">
26         <memo>Refocusing needed</memo>
27        </data>
28       </sc:data>
29      </sc:datamodel>
30      ⊞ ...
31     </sc:scxml>
32    </elements>
33    ⊞ <childLevel name="renterType" ...
34   </topLevel>
35   ⊞ <concretizations ...
36  </mba>
```

system variable in an mba element's active top-level scxml element. Listing 7.1 contains the logical representation of the data model of MBA Rental
from previous examples, storing the currently active states of the MBA
under the currentStatus (Line 13) child of the data element with value
"_x" as id. Note that the state children of the currentStatus element
are from the empty namespace, as opposed to the state descendants of
the scxml element, which are in the SCXML namespace. The children
of currentStatus refer in their ref attribute to identifiers of state
and parallel elements from the MBA's active top-level scxml element.
The getConfiguration function resolves these references and returns the
state and parallel elements from the MBA's active top-level scxml
element that correspond to the references in the currentStatus element.
This set of state and parallel elements may then serve as the input for
an SCXML interpreter.

7.1.2 XQuery-based Interpreter for State Chart XML

A business process engine for the MBA-based automation of multilevel
business processes must handle SCXML. The logical representation of MBAs
employs SCXML as the representation language for the life cycle models
at the various abstraction levels. With SCXML being an XML-based state
machine language, a business process engine that deals with SCXML must
query and manipulate XML documents. Thus, it is logical to have an SCXML
implementation based on XQuery, the standard query, manipulation, and
programming language for XML.

An SCXML implementation using XQuery allows for a convenient integration of the multilevel business process engine in an XML database environment. Table 7.2 describes XQuery functions for the interpretation of SCXML
documents. The XQuery functions derive from the informative pseudo-code
algorithm described in the SCXML standard [130, #AlgorithmforSCXML-
Interpretation]; this algorithm may serve as a guide for the implementation
of an XQuery-based interpreter. Taking advantage of the XQuery and XPath
data model (XDM), an XQuery-based SCXML interpreter may operate on
the elements of an SCXML document in an object-oriented fashion.

The selectTransitions and selectEventlessTransitions
functions retrieve the set of enabled transitions given a configuration
of active states. The argument configuration must consist of a set of
state and parallel elements from the scxml element that is to be
interpreted. Due to the preservation of node identity, using a simple

Table 7.2: Main XQuery functions for SCXML interpretation

FUNCTION	PARAMETERS	DESCRIPTION
selectEventless-Transitions	$configuration element()*, $dataModels element()*	Returns set of enabled transition elements not associated with any event.
selectTransitions	$configuration element()*, $dataModels element()*, $event xs:string	Returns set of enabled transition elements associated with given event.
computeExitSet	$configuration element()*, $transitions element()*	Returns set of state elements from configuration to be exited given set of enabled transitions.
computeEntrySet	$transitions element()*	Returns set of state elements to be entered given set of enabled transitions.
selectDataModels	$configuration element()*	Returns set of datamodel elements that are valid under given configuration.
eval	$expr xs:string, $dataModels element()*	Dynamically evaluates a given expression over the argument datamodel elements.

(continues on next page)

Table 7.2 (continued): XQuery functions for SCXML interpretation

FUNCTION	PARAMETERS	DESCRIPTION
assign	$dataModels element()*, $location xs:string, $expression xs:string?, $type xs:string?, $attribute xs:string?, $nodelist node()*	Updates data elements, identified by an XPath expression, from a given set of data models. Different types of operations require different parameters. See SCXML [130, #xpath_assign].

XPath expression, the SCXML interpreter may access the enclosing scxml element that contains the states in the configuration; a separate parameter for passing the scxml element is not necessary in this case. The selectTransitions function takes as additional parameter the name of an event, selecting those transitions that are triggered by the argument event. The selectEventlessTransitions function selects enabled transitions without an associated event.

The computeExitSet and computeEntrySet functions retrieve, given a set of transitions, those states of an SCXML document that are to be entered and exited, respectively. Under preservation of node identity, both functions take a set of transition elements as parameter and return a set of state and parallel elements from the interpreted SCXML document as result. Due to the preservation of node identity, the SCXML interpreter may access the enclosing scxml element through the argument set of transition elements. The computeExitSet function takes a configuration of active states as additional parameter; only currently active states may be removed from the configuration. Again, the function must receive the argument configuration under preservation of node identity.

The selectDataModels function is an auxiliary that retrieves those datamodel elements that are valid under a given configuration of active states. Besides the global datamodel, each state and parallel element in an SCXML document may itself contain a datamodel element. These local datamodel elements are only valid when the containing state is currently active. The `selectDataModels` function expects an argument configuration to be passed under preservation of node identity in order to access the enclosing `scxml` element.

The `eval` function allows for the dynamic evaluation of an argument string as non-updating XQuery expression which may refer to the contents of the `data` elements in the argument SCXML data models. For the evaluation of the argument string, the `eval` function binds the contents of each `data` element in one of the argument data models to a variable bearing the `data` element's `id` value as name.

The functionality of executable content [130, #executable], or action elements, may be implemented using XQuery. These functions have a parameter for each potential attribute and child element of the corresponding action element. The `assign` function realizes the `assign` element [130, #xpath_assign]. The `$location`, `$expression`, `$type`, and `$attribute` parameters each correspond to an attribute of the `assign` element; the `$nodelist` parameter represents potential child elements for inline specification of content. The `assign` element's derivations for multilevel synchronization (see Chapter 6) take additional parameters. The implementation of the `send` element and its derivations for multilevel synchronization depend on the event processor.

7.1.3 Event Processor

Events drive the automated business process, causing changes in the state of the involved MBAs and in their data models. The event processor dispatches occurring events, including the payload, to the MBAs and invokes the SCXML interpreter. Table 7.3 describes the functions for the management of the event queues of the MBAs in the database. The `enqueueExternal-Event` function takes as arguments an `mba` element and the serialization of an event, and appends the event serialization to the argument MBA's event queue. Conversely, the `dequeueExternalEvent` function removes the first event serialization from an MBA's event queue. The `loadNext-ExternalEvent` function takes the first event serialization and loads it into the `data` element with value "_event" as `id`.

Listing 7.2 illustrates how the event processor may invoke, upon an event occurrence, the MBA management and SCXML interpretation functions in order to change an MBA's current states based on its configuration and the active top-level `scxml` element. As a pre-condition, the event processor must enqueue the events in order of their occurrence and load the serialization

Table 7.3: Main XQuery functions for management of events sent to MBAs

FUNCTION	PARAMETERS	DESCRIPTION
enqueue- ExternalEvent	$mba element(), $event element()	Appends event with payload to a given MBA's event queue.
dequeue- ExternalEvent	$mba element()	Removes the first event from a given MBA's event queue.
loadNext- ExternalEvent	$mba element()	Loads first event and payload from given MBA's event queue into data element with "_event" as id.

of the next event from the queue into the processed SCXML document's datamodel prior to the execution of the code in Listing 7.2. Note that out-of-order event arrival as well as differences in occurrence and detection time [46] are orthogonal issues which must be investigated separately; the development of a complex event processing system is not the focus of this work. Based on the enabled transitions, the sets of states to be exited and entered are calculated by the SCXML interpretation functions. Subsequently, the previously calculated sets of states are added and removed, respectively, from the MBA's configuration.

The execution of SCXML documents requires event queue management. The data element for storing custom system variables may serve as the storage location for the event queue. The contents of the externalEvent-Queue element from the empty namespace under the data element with value "_x" as id contains serializations of the events raised for a particular MBA in order of their occurrence. When starting the processing of a particular event, the event processor removes the entry for the respective event from the event queue and loads the event's description into the data element with value "_event" as id. For example, the event queue for MBA Rental in Listing 7.1 consists of two events with the names "set-Mission" (Line 17) and "reopen" (Line 20). Note that the child elements that describe the events in the queue are from the empty rather than the SCXML namespace. In this example, the content of the first event element

Listing 7.2: The XQuery code for changing an MBA's current states

```
 1 declare variable $db external;
 2 declare variable $collection external;
 3 declare variable $name external;
 4
 5 let $mba := mba:getMBA($db, $collection, $name)
 6 let $scxml := mba:getSCXML($mba)
 7
 8 let $currentEvent :=
 9 $scxml/sc:datamodel/sc:data[@id = '_event']
10 let $eventName := $currentEvent/name
11
12 let $configuration := mba:getConfiguration($mba)
13 let $dataModels :=
14  sc:selectDataModels($configuration)
15
16 let $transitions :=
17  sc:selectTransitions($configuration,
18                       $dataModels,
19                       $eventName)
20
21 let $exitSet :=
22  sc:computeExitSet($configuration, $transitions)
23 let $entrySet :=
24  sc:computeEntrySet($transitions)
25
26 return (
27   mba:removeCurrentStates($mba, $exitSet),
28   mba:addCurrentStates($mba, $entrySet)
29 )
```

(from empty namespace) constitutes the payload of the occurrence of the setMission event, which during processing becomes the contents of the data child (from empty namespace) of the sc:data element with value "_event". When an event is raised for a particular MBA, the event processor enqueues the serialization of the event occurrence in the MBA's event queue.

Listing 7.3: A possible implementation of the custom action element for sending events to descendants at a particular level

```
1 declare updating function sync:sendDescendants(
2   $mba as element(), $level as xs:string,
3   $eventId as xs:string, $stateId as xs:string?,
4   $cond as xs:string?, $param as element()*,
5   $content as element()?
6 ) {
7   let $descendants :=
8    mba:getDescendantsAtLevel($mba, $level)
9
10  let $descendantsInState :=
11   if($stateId and not($stateId = '')) then
12    $descendants[mba:isInState(., $stateId)]
13   else $descendants
14
15  let $filteredDescendants :=
16   if($cond and not($cond = '')) then
17    for $descendant in $descendantsInState
18     let $dataModels :=
19      sc:selectDataModels(
20       mba:getConfiguration($descendant)
21      )
22     return
23      if (sc:eval($cond, $dataModels)) then
24       $descendant
25      else ()
26   else $descendantsInState
27
28  let $event :=
29   <event xmlns="" name="{$eventId}">{
30    let $dataModels :=
31     sc:selectDataModels(
32      mba:getConfiguration($mba)
33     )
34    return if ($content) then (
35     if ($content/@expr) then
36      sc:eval($content/@expr, $dataModels)
37     else $content/*
```

```
38    ) else if($param) then (
39      for $p in $param
40      return element{$p/@name}{
41        if($p/@expr) then
42        sc:eval($p/@expr, $dataModels)
43        else if($p/@location) then
44        sc:eval($p/@location, $dataModels)
45        else ()
46      }
47    ) else ()
48    }</event>
49
50  for $descendant in $filteredDescendants
51    return mba:enqueueExternalEvent(
52    $descendant, $event
53    )
54 }
```

The custom action elements for modeling multilevel synchronization dependencies as described in Chapter 6 may also be realized using XQuery functions. Consider, for example, the sendDescendants element which signals the dispatch of a given event to descendants of an MBA at a particular level. The sendDescendants element has an attribute that defines the level of the considered descendants as well as an attribute that contains the name of the dispatched event. The set of descendants that receive an event notification may further be restricted to MBAs in a particular state and MBAs that satisfy an additional condition; the sendDescendants element has optional attributes for specifying these additional restrictions. Furthermore, the sendDescendants element may have child elements specifying the event payload. The corresponding XQuery function, which is in the synchronization namespace, prefixed sync, has parameters for the potential attributes and child elements of the sendDescendants element. The signature of the sendDescendants function in Listing 7.3 defines these parameters. The optional $stateId and $cond parameters allow for the further restriction of considered descendants. The optional $param parameter, which takes a list of param elements, and the optional $content parameter contain payload specifications. The function evaluates either $param or $content, but never both parameters.

Listing 7.4: The logical representation of top-level life cycle model of MBA Rental

```
 1  ⊟ <mba name="Rental" ⊞ xmlns=...>
 2    ⊟ <topLevel name="business">
 3      ⊟ <elements>
 4        ⊟ <sc:scxml>
 5          ⊞ <sc:datamodel ...
 6          ⊟ <sc:initial>
 7            ⊟ <sc:transition target="Restructuring"/>
 8            └ </sc:initial>
 9          ⊞ <sc:state id="Restructuring" ...
10          ⊟ <sc:state id="Running">
11            ⊟ <sc:transition event="restructure"
12                    target="Restructuring">
13              ⊟ <sync:sendDescendants
14                  level="renterType"
15                  event="cancel"
16                  state="OnOffer">
17                ⊟ <sc:param name="memo"
18                    expr="$_event/memo/text()"/>
19                └ </sync:sendDescendants>
20              └ </sc:transition>
21            └ </sc:state>
22          └ </sc:scxml>
23        └ </elements>
24      ⊞ <childLevel name="renterType" ...
25      └ </topLevel>
26    ⊞ <concretizations ...
27  └ </mba>
```

Listing 7.3 contains a possible implementation of the sendDescendants function which employs the previously defined MBA management and SCXML interpretation functions. From the argument MBA's descendants at the argument level, only those descendants are selected that presently are in the given state, provided such a state was passed to the function. The list of descendants is further reduced by evaluating the optional condition using the eval function. Finally, the function marshals the event, taking into account the parameters for the definition of the payload.

The action element in Listing 7.4, Line 13, has values for the `level`, `event`, and `state` attributes, as well as a `param` child. The action element signals the dispatch of a cancel event to all descendants at the renterType level that are in the OnOffer state. The dispatched event contains a memo message as payload. The corresponding function call provides argument values that determine the name of the dispatched event as well as level and state of the considered descendants while passing an empty list for the parameter that holds the additional constraint condition; a `param` element rather than a `content` element defines the event payload. Therefore, the action element translates into the following function call, where the $mba variable holds the logical representation of MBA Rental:

```
sync:sendDescendants(
  $mba, 'renterType', 'cancel', 'OnOffer', (),
  <sc:param name="memo" expr="$_event/memo/text()"/>, ()
)
```

The previous function call enqueues the following event serialization in the external event queues of the selected descendant MBAs:

```
<event xmlns="" name="cancel">
  <memo>Refocusing on core competencies needed</memo>
</event>
```

For each action element under an activated transition, the event processor calls the corresponding XQuery function. Listing 7.5 shows the XQuery code for the execution of a given action element. The $content variable is provided by the event processor and contains a copy of the action element that is to be processed. Depending on the dynamic type of the $content variable, a different XQuery function is invoked with the attributes and children of the respective action element as arguments. The action elements are processed in document order, the processing being iterative. The invoked XQuery functions that implement the action elements are updating. The updates of one iteration step should be visible to the next. An event processor implementation may retrieve the action elements of a fired transition and invoke the XQuery code in Listing 7.5 in a loop, with varying values bound to the $content variable. The XQuery functions that implement the action elements do not manipulate the argument values that originate from the action element's attributes and children. The requirement of preservation of node identity, in this case, applies only to the passing of the mba element itself and its data models.

Listing 7.5: The XQuery code for inducing the processing of executable content

```
1 declare variable $db external;
2 declare variable $collection external;
3 declare variable $name external;
4
5 declare variable $content external;
6
7 let $mba := mba:getMBA($db, $collection, $name)
8
9 return
10  typeswitch($content)
11    case element(sc:assign) return
12     let $dataModels := sc:selectDataModels(
13       mba:getConfiguration($mba)
14     )
15     return sc:assign(
16      $dataModels, $content/@location,
17      $content/@expr, $content/@type,
18      $content/@attr, $content/*
19     )
20    case element(sync:assignAncestor) return
21     sync:assignAncestor(
22      $mba, $content/@level,
23      $content/@location, $content/@expr,
24      $content/@type, $content/@attr,
25      $content/*
26     )
27    case element(sync:sendAncestor) return
28     sync:sendAncestor(
29      $mba, $content/@level,
30      $content/@event, $content/sc:param,
31      $content/sc:content
32     )
33    case element(sync:assignDescendants) return
34     sync:assignDescendants(
35      $mba, $content/@level,
36      $content/@location, $content/@expr,
37      $content/@type, $content/@attr,
```

```
38      $content/*, $content/@inState,
39      $content/@satisfying
40    )
41    case element(sync:sendDescendants) return
42      sync:sendDescendants(
43        $mba, $content/@level,
44        $content/@event, $content/@inState,
45        $content/@satisfying, $content/sc:param,
46        $content/sc:content
47      )
48    case element(sync:newDescendant) return
49      sync:newDescendant(
50        $mba, $content/@level,
51        $content/@name, $content/@parents,
52        $content/*
53      )
54    default return ()
```

MULTILEVEL BUSINESS PROCESS AUTOMATION WITH CONCEPTBASE

The ConceptBase system is a possible alternative for the implementation of a multilevel business process management system. In this case, the ConceptBase system may serve as the business process model repository and, by leveraging the feature for the definition of graphical notations, the modeling component. Furthermore, the ConceptBase system supports the formulation of active rules as event-condition-action (ECA) rules [54, p. 60 et seq.]. Using ECA rules, the ConceptBase system may serve as an execution engine for business processes, which other work has demonstrated for Petri nets [51].

7.2 Application Development

The MBA-based development of software solutions yields data-centric, event-driven applications. These applications are organized around the data of interest; events trigger operations on these data of interest. The application logic is defined by the SCXML documents at the various abstraction levels.

The specification of web-service calls in these SCXML documents allows for the modular development of software solutions.

Using MBAs, modelers specify the attributes and behavior of data objects in a top-down fashion. For an entire hierarchy of data objects modelers specify common attributes, business rules and policies. Then, for specific sub-hierarchies, heterogeneities are introduced. These heterogeneities, in turn, become part of the homogeneous model of the data objects in the sub-hierarchy. Applications that work with a particular sub-hierarchy of data objects may rely on the homogeneous model, with potentially positive implications on code reusability.

The hetero-homogeneous nature of MBA-based conceptual and logical models allows for a decentralized development process. Developers at different organizational levels or local branches and divisions within the company may be granted access and manipulation rights to the appropriate MBAs in the database, or rights for the creation of MBAs at a specific level of abstraction within a sub-hierarchy. These developers may then autonomously adapt, create, manipulate, and access data objects in their sphere of responsibility. Yet, the semantics of multilevel concretization limits the freedom of developers. Thus, the MBA-based development process allows developers to enforce compliance with the homogeneous model for changes to the schema at lower levels in the sub-hierarchy.

7.3 Event Logs

The automated execution of business processes produces *event logs* [27, p. 353 et seq.] which, in the case of artifact-centric business processes, document the manipulation of the involved data objects and their change of states. The recording of such event logs, especially the data about time, constitutes a basic requirement for the quantitative analysis of business process performance. Event logs allow for the reconstruction of object life cycles and the calculation of cycle times.

We propose the use of XES event logs for tracing the execution of multilevel business processes. The XES (eXtensible Event Stream) standard specifies an XML-based representation format for event logs [39]. The XML representation format makes XES particularly convenient for logging the execution of SCXML documents; XES event logs seamlessly integrate into SCXML documents with XPath data models.

An MBA's active top-level scxml element contains a custom system variable for storing event logs. These event logs then reside in a log element from the XES namespace, prefixed xes, under the data element with "_x" as the value for the id attribute. Listings 7.6 and 7.7 show an XES event log embedded in the data element with value "_x" as id from the logical representation of MBA Rental. The log element (Listing 7.6, Line 8) has a trace child which contains a number of logged event occurrences, each represented as an event element. An event element captures the characteristics of an event occurrence as key/value pairs which are referred to as the *attributes* of the event occurrence. Each key/value pair is an element with a key attribute which determines the name of the represented attribute of the event occurrence. The attribute value is either defined by the element's value attribute or by the element's children, depending on the type of the element. The type of the element itself, that is, the tag name, determines the expected data type of the attribute value.

For an SCXML document, each event element in the XES log data represents a successfully taken transition. Although in many cases a transition is triggered by an event, there are also "eventless" transitions. The XES event elements must therefore be distinguished from the events that trigger the transitions. The event log in Listings 7.6 and 7.7 records three successfully taken transitions for MBA Rental.

The "time:timestamp" attribute [39, p. 11] and the "concept:name" attribute [39, p. 14] are standard XES attributes. The former records the time of an event occurrence, the latter the name of the event that triggered the transition. In Listing 7.6, the event log for MBA Rental shows a taken transition not triggered by any event (Line 11) and a transition triggered by an event named "setMission" (Line 19). In Listing 7.7, the event log shows a transition triggered by an event named "reopen.1" (Line 12).

The XES event model is extensible by design, allowing for the introduction of attributes for specific applications such as SCXML. Extensions allow for the definition of attributes and their semantics [39, p. 7 et seq.]. Technically, even the previously used standard attributes, "time:timestamp" and "concept:name", are defined in extensions, albeit standard extensions. Each extension has a name, URL, and prefix. When referring to an attribute from an extension in an event log, the prefix of the extension precedes the attribute's name. For example, "time:timestamp" refers to the attribute named "timestamp" from an extension with prefix "time"; an extension element in the event log must declare the corresponding extension (not shown in Listings 7.6 and 7.7).

Listing 7.6: The event log of MBA Rental – Part 1

```
 1  <sc:data id="_x">
 2    <db xmlns="">myMBAse</db>
 3    <collection xmlns="">
 4      CarRentals
 5    </collection>
 6    <mba xmlns="">Rental</mba>
 7    ...
 8    <xes:log
 9      xmlns:xes="http://www.xes-standard.org/">
10      <xes:trace>
11        <xes:event>
12          <xes:date key="time:timestamp"
13            value="2014-07-21T16:31:32.505+02:00"/>
14          <xes:string key="sc:initial"
15            value="Rental"/>
16          <xes:string key="sc:target"
17            value="Restructuring"/>
18        </xes:event>
19        <xes:event>
20          <xes:string key="concept:name"
21            value="setMission"/>
22          <xes:date key="time:timestamp"
23            value="2014-08-24T11:51:26.839+02:00"/>
24          <xes:container key="payload">
25            <xes:string key="mission"
26              value="Moving people"/>
27          </xes:container>
28          <xes:string key="sc:state"
29            value="Restructuring"/>
30          <xes:string key="sc:event"
31            value="setMission"/>
32        </xes:event>
33        ...
34      </xes:trace>
35    </xes:log>
36  </sc:data>
```

Listing 7.7: The event log of MBA Rental – Part 2

```
 1  <sc:data id="_x">
 2    <db xmlns="">myMBAse</db>
 3    <collection xmlns="">
 4      CarRentals
 5    </collection>
 6    <mba xmlns="">Rental</mba>
 7    ...
 8    <xes:log
 9      xmlns:xes="http://www.xes-standard.org/">
10      <xes:trace>
11        ...
12        <xes:event>
13          <xes:string key="concept:name"
14            value="reopen.1"/>
15          <xes:date key="time:timestamp"
16            value="2014-09-29T12:21:51.623+02:00"/>
17          <xes:string key="sc:state"
18            value="Restructuring"/>
19          <xes:string key="sc:event"
20            value="reopen"/>
21          <xes:string key="sc:target"
22            value="Running"/>
23        </xes:event>
24      </xes:trace>
25    </xes:log>
26  </sc:data>
```

We introduce additional variables which relate an XES `event` element with the corresponding `transition` element in the SCXML document. The corresponding extension uses "sc" as prefix and employs the SCXML namespace URI as extension URL. The names of the variables are "sc:state", "sc:initial", "sc:target", "sc:event", and "sc:cond". The variables named "sc:state" and "sc:initial" relate to the element in the SCXML document that contains the taken transition; an `event` element must not have both variables simultaneously. The "sc:state" variable refers to the `id` value of the `state` or `parallel` element that contains the transition. The "sc:initial" variable applies to transitions under an `initial` element; the variable refers to the `id` value of the `state` or `parallel` element that contains the `initial` element, or the name of the `scxml` element. The "sc:target", "sc:event", and "sc:cond" attributes contain the values of the taken transition's attributes with the same name.

According to the event log for MBA Rental, the first successfully taken transition (Listing 7.6, Line 11) is from the `initial` element under the `scxml` element, the name of which is "Rental", and not triggered by any event but fired automatically in the beginning of the execution; the target of this transition is a state named "Restructuring". The second transition (Listing 7.6, Line 19) originates from the state named "Restructuring", has no target state, and the name of triggering events must conform to the "setMission" descriptor. Furthermore, the triggering event had a payload attached, represented in the event log as a `container` element with "payload" as `key` (see Günther et al. [38, p. 8]). The third transition (Listing 7.7, Line 12) also originates from the state named "Restructuring", has a target state named "Running", and the name of triggering events must conform to the "reopen" descriptor. Notice the difference between the "concept:name" and the "sc:event" attribute. The former contains the name of the event that actually triggered the transition, the latter contains a descriptor for events that potentially trigger the transition. An event must conform to the event descriptor specified by the transition in order to trigger the event [130, #EventDescriptors], "reopen.1" conforms to the "reopen" descriptor.

In conjunction with the SCXML document, an event log allows for the reconstruction of the sequence of states that an MBA entered during its life cycle. A *state log* derives from an MBA's event log and contains timestamps for the entry and exit of each state in an MBA's life cycle. Listing 7.8 shows an XQuery function that derives from an MBA's event log the state log containing the timestamps for entry and exit of states. For example, the event log in Listings 7.6 and 7.7 translates into the following state log:

```
<state xmlns=""
       ref="Restructuring"
       from="2014-07-21T16:31:32.505+02:00"
       until="2014-09-29T12:21:51.623+02:00"/>
<state xmlns=""
       ref="Running"
       from="2014-09-29T12:21:51.623+02:00"/>
```

The state log consists of a set of state elements. The ref attribute refers to the name of a state in the state machine. The from attribute contains the timestamp of state entry, the until attribute contains the timestamp of state exit. Entries for currently active states of the state machine do not have an until attribute. Consequently, in the previous example state log, the entry with value "Running" as ref refers to a currently active state, namely Running.

The getStateLog function in Listing 7.8 first obtains a chronologically-ordered list of XES event elements (Line 5) from the event log of the argument mba element. A *fold* (Line 11) then iterates over the previously obtained list of events in order to construct the state log. The fold also reconstructs the historic configuration during each iteration step. For each XES event element, the fold operation determines whether and when the event caused any state changes. Using the SCXML interpreter functions, the fold operation computes entry and exit sets (Lines 37 and 39) given the historic events in the event log. For every state in the entry set, the fold constructs a new entry in the state log (Line 41). For every already existing entry in the state log, the fold determines whether an until value must be added given the exit set. The fold passes a map between iteration steps containing the preliminary state log and the current configuration after taking into account the event log entry from the just finished iteration step. The map constitutes the result of the fold. Listing 7.8 employs XQuery 3.1 functions [133] for management of maps.

Listing 7.8: The XQuery code for the derivation of the state log from an MBA's event log

```
1 declare function mba:getStateLog(
2   $mba as element()
3 ) as element()* {
4   let $eventLog := mba:getAttribute('_x')/xes:log
5   let $events :=
6    for $event in $eventLog/xes:trace/xes:event
7    order by
8     $event/xes:date[@key='time:timestamp']/@value
9    return $event
10
11   let $stateLog := fn:fold-left($events, map:merge((
12    map:entry('configuration', ()),
13    map:entry('stateLog', ())
14   )), function($result, $event) {
15    let $configuration :=
16     map:get($result, 'configuration')
17    let $stateLog := map:get($result, 'stateLog')
18    let $eventTimestamp :=
19     xs:dateTime(
20      $event/xes:date[@key = 'time:timestamp']/@value
21     )
22    let $eventState :=
23     $event/xes:string[@key = 'sc:state']/@value
24    let $eventInit :=
25     $event/xes:string[@key = 'sc:initial']/@value
26    let $eventEvent :=
27     $event/xes:string[@key = 'sc:event']/@value
28    let $eventTarget :=
29     $event/xes:string[@key = 'sc:target']/@value
30    let $eventCond :=
31     $event/xes:string[@key = 'sc:cond']/@value
32    let $transition := sc:getTransition(
33     $scxml, $eventState, $eventInit,
34     $eventEvent, $eventTarget, $eventCond
35    )
36    let $entrySet :=
37     sc:computeEntrySet($transition)
```

```
38    let $exitSet :=
39     sc:computeExitSet($configuration, $transition)
40
41    let $newStateLogEntries :=
42     for $state in $entrySet return
43      <state xmlns="" ref="{$state/@id}"
44                       from="{$eventTimestamp}"/>
45    let $stateLog :=
46     for $entry in $stateLog return
47      if(
48       not($entry/@until) and (
49       some $state in $exitSet satisfies
50        $state/@id = $entry/@ref
51       )
52      ) then
53       copy $new := $entry modify (
54        insert node attribute until{$eventTimestamp}
55        into $new
56       ) return $new
57      else $entry
58    let $newConfiguration := (
59     $configuration[not(
60       some $s in $exitSet satisfies $s is .
61     )],
62     $entrySet
63     )
64
65    return map:merge((
66     map:entry('configuration', $newConfiguration),
67     map:entry(
68      'stateLog',
69      ($stateLog, $newStateLogEntries)
70     )
71    ))
72   }
73  )
74
75  return map:get($stateLog, 'stateLog')
76 }
```

8 Multilevel Business Process Intelligence

The automation of business processes using information technology produces event logs serving as the basis for performance analysis. For the top-level life cycle model, a multilevel business artifact (MBA) records performance data. For the lower-level life cycle models, an MBA aggregates performance data from descendants. Then, pre- and post-conditions of transitions in the life cycle models of an MBA's different abstraction levels may refer to performance data from ancestors and descendants, thereby expressing multilevel synchronization dependencies over performance data.

Hetero-homogeneous models of multilevel business processes present considerable advantages for performance analysis. For each abstraction level, an MBA describes a life cycle model that applies to every descendant at this level. When aggregating performance data of these descendants, the homogeneous life cycle models of the respective levels serve as the basis. Nevertheless, a concretization may refine and extend the life cycle models according to the rules of observation-consistent specialization, the specialized life cycle models being a homogeneous schema for the sub-hierarchy represented by the concretization. When analyzing performance data of the sub-hierarchy, analysts may leverage additional data from the specialized life cycle models.

8.1 Data Analysis with Multilevel Business Artifacts

Conceptually, performance measures are attributes in the data models of MBAs. Depending on the abstraction level of the data model that contains the performance measure, the attribute value either is asserted or derives from the data models of descendant MBAs. The *cycle time*, for example, is a basic metric in process analysis [74, 27]. Then, for the top-level life cycle model, an MBA records in the data model the actual cycle time of each individual state, that is, the amount of time spent in the respective state. For the lower-level life cycle models, in turn, an MBA applies an aggregation function on the measure values recorded by the descendants in order to obtain a condensed value, in this case, the average cycle time. In practice, when working with the logical representation of MBAs, performance measures are calculated from event logs.

8.1.1 Flow Analysis

Using flow analysis, business analysts may assess the overall performance of a process instance by exploiting performance data of its individual activities (cf. [27, p. 219 et seq.]). A common measure for the performance of a process instance is the (actual) cycle time [74]. For artifact-centric business process models, the cycle time may refer to the amount of time that a data object spends in a particular state. Through summation of the actual cycle times of the individual states, the analyst may obtain the overall cycle time of the data object's life cycle.

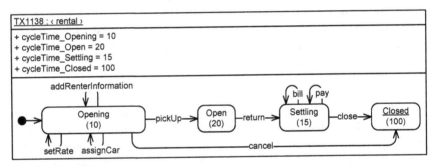

Figure 8.1: An MBA with actual cycle times for the different states of its top-level life cycle model

Figure 8.1 shows an MBA named TX1138 which records cycle times for the states in its life cycle model. For each state, the MBA has an attribute in the data model which holds the amount of time spent in the respective state. By convention, the names of these attributes are composed of the name of the measure, in this case, the (actual) cycle time, and the name of the state of which they describe the performance: "cycleTime_*state*". For example, the cycleTime_Opening attribute records the amount of time spent in the Opening state. We also adopt the notational convention of placing a state's cycle time in parentheses directly under or next to the name of the state in the state machine diagram. Thus, MBA TX1138 in Figure 8.1, which currently is in the Closed state, spent ten time units in the Opening state, twenty in Open, fifteen in Settling, and already a hundred time units, and still counting, in the Closed state.

The sum of the actual cycle times of the individual states constitutes the overall cycle time of the data object's entire life cycle. For example, the actual cycle time of the life cycle of MBA TX1138 in Figure 8.1 amounts to 145 time units. When considering Closed as a final archival state, it is more practical to consider the overall cycle time as the amount of time passed until entering the Closed state, which in the case of MBA TX1138 amounts to 45 time units. Thus, in practice, the operation for the calculation of the overall cycle time of the data object's life cycle may take as parameter a final state up to which the cycle times of the individual states are summarized. The explicit specification of a final state for the calculation allows for the comparison of data objects in different phases of their life cycle, that is, different current states.

8.1.2 Aggregation of Measures

An MBA only asserts cycle times for the states in its top-level life cycle model whereas for the non-top levels the MBA aggregates values from the descendants at the respective level. For example, Figure 8.2 shows an MBA named Private which records actual cycle times for the states in its top-level life cycle model and average cycle times for the second-level life cycle model. The cycleTime_InDevelopment, cycleTime_OnOffer, cycleTime_Canceled, and cycleTime_Discontinued attributes capture the amount of time spent in the InDevelopment, OnOffer, Canceled, and Discontinued state, respectively. Being currently in the OnOffer state, MBA Private spent 145 time units in the InDevelopment state and 220 time units in the OnOffer state. Since MBA Private has not yet spent any time in the Canceled and Discontinued states, the respective attributes contain a NULL value. The averageCycleTime_Rental-Opening, averageCycleTime_RentalOpen, averageCycleTime_RentalSettling, and averageCycleTime_RentalClosed attributes represent the average amount of time spent by the descendants of MBA Private in the Opening, Open, Settling, and Closed state, respectively. The slash before the attribute name indicates a derived attribute. As a notational convention, we place a state's average cycle time in parentheses directly under or next to the name of the state in the lower-level state machine diagrams of an MBA. So, for example, the value of the derived averageCycleTime_RentalOpening attribute at the renterType level, which is 8, corresponds to the value in parentheses

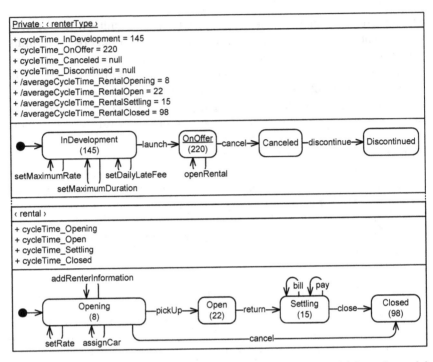

Figure 8.2: An MBA with actual cycle times for the top-level life cycle model and average cycle times for the second-level life cycle model

under the name of the Opening state at the rental level. Similarly, the value of the derived averageCycleTime_RentalOpen attribute corresponds to the value in parentheses under the name of the Open state. The same holds true for the other derived attributes averageCycleTime_RentalSettling and averageCycleTime_RentalClosed.

There are different possibilities for the calculation of average cycle times of individual states. First, the calculation rule for the average cycle time of a specific state may take into account only those descendants of an MBA that assign a non-NULL value to the actual cycle time of the respective state. Consider, for example, the derivation rule for the average cycle time of the Opening state of descendants at the rental level of MBA Private (Listing 8.1). Assume that MBA Private associates the PrivateRenterType class with the rental level. Then, the calculation rule sums up the individual cycle times for the Opening state from each descendant and divides the sum by the

Listing 8.1: The derivation rule for the average cycle time for the Opening state from the descendants of MBA Private in Figure 8.1

```
1  context PrivateRenterType::
2  averageCycleTime_RentalOpening : Integer derive:
3    let classOfLevel : Class =
4      self.MBA.MBAToLevel->select(l |
5        l.level = <rental>
6      ).dataModel in
7    let descendants : MBA =
8      self.MBA.descendants(<rental>) in
9    descendants.instanceData->collect(
10     oclAsType(classOfLevel)
11   ).cycleTime_Opening->sum() /
12   descendants.instanceData->collect(
13     oclAsType(classOfLevel)
14   ).cycleTime_Opening->select(v |
15     not v.oclIsUndefined()
16   )->size()
```

number of descendants with a non-NULL cycle time for the Opening state (Line 16); the standard oclIsUndefined method tests for NULL values. On the other hand, the calculation rule may take into account only those descendants of an MBA that currently are in a specific state. Now consider a different derivation rule for the average cycle time of the Opening state (Listing 8.2). The alternative calculation rule sums up the individual cycle times for the Opening state from all descendants that are currently in the Closed state (Line 11), and divides this sum by the number of descendants in the Closed state with a non-NULL cycle time of the Opening state.

For an accurate interpretation of average cycle times as an indicator for the expected actual cycle times of future process instances, business analysts must be aware of the applied calculation rule. A business analyst that takes into account all descendants for the calculation of average cycle times, but only counts non-NULL values, may be confronted with varying degrees of significance between the average values for different states. Average cycle times for early states in the life cycle model, due to the expectedly larger number of considered values, may tend to be more accurate predictions. In turn, average cycle times for late states, due to the expectedly smaller

Listing 8.2: The derivation rule for the average cycle time for the Opening state
from the descendants of MBA Private (Figure 8.1) that are in the Closed state

```
1  context PrivateRenterType::
2  averageCycleTime_RentalOpening : Integer derive:
3  let classOfLevel : Class =
4   self.MBA.MBAToLevel->select(l |
5    l.level = <rental>
6   ).dataModel in
7  let descendants : MBA =
8   self.MBA.descendants(<rental>)->select(d |
9    d.instanceData.oclAsType(
10     classOfLevel
11    ).oclIsInState(Closed)
12   ) in
13  descendants.instanceData->collect(
14   oclAsType(classOfLevel)
15  ).cycleTime_Opening->sum() /
16  descendants.instanceData->collect(
17   oclAsType(classOfLevel)
18  ).cycleTime_Opening->select(v |
19   not v.oclIsUndefined()
20  )->size()
```

number of considered values, are more easily biased by outliers. By taking
into account only those descendants that currently are in a particular state,
a business analyst receives the same degree of significance for the prediction
from each state, but lags behind current trends in earlier states which
potentially could benefit the analysis. The differences between the derivation
methods diminish with an increasing number of process instances.

For sequential life cycle models and those with parallel forks, a restriction
to non-NULL values, as in the calculation rule in Listing 8.2, will not alter
an average value obtained from the descendants that are in a given state,
since all descendants in this state will have entered the exact same states
during their life cycle. With alternative paths, however, two descendants X
and X' of an MBA at the same level that are in the same state S may have
entered different states during their life cycle, and thus assign NULL values
to different states. For example, descendant X may have entered state Q

prior to entering S whereas descendant X' may have entered state R before entering S. Consequently, descendant X assigns a NULL value to the cycle time attribute for state R whereas descendant X' assigns a NULL value to the cycle time attribute for state Q. In this case, for the calculation of the average cycle time of states R and S, a business analyst may wish to consider only those data objects that actually entered the particular state. Then, taking into account only the non-NULL values for average calculation leads to more accurate results.

A concretization hierarchy of MBAs already constitutes a data warehouse dimension which enables slice operations for the analysis of performance data for the associated life cycle models. The navigation from a given MBA to one of its descendants restricts the value base for the calculation of average cycle times, taking into account only the values from the particular sub-hierarchy that the descendant represents; the business analyst receives more concrete numbers for the analysis. Conversely, the navigation from a concretization to its abstraction widens the value base, with the analyst receiving more abstract, condensed numbers.

Consider, for example, MBA Rental as the root of a concretization hierarchy which also comprises MBAs Private and TX1138 (Figure 8.3). A business analyst may use MBA Rental as a starting point for the analysis. For the top level of MBA Rental, the business analyst receives concrete performance data, namely the actual cycle times for the Restructuring and Running states. For the renterType and rental levels, the business analyst receives summarized performance data, namely the average cycle times. The calculation of the renterType-level average cycle times for MBA Rental considers the actual cycle times of descendants of MBA Rental at the renterType level. The calculation of the rental-level average cycle times for MBA Rental considers the actual cycle times of descendants of MBA Rental at the rental level. Notice that the average cycle times of the rental-level states for MBA Rental differ from the average values given by MBA Private in Figure 8.2, a difference stemming from the restriction of the set of values considered for the calculation. By navigating from MBA Rental to Private, the business analyst receives concrete performance data for the renterType level and summarized performance data for the rental level with a restricted value base. The calculation of the rental-level average cycle times for MBA Private considers only the actual cycle times of descendants of MBA Private at the rental level.

Furthermore, the navigation from a given MBA to all of its descendants at a particular level corresponds to a drill-down operation. Rather than a single aggregate value, the business analyst then considers multiple values

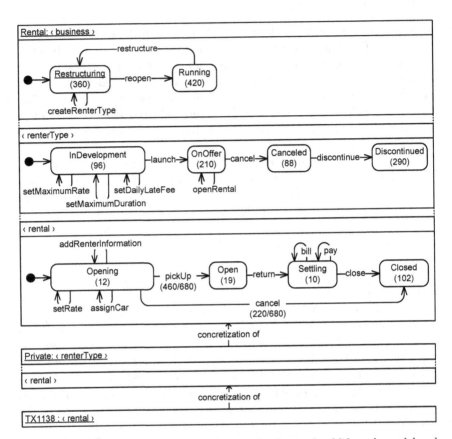

Figure 8.3: An MBA with actual cycle times for the top-level life cycle model and average cycle times for the non-top level life cycle models as well as probabilities for alternative paths

for the analysis. In this context, summarizability issues may arise with respect to the aggregation of average values [61]. Consider, for example, the rental-level state machine of MBA Rental in Figure 8.3. When obtaining the cycle times of a particular state, for example, Opening, as recorded by the renterType-level descendants of MBA Rental, the cycle times are average values. The average of these average values, however, will not yield the same result for the average cycle time of the Opening state as a derivation from the base data. Rather than storing average values, MBAs may record the sum of the actual cycle times and the count of descendants for non-top levels.

The average cycle times of individual states may be aggregated in order to calculate the average cycle time of an entire object life cycle. In case of a purely sequential life cycle model, the average cycle time of the entire object life cycle corresponds to the sum of the average cycle times of the individual states. An archival, final state such as Closed may be excluded from the summarization. In case of the existence of non-parallel forks and rework loops in the life cycle model, that is, alternative paths, the different paths must be weighted according to their probability of occurrence (see Dumas et al. [27, p. 219 et seq.]). In a state machine, alternative paths occur when two or more transitions with a different target state share the same source state. Consider, for example, the Opening state in the rental-level state machine of MBA Rental (Figure 8.3). Both the pickUp and cancel method may trigger a state change, each resulting in a different path. The probability of a given path then corresponds to the ratio between the number of taken transitions starting this particular path and the total number of taken transitions leaving the same source state; occurrences of transitions not leaving the state are not taken into account. For example, in Figure 8.3, the transitions with pickUp and cancel as triggering methods are the only transitions leaving the Opening state. In the example, out of 680 taken transitions that originated from the Opening state, 460 occurrences were triggered by the pickUp method whereas 220 occurrences were triggered by the cancel method.

When working with the XML representation of an MBA, the average cycle times of individual states are obtained through summarization from the state logs (see Section 7.3) of the MBA's descendants. Listing 8.3 defines an XQuery function for the calculation of the average cycle time of a given state from the event logs of an MBA's descendants. The average-CycleTime function takes an mba element as argument and calculates the average cycle time of an argument state of interest ($stateId) over the descendants of the argument MBA at a given level ($level) that are in a given state ($inState); the averageCycleTime function returns a result of XML Schema built-in data type xs:duration. For each descendant satisfying the conditions, the averageCycleTime function retrieves the state log using the getStateLog function (see Section 7.3, Listing 7.8). For each entry in a descendant's state log that concerns the state of interest (Listing 8.3, Line 16), the averageCycleTime function then calculates a duration by subtracting from the exit timestamp the timestamp of entry in the state, and sums up these durations using the fn:sum function. For currently active states, the function takes the current system date/time as

Listing 8.3: An XQuery implementation of the calculation rule for the average cycle time of a given state

```
1  declare function analysis:averageCycleTime(
2    $mba as element(),
3    $level as xs:string,
4    $inState as xs:string,
5    $stateId as xs:string
6  ) as xs:duration {
7    let $descendants :=
8      mba:getDescendantsAtLevel($mba, $level)
9        [mba:isInState(.,$inState)]
10
11   let $cycleTimes :=
12     for $descendant in $descendants
13       let $stateLog := mba:getStateLog($descendant)
14       return fn:sum(
15         (
16           for $entry in $stateLog[@ref = $stateId]
17           return
18             if($entry/@until) then
19               xs:dateTime($entry/@until) -
20               xs:dateTime($entry/@from)
21             else fn:current-dateTime -
22               xs:dateTime($entry/@from)
23         ),
24         ()
25       )
26
27   return fn:avg($cycleTimes)
28 }
```

exit timestamp. The fn:sum function call's second argument (Line 24) is the empty sequence, which indicates that a non-existent value in the state log of a particular descendant for the actual cycle time of the given state of interest should not count as zero but remain an empty sequence [132, #func-sum]. The fn:avg function then ignores these values for the calculation of the average value over all individual values obtained from the descendants.

8.2 Hetero-Homogeneous Data Analysis

Multilevel concretization allows for the extension and refinement of life cycle models at inherited levels according to rules of observation-consistent specialization. When working with hetero-homogeneous models, a business analyst may potentially leverage more finely-grained performance data with additional measures after performing a slice operation which puts the emphasis on a sub-hierarchy. In this section, we apply the principle of hetero-homogeneous data warehouses [80] to business process analysis.

In case a concretization refines inherited states in its life cycle models, a navigation from an ancestor MBA to this concretization corresponds to a combination of slice and drill-down operation. In the sub-hierarchy represented by the concretization, performance measures for the individual states are then available at a more specific granularity, which allows for a more in-depth analysis of process performance. Consider, for example, the concretization hierarchy in Figure 8.4 with MBAs Rental at the business level and Private at the renterType level. The navigation from MBA Rental to Private performs a zoom-in which retrieves actual performance data for the renterType level and restricts the set of actual cycle times of the rental-level states considered for the calculation of average cycle times to the descendants of Rental. Since MBA Rental refines the OnOffer state at the renterType level as well as the Opening and Closed states at the rental level, the navigation from Rental to Private corresponds to a drill-down operation. The business analyst may view the average cycle times of these refined states at a finer level of granularity.

Drill-down along the sub-state relationships at a single level must be distinguished from drill-down along the concretization hierarchy. The former leverages observation-consistent specialization in order to obtain a more finely-grained view on the life cycle model in a particular sub-hierarchy. The latter breaks down an aggregate value into a set of individual values for the states in the homogeneous model. These flavors of drill-down are analogous to topological and informational drill-down in graph OLAP [22] or merge and abstract in business model intelligence [113].

Depending on the employed notion of observation consistency, a concretization may also specialize transitions. Consider, for example, the transitions originating from the OnOffer sub-states in the rental-level state machine of MBA Private (Figure 8.4). The transition that originates from the Ready state and is triggered by the pickUp call event refines the inherited transition that is triggered by the pickUp call event as well and originates from the

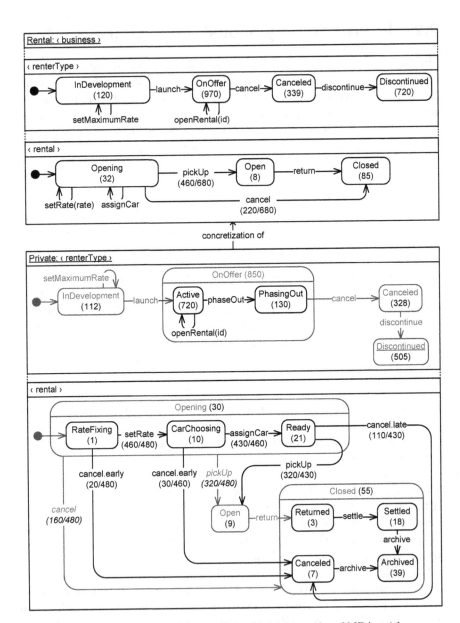

Figure 8.4: A hetero-homogeneous concretization hierarchy of MBAs with average cycle times and probabilities for alternative paths

Opening state, the super-state of Ready. When adopting the SCXML matching rules for event descriptors [130, #EventDescriptors], the cancel.early and cancel.late call events both match the cancel call event, and thus the transitions triggered by the cancel.early and cancel.late call events refine the inherited transition between Opening and Closed that is triggered by the cancel call event. The refinements put the data object in the Canceled state, a sub-state of Closed.

The occurrences of the refinements of a transition count towards the total number of occurrences of the general transition. Each refinement has its own number of occurrences in a particular sub-hierarchy. Consider, for example, the transition between RateFixing and Canceled triggered by the cancel.early call event has 20 occurrences in the Private sub-hierarchy (Figure 8.4). This number counts towards the total number of occurrences of the inherited transition between Opening and Closed triggered by the cancel call event. Likewise, the numbers of occurrences of the transition between CarChoosing and Canceled as well as the transition between Ready and Canceled also count towards the number of 160 occurrences of the inherited transition between Opening and Closed triggered by the cancel call event.

Note that average cycle times of sub-states may not add up to the average cycle time of the super-state. For example, in the rental-level state machine of MBA Private (Figure 8.4), the sum of the average cycle times of the RateFixing, CarChoosing, and Ready state does not correspond to the average cycle time of the Opening state. Likewise, the sum of the average cycle times of the Returned, Settled, Canceled, and Archived states does not correspond to the average cycle time of the Closed state. Rather, the average cycle times of the Opening and the Closed state derive directly from the base data, that is, the state log. This kind of summarizability issue related to the aggregation of sub-states of a super-state stems from the possibility of multiple outgoing transitions from and incoming transitions to the various sub-states of the super-state. In the absence of alternative paths, the average cycle times of the sub-states simply add up to the average cycle time of the super-state. By using path probabilities as weights, the average cycle time of a super-state may be calculated from the sub-states. For further information about the calculation of the cycle time of a sequence of nodes, possibly with alternative paths, we refer to Dumas et al. [27, p. 219 et seq.].

Conceptually, with performance measures viewed as attributes of MBAs, a concretization may introduce additional performance measures with respect to its abstraction. In this case, the sub-hierarchy represented by the concretization measures business process performance along additional criteria not applicable to the general case. For example, in a manufacturing company, measures of process quality may differ between types of products. While there may exist some standard quality measure that applies to the manufacturing process of all products, for specific products the company may examine additional indicators of process quality.

8.3 Multilevel Synchronization over Performance Data

In many companies, business rules will trigger specific actions for cases of goal achievement or failure thereof. Typically, business executives will be notified and automatically prompted to act when their subordinates fail at achieving specified performance goals. The corresponding business rules trigger actions on one hierarchy level based on performance data of another level. Thus, these business rules constitute multilevel synchronization dependencies.

Conceptually, multilevel synchronization dependencies over performance data are expressed as pre-conditions that refer to performance data attributes. For example, in case the average time spent for settling a car rental exceeds a specified threshold value, management may be notified and the business automatically put in a state of Restructuring in order to improve processes and lower cycle times. In order to model such a behavior, a necessary and sufficient pre-condition of an eventless transition at the business level may express a condition over the derived averageCycleTime_Settling attribute, which holds the average cycle time of the Settling state at the rental level obtained through summarization of actual cycle times from the descendants at the rental level.

In the logical representation, multilevel synchronization dependencies are function calls in the cond attributes of transition elements. The $_averageCycleTime function returns the average cycle time of a given state at a particular level, obtained from the actual cycle times of all descendants that are in a given state. Modelers may use the XML Schema duration data type [131, #duration] and its derivations, dayTimeDuration and yearMonthDuration, for expressing conditions over cycle times. Consider, for example, a transition element that logically represents a transition to the Restructuring state at the business level which fires when the average cycle time of the Settling state over all descendants at the rental level that are in the Closed state exceeds 21 days:

```
<sc:transition
 cond="xs:dayTimeDuration(
   $_averageCycleTime(
     'rental', 'Closed', 'Settling'
   )
 ) > xs:dayTimeDuration('P21D')"
 target="Restructuring"
/>
```

The $_averageCycleTime function as used in the cond attribute of a transition element translates into an averageCycleTime function call (Listing 8.3, see also Section 7.3). The first parameter of the average-CycleTime function, which upon execution receives the mba element the descendants of which serve as the basis for average calculation, is fixed to the mba element which the SCXML document is executed for. Thus, when evaluating the cond attribute of the previous transition element, the SCXML interpreter will evaluate XQuery code equivalent to the following:

```
let $mba := mba:getMBA(
 $_x/db, $_x/collection, $_x/mba
)
let $_averageCycleTime :=
 analysis:averageCycleTime($mba, ?, ?, ?)
return xs:dayTimeDuration(
 $_averageCycleTime(
   'rental', 'Closed', 'Settling'
 )
) > xs:dayTimeDuration('P21D')
```

Just like other kinds of pre-conditions of transitions, multilevel synchronization dependencies over performance data may be strengthened upon concretization. Consequently, company-wide performance goals may be tightened for a particular sub-entity. For example, whereas rentals in general must achieve an average duration of 21 days for settling the accounts, corporate rentals may have a smaller tolerance with respect to the average cycle time of the Settling state. Furthermore, a sub-entity may define additional pre-conditions over the average cycle times of states that are not part of the life cycle models in other sub-hierarchies. Thus, the hetero-homogeneous modeling approach allows for the definition of company-wide goals which may be tailored to the particularities of sub-entities.

9 Conclusion

In this book we have explored the conceptual and logical modeling of multi-level business processes. We have examined the automation of multilevel business processes and the use of the generated event log data for performance analysis. With respect to existing methodologies, the multilevel business artifact (MBA) allows for a better representation of dependencies between the various hierarchy levels within a company; the concretization mechanism provides flexibility while preserving the advantages of homogeneous models. The fundamentals of multilevel business process management being established, future work will further extend multilevel business process modeling techniques and investigate applications.

9.1 Summary

Companies perform value-creating activities at various hierarchy levels within an organization. These activities are interconnected and depend on each other, constituting a multilevel business process. At each hierarchy level, different data objects are involved in the multilevel business process. These data objects are hierarchically-organized, their order reflecting, to a certain extent, the organization hierarchy. The MBA modeling approach adopts a multilevel modeling technique in order to obtain an artifact-centric representation of multilevel business processes. This representation makes explicit, in the form of multilevel predicates, the synchronization dependencies between the activities at different levels within the hierarchy.

Rather than imposing a single fixed process, process models must account for the variability of real-world business problems. Each MBA represents the homogeneous schema of an entire hierarchy of business artifacts. Multilevel concretization allows for the introduction of heterogeneities in sub-hierarchies of business artifacts, which still comply with the homogeneous global schema. A concretizing MBA then constitutes a variant of an entire sub-hierarchy of business artifacts. The concretizing MBA also becomes the homogeneous model for this sub-hierarchy, which may again be concretized. At the same time, an MBA may associate different variants of life cycle models at different levels. By modeling meta-process activities in the life cycle models, the flexibility of the concretization mechanism may be deliberately restricted in order to enforce compliance with company-wide business policies.

A conceptual MBA model translates into an XML-based logical representation, using State Chart XML as the modeling language for the life cycle models at the different levels. The logical representation serves as the basis for the (semi-)automated execution of multilevel business processes, thereby producing event log data which enable performance analysis for multilevel business processes. Business analysts conduct slice and drill-down operations along a concretization hierarchy. Different sub-hierarchies may capture process performance data at a finer granularity.

9.2 Discussion

Multilevel modeling relaxes the restriction to two-level instantiation of traditional conceptual modeling, allowing for an arbitrary number of metalevels [59]. Adopting a *multilevel modeling* approach may prove beneficial in many practical, real-world situations. To multilevel business processes, the following patterns (see [59]) apply: (1) *type-object*, the dynamic introduction of types, (2) *dynamic features*, the dynamic introduction of features for a type, (3) *element classification*, application of specialization in the presence of the type-object pattern. More specifically, multilevel concretization, with its aggregation, instantiation, and specialization facets, embodies the type-object and element classification pattern. By explicitly representing meta-process activities in the life cycle model, MBAs realize the dynamic features pattern.

In general, an operational business process has a corresponding *management process* [42, p. 297 et seq.]. In analogy to the arbitrary number of metalevels in multilevel data modeling, multilevel business process modeling enables modeling of an arbitrary number of management levels. Each level of an MBA represents a management process for the lower levels. Furthermore, MBAs also represent the *process management processes* [42, p. 299 et seq.] for each level, meta-processes the output of which are again process models [101]. Each level of an MBA may represent, by modeling transitions with reflective methods as trigger, a meta-process for the lower levels.

With respect to the four-worlds framework for process engineering [101], we characterize multilevel business process management as follows. The *subject world* of multilevel business process management consists of business processes at various organizational levels within a company as well as the interactions between processes at different levels. Concerning the *usage world*, in the process model domain, MBAs represent the conceptual model of multilevel business process management. MBA-based business process models have a descriptive purpose in the sense that they aim for a better description of the interdependencies between organizational levels; they have a prescriptive purpose in the sense that they describe legal execution orders of the methods of data objects. The XML representation of MBAs serves as the logical format in the model enactment domain and as the fundamental for the business process management activities associated with the process performance domain. Concerning the *system world*, the MBA-based representation adopts a data- or artifact-centric view. The level of detail of the business process descriptions as well as the modeling language may vary. Concerning the *development world*, MBA-based modeling is a top-down, hetero-homogeneous approach for the representation of abstraction hierarchies of data objects as well as their life cycle models, allowing for the local introduction of heterogeneities in an otherwise homogeneous model.

In practice, a multitude of use cases for business process management exist. The multilevel approach to business process modeling covers the following use cases (see [2] for use cases): (1) *design model*, the MBA serves as the conceptual representation, (2) *refine and enact model*, an XML representation of MBAs allows for multilevel business process automation, (3) *select model from collection*, concretization hierarchies organize business process models, (4) *design configurable model*, an MBA may associate several business process model variants with each level, (5) *log event data and analyze performance using event data*, the (semi-)automated MBA-based execution of business processes produces event data which can be used for analysis.

The PHILharmonicFlows framework [57, 56] provides an integrated perspective on data and business process. Object-relational data models represent the data. From the relationships between data objects in the data model derives a classification of data objects into *data levels* which are similar to the levels of abstraction in the MBA approach. The coordination concepts of process context and aggregation [56, p. 245] correspond to the use of multilevel predicates over states of ancestors and descendants in pre-conditions of the transitions of an MBA's life cycle models. The MBA approach, in addition, provides a mechanism and guidelines for handling heterogeneities in the hierarchical organization of data objects as well as in data and life cycle models. For specific partitions of data objects, the level hierarchy may comprise additional levels with specialized data and life cycle models. As opposed to data levels in PHILharmonicFlows, which are determined by relationships between data objects, level hierarchies of MBAs result from an explicit top-down definition of levels.

The map-driven approach towards business process modeling is goal-oriented, a map consisting of intentions and sections [103]. An intention specifies what is to be achieved by performing the process, a section models the application of a strategy to a particular situation in order to achieve an intention. The map approach relies on stepwise refinement for the modeling of business processes [83]: Another map may refine an individual section of a map. In a spiral, maps are recursively refined. A map of the current situation and a map of the desired situation serve as the basis for the identification of sections that need refinement. Each of these sections is then refined by a map which serves as the input for a new spiral iteration. In the course of such an iteration, individual sections of the map are further refined. In connection with the MBA-based modeling approach, the map approach may assist with the definition of the life cycle models of the individual levels of an MBA, recursively refining the various states of a level. In this sense, the map approach is orthogonal to the MBA-based approach. On the other hand, the MBA-based modeling approach allows for an incremental specification of business process models. The MBA-based approach, however, places focus on the preservation of heterogeneities in well-defined partitions of the data while, at the same time, describing the common elements of all data objects.

9.3 Future Work

In many cases, a company will already have some sort of representation of their business processes. Therefore, *multilevel business process discovery* techniques will obtain multilevel business process models from existing process descriptions. The thus obtained multilevel business process models constitute views over existing models. The advantage of these views is twofold. First, they provide an explicit representation of synchronization dependencies between life cycle models at different levels of abstraction. Second, the hetero-homogeneous nature of the obtained data models may present advantages for performance analysis.

A process cube organizes event log data in a multidimensional space, allowing for slice, roll-up, and drill-down operations on the business process models obtained through process mining [4]. Process cubes present similarities to previous work [113] on ontology-valued measures in OLAP cubes, which organizes business models in the cells of an OLAP cube, thereby allowing for the combination of knowledge from different contexts. Future work will introduce the notion of *hetero-homogeneous process cube*, building on existing work about hetero-homogeneous OLAP cubes [80].

Game development and graphics programming are other potential application areas for the MBA-based modeling approach. More specifically, the representation of action state machines [35, p. 621 et seq.] may benefit from the use of MBAs and hetero-homogeneous models. Action state machines abstract from low-level programming of animations, for example, of bodies and body parts, and allow for a more model-driven approach towards graphics programming. As many complex animated objects are composed of multiple individual components with different kinds of movement which interact with each other, the representation of such objects using multilevel models seems only logical. The hetero-homogeneous nature of MBAs may increase flexibility and code reusability in graphics programming.

References

[1] van der Aalst, W., Weske, M., Grünbauer, D.: Case handling: A new paradigm for business process support. Data & Knowledge Engineering 53(2), 129–162 (2005)

[2] van der Aalst, W.M.P.: Business process management: a comprehensive survey. ISRN Software Engineering 2013 (2013), http://dx.doi.org/10.1155/2013/507984

[3] van der Aalst, W.M.P., van Hee, K.M., van der Toorn, R.A.: Component-based software architectures: a framework based on inheritance of behavior. Science of Computer Programming 42(2-3), 129–171 (2002)

[4] van der Aalst, W.: Process cubes: Slicing, dicing, rolling up and drilling down event data for process mining. In: Song, M., Wynn, M., Liu, J. (eds.) AP-BPM 2013, LNBIP, vol. 159, pp. 1–22. Springer (2013)

[5] van der Aalst, W., Barthelmess, P., Ellis, C., Wainer, J.: Workflow modeling using proclets. In: Scheuermann, P., Etzion, O. (eds.) CoopIS 2000, LNCS, vol. 1901, pp. 198–209. Springer (2000)

[6] van der Aalst, W., Barthelmess, P., Ellis, C., Wainer, J.: Proclets: A framework for lightweight interacting workflow processes. International Journal of Cooperative Information Systems 10(4), 443–481 (2001)

[7] Abiteboul, S., Bourhis, P., Galland, A., Marinoiu, B.: The AXML artifact model. In: Proceedings of the 16th International Symposium on Temporal Representation and Reasoning. pp. 11–17 (2009)

[8] Abiteboul, S.: On views and XML. In: Proceedings of the 18th ACM SIGMOD-SIGACT-SIGART Symposium on Principles of Database Systems. pp. 1–9 (1999)

[9] Atkinson, C.: Meta-modeling for distributed object environments. In: Proceedings of the 1st International Enterprise Distributed Object Computing Conference. pp. 90–101 (1997)

[10] Atkinson, C., Grossmann, G., Kühne, T., de Lara, J. (eds.): Proceedings of the Workshop on Multi-Level Modelling co-located with ACM/IEEE 17th International Conference on Model Driven Engineering Languages & Systems, CEUR Workshop Proceedings, vol. 1286. CEUR-WS.org (2014), http://ceur-ws.org/Vol-1286

[11] Atkinson, C., Kühne, T.: The essence of multilevel metamodeling. In: Gogolla, M., Kobryn, C. (eds.) UML 2001. LNCS, vol. 2185, pp. 19–33. Springer (2001)

[12] Atkinson, C., Kühne, T.: Model-driven development: A metamodeling foundation. IEEE Software 20(5), 36–41 (2003)

[13] Atkinson, C., Kühne, T.: Reducing accidental complexity in domain models. Software & Systems Modeling 7(3), 345–359 (2008)

[14] Bencomo, N., Bennaceur, A., Grace, P., Blair, G.S., Issarny, V.: The role of models@run.time in supporting on-the-fly interoperability. Computing 95(3), 167–190 (2013)

[15] Blair, G., Bencomo, N., France, R.B.: Models@run.time. IEEE Computer 42(10), 22–27 (2009)

[16] Briol, P.: The Business Process Modeling Notation BPMN 2.0 Distilled. Lulu.com (2010)

[17] Buneman, P., Davidson, S.B., Kosky, A.: Theoretical aspects of schema merging. In: Pirotte, A., Delobel, C., Gottlob, G. (eds.) EDBT 1992, LNCS, vol. 580, pp. 152–167. Springer (1992)

[18] Cabot, J.: From declarative to imperative UML/OCL operation specifications. In: Parent, C., Schewe, K., Storey, V.C., Thalheim, B. (eds.) ER 2007. LNCS, vol. 4801, pp. 198–213. Springer (2007)

[19] Calvanese, D., Montali, M., Estañol, M., Teniente, E.: Verifiable UML artifact-centric business process models (extended version). The Computing Research Repository (CoRR) abs/1408.5094 (2014), http://arxiv.org/abs/1408.5094

[20] Cardelli, L.: Structural subtyping and the notion of power type. In: Proceedings of the 15th ACM SIGPLAN-SIGACT Symposium on Principles of Programming Languages. pp. 70–79 (1988)

[21] Castellanos, M.M., de Medeiros, A.K.A., Mendling, J., Weber, B., Weijters, A.J.M.M.: Business process intelligence. In: Handbook of research on business process modeling, pp. 456–480. IGI Global (2009)

[22] Chen, C., Zhu, F., Yan, X., Han, J., Yu, P., Ramakrishnan, R.: InfoNetOLAP: OLAP and mining of information networks. In: Yu, P.S., Han, J., Faloutsos, C. (eds.) Link Mining: Models, Algorithms, and Applications, pp. 411–438. Springer (2010)

[23] Cohn, D., Dhoolia, P., Heath, F.T., Pinel, F., Vergo, J.: Siena: From PowerPoint to web app in 5 minutes. In: Bouguettaya, A., Krüger, I., Margaria, T. (eds.) ICSOC 2008. LNCS, vol. 5364, pp. 722–723 (2008)

[24] Cohn, D., Hull, R.: Business artifacts: A data-centric approach to modeling business operations and processes. Bulletin of the IEEE Computer Society Technical Committee on Data Engineering 32(3) (2009)

[25] Dahchour, M., Pirotte, A., Zimányi, E.: Materialization and its meta-class implementation. IEEE Transactions on Knowledge and Data Engineering 14(5), 1078–1094 (2002)

[26] Dori, D.: Object-Process Methodology – A Holistic Systems Paradigm. Springer (2002)

[27] Dumas, M., La Rosa, M., Mendling, J., Reijers, H.A.: Fundamentals of Business Process Management. Springer (2013)

[28] Embley, D.W., Mok, W.Y.: Mapping conceptual models to database schemas. In: Embley, D.W., Thalheim, B. (eds.) Handbook of Conceptual Modeling, pp. 123–163. Springer (2011)

[29] Eriksson, O., Henderson-Sellers, B., Ågerfalk, P.J.: Ontological and linguistic metamodelling revisited: A language use approach. Information and Software Technology 55(12), 2099 – 2124 (2013)

[30] Estañol, M., Queralt, A., Sancho, M., Teniente, E.: Artifact-centric business process models in UML. In: Rosa, M.L., Soffer, P. (eds.) BPM 2012 Workshops. LNBIP, vol. 132, pp. 292–303. Springer (2013)

[31] Felden, C., Chamoni, P., Linden, M.: From process execution towards a business process intelligence. In: Abramowicz, W., Tolksdorf, R. (eds.) BIS 2010. LNBIP, vol. 47, pp. 195–206. Springer (2010)

[32] Genesys: Orchestration Server Developer's Guide, Orchestration Server 8.1.3, http://docs.genesys.com/Documentation/OS/8.1.3/Developer/

[33] Gonzalez-Perez, C., Henderson-Sellers, B.: A powertype-based meta-modelling framework. Software & Systems Modeling 5(1), 72–90 (2006)

[34] Gordijn, J., Akkermans, H., van Vliet, H.: Business modelling is not process modelling. In: Liddle, S., Mayr, H., Thalheim, B. (eds.) ER 2000 Workshop, LNCS, vol. 1921, pp. 40–51. Springer (2000)

[35] Gregory, J.: Game Engine Architecture. CRC Press, Boca Raton, FL, 2nd edn. (2014)

[36] Grigori, D., Casati, F., Castellanos, M., Dayal, U., Sayal, M., Shan, M.C.: Business process intelligence. Computers in Industry 53(3), 321–343 (2004)

[37] Gröner, G., Boskovic, M., Silva Parreiras, F., Gasevic, D.: Modeling and validation of business process families. Information Systems 38(5), 709–726 (2013)

[38] Günther, C.W., Verbeek, E.: OpenXES: Developer Guide – Version 2.0, March 28, 2014. IEEE Task Force on Process Mining (2014), http://www.xes-standard.org/openxes/developerguide

[39] Günther, C.W., Verbeek, E.: XES: Standard Definition – Version 2.0, March 28, 2014. IEEE Task Force on Process Mining (2014), http://www.xes-standard.org/xesstandarddefinition

[40] Hallerbach, A., Bauer, T., Reichert, M.: Capturing variability in business process models: the Provop approach. Journal of Software Maintenance and Evolution: Research and Practice 22(6-7), 519–546 (2010)

[41] Hallerbach, A., Bauer, T., Reichert, M.: Configuration and management of process variants. In: vom Brocke, J., Rosemann, M. (eds.) Handbook on Business Process Management 1, pp. 237–255. International Handbooks on Information Systems, Springer (2010)

[42] Harmon, P.: Business process change: A guide for business managers and BPM and Six Sigma professionals. Morgan Kaufmann, Burlington, 2nd edn. (2007)

[43] Heath, F.T., Boaz, D., Gupta, M., Vaculín, R., Sun, Y., Hull, R., Limonad, L.: Barcelona: A design and runtime environment for declarative artifact-centric BPM. In: Basu, S., Pautasso, C., Zhang, L., Fu, X. (eds.) ICSOC 2013. LNCS, vol. 8274, pp. 705–709. Springer (2013)

[44] ter Hofstede, A.H.M., van der Aalst, W.M.P., Adams, M., Russell, N. (eds.): Modern Business Process Automation: YAWL and its support environment. Springer (2010)

[45] Hruby, P.: Model-driven design using business patterns. Springer (2006)

[46] Huemer, M.: Bitemporal complex event processing of web event advertisements. Ph.D. thesis, Johannes Kepler University Linz, Austria (2014)

[47] Hull, R.: Artifact-centric business process models: Brief survey of research results and challenges. In: Meersman, R., Tari, Z. (eds.) OTM 2008, Part II. LNCS, vol. 5332, pp. 1152–1163. Springer (2008)

[48] Hull, R., Damaggio, E., Fournier, F., Gupta, M., Heath, F.T., Hobson, S., Linehan, M.H., Maradugu, S., Nigam, A., Sukaviriya, P., Vaculín, R.: Introducing the guard-stage-milestone approach for specifying business entity lifecycles. In: Bravetti, M., Bultan, T. (eds.) WS-FM 2010. LNCS, vol. 6551, pp. 1–24. Springer (2011)

[49] Hull, R., Damaggio, E., Masellis, R.D., Fournier, F., Gupta, M., Heath, F.T., Hobson, S., Linehan, M.H., Maradugu, S., Nigam, A., Sukaviriya, P.N., Vaculín, R.: Business artifacts with guard-stage-milestone lifecycles: managing artifact interactions with conditions and events. In: Proceedings of the 5th ACM International Conference on Distributed Event-Based Systems. pp. 51–62 (2011)

[50] Hürsch, W.L.: Should superclasses be abstract? In: Tokoro, M., Pareschi, R. (eds.) ECOOP 1994. LNCS, vol. 821, pp. 12–31. Springer (1994)

[51] Jarke, M., Jeusfeld, M.A., Nissen, H.W., Quix, C., Staudt, M.: Meta-modelling with datalog and classes: ConceptBase at the age of 21. In: Norrie, M.C., Grossniklaus, M. (eds.) ICOODB 2009. LNCS, vol. 5936, pp. 95–112. Springer (2010)

[52] Jeusfeld, M.A.: A deductive view on process-data diagrams. In: Ralyté, J., Mirbel, I., Deneckère, R. (eds.) ME 2011. IFIP AICT, vol. 351, pp. 123–137. Springer (2011)

[53] Jeusfeld, M.A., Jarke, M., Mylopoulos, J.: Metamodeling for Method Engineering. The MIT Press (2009)

[54] Jeusfeld, M.A., Quix, C., Jarke, M.: Concept-Base.cc User Manual Version 7.7. University of Skövde, RWTH Aachen (2014), http://merkur.informatik.rwth-aachen.de/pub/bscw.cgi/d2745581/CB-Manual.pdf

[55] Kappel, G., Schrefl, M.: Object/behavior diagrams. In: Proceedings of the 7th International Conference on Data Engineering. pp. 530–539 (1991)

[56] Künzle, V.: Object-Aware Process Management. Ph.D. thesis, University of Ulm, Germany (2013), http://dbis.eprints.uni-ulm.de/1010/

[57] Künzle, V., Reichert, M.: PHILharmonicFlows: towards a framework for object-aware process management. Journal of Software Maintenance and Evolution: Research and Practice 23(4), 205–244 (2011)

[58] La Rosa, M.: Managing variability in process-aware information systems. Ph.D. thesis, Queensland University of Technology, Brisbane, Australia (2009)

[59] de Lara, J., Guerra, E., Cuadrado, J.S.: When and how to use multilevel modelling. ACM Transactions on Software Engineering and Methodology 24(2), 12:1–12:46 (2014)

[60] Leavenworth, B.M.: Syntax macros and extended translation. Communications of the ACM 9(11), 790–793 (1966)

[61] Lenz, H.J., Shoshani, A.: Summarizability in OLAP and statistical data bases. In: Proceedings of the 9th International Conference on

Scientific and Statistical Database Management. pp. 132–143. IEEE (1997)

[62] van Lessen, T., Lübke, D., Nitzsche, J.: Geschäftsprozesse automatisieren mit BPEL. dpunkt.verlag, Heidelberg (2011), in German. Automating business processes using BPEL.

[63] List, B., Bruckner, R., Machaczek, K., Schiefer, J.: A comparison of data warehouse development methodologies case study of the process warehouse. In: Hameurlain, A., Cicchetti, R., Traunmüller, R. (eds.) DEXA 2002, LNCS, vol. 2453, pp. 203–215. Springer (2002)

[64] List, B., Schiefer, J., Tjoa, A., Quirchmayr, G.: Multidimensional business process analysis with the process warehouse. In: Abramowicz, W., Zurada, J. (eds.) Knowledge Discovery for Business Information Systems, The International Series in Engineering and Computer Science, vol. 600, pp. 211–227. Springer (2002)

[65] Liu, E., Wu, F.Y., Pinel, F., Shan, Z.: A two-tier data-centric framework for flexible business process management. In: 18th Americas Conference on Information Systems. Association for Information Systems (2012)

[66] Lohmann, N., Nyolt, M.: Artifact-centric modeling using BPMN. In: Pallis, G., Jmaiel, M., Charfi, A., Graupner, S., Karabulut, Y., Guinea, S., Rosenberg, F., Sheng, Q.Z., Pautasso, C., Mokhtar, S.B. (eds.) ICSOC 2011. LNCS, vol. 7221, pp. 54–65. Springer (2012)

[67] Mafazi, S., Grossmann, G., Mayer, W., Stumptner, M.: On-the-fly change propagation for the co-evolution of business processes. In: Meersman, R., Panetto, H., Dillon, T.S., Eder, J., Bellahsene, Z., Ritter, N., Leenheer, P.D., Dou, D. (eds.) OTM 2013. LNCS, vol. 8185, pp. 75–93. Springer (2013)

[68] Malinowski, E., Zimányi, E.: Hierarchies in a multidimensional model: From conceptual modeling to logical representation. Data and Knowledge Engineering 59(2), 348–377 (2006)

[69] Mansmann, S., Neumuth, T., Scholl, M.H.: Multidimensional data modeling for business process analysis. In: Parent, C., Schewe, K.D., Storey, V.C., Thalheim, B. (eds.) ER 2007. LNCS, vol. 4801, pp. 23–38. Springer (2007)

[70] Mansmann, S., Neumuth, T., Scholl, M.H.: OLAP technology for business process intelligence: Challenges and solutions. In: Song, I.Y., Eder, J., Nguyen, T.M. (eds.) DaWaK 2007. LNCS, vol. 4654, pp. 111–122. Springer (2007)

[71] Marin, M., Hull, R., Vaculín, R.: Data centric BPM and the emerging case management standard: A short survey. In: Rosa, M.L., Soffer, P. (eds.) BPM 2012 Workshops. LNBIP, vol. 132, pp. 24–30. Springer (2013)

[72] Meyer, A., Pufahl, L., Fahland, D., Weske, M.: Modeling and enacting complex data dependencies in business processes. In: Daniel, F., Wang, J., Weber, B. (eds.) BPM 2013, LNBIP, vol. 8094, pp. 171–186. Springer (2013)

[73] Meyer, B.: Object-Oriented Software Construction. Prentice Hall, Upper Saddle River, 2nd edn. (1997)

[74] zur Mühlen, M., Shapiro, R.: Business process analytics. In: vom Brocke, J., Rosemann, M. (eds.) Handbook on Business Process Management 2, pp. 137–157. Springer (2010)

[75] Mylopoulos, J., Borgida, A., Jarke, M., Koubarakis, M.: Telos: Representing knowledge about information systems. ACM Transactions on Information Systems 8(4), 325–362 (1990)

[76] Neumayr, B.: Multi-level modeling with m-objects and m-relationships. Ph.D. thesis, Johannes Kepler University Linz, Austria (2010)

[77] Neumayr, B., Grün, K., Schrefl, M.: Multi-level domain modeling with m-objects and m-relationships. In: Proceedings of the 6th Asia-Pacific Conference on Conceptual Modelling. pp. 107–116 (2009)

[78] Neumayr, B., Jeusfeld, M.A., Schrefl, M., Schütz, C.: Dual deep instantiation and its ConceptBase implementation. In: Jarke, M., Mylopoulos, J., Quix, C., Rolland, C., Manolopoulos, Y., Mouratidis, H., Horkoff, J. (eds.) CAiSE 2014. LNCS, vol. 8484, pp. 503–517. Springer (2014)

[79] Neumayr, B., Schrefl, M.: Multi-level conceptual modeling and OWL. In: Heuser, C.A., Pernul, G. (eds.) ER 2009 Workshops. LNCS, vol. 5833, pp. 189–199. Springer (2009)

[80] Neumayr, B., Schrefl, M., Thalheim, B.: Hetero-homogeneous hierarchies in data warehouses. In: Proceedings of the 7th Asia-Pacific Conference on Conceptual Modelling. pp. 61–70 (2010)

[81] Neumayr, B., Schrefl, M., Thalheim, B.: Modeling techniques for multi-level abstraction. In: Kaschek, R., Delcambre, L.M.L. (eds.) The Evolution of Conceptual Modeling. LNCS, vol. 6520, pp. 68–92. Springer (2011)

[82] Nigam, A., Caswell, N.S.: Business artifacts: An approach to operational specification. IBM Systems Journal 42(3), 428–445 (2003)

[83] Nurcan, S., Etien, A., Kaabi, R.S., Zoukar, I., Rolland, C.: A strategy driven business process modelling approach. Business Process Management Journal 11(6), 628–649 (2005)

[84] OASIS: Web Services Business Process Execution Language Version 2.0, Primer, 9 May 2007 (2007), https://www.oasis-open.org/committees/download.php/23974/wsbpel-v2.0-primer.pdf

[85] Odell, J.J.: Advanced object-oriented analysis and design using UML, chap. Power types, pp. 23–32. Cambridge University Press (1998)

[86] Olivé, A.: Conceptual modeling of information systems. Springer (2007)

[87] OMG: OMG Ontology Definition Metamodel (ODM), Version 1.0 (2009), http://www.omg.org/spec/ODM/1.0/

[88] OMG: OMG Unified Modeling Language (OMG UML), Superstructure, Version 2.4.1 (2011), http://www.omg.org/spec/UML/2.4.1/

[89] OMG: Business Process Model and Notation (BPMN), Version 2.0.2 (2013), http://www.omg.org/spec/BPMN/2.0.2/

[90] OMG: Semantics of Business Vocabulary and Business Rules (SBVR), Annex G – EU-Rent Example, Version 1.2 (2013), http://www.omg.org/cgi-bin/doc?formal/2013-11-08

[91] OMG: OMG Meta Object Facility (MOF) Core Specification, Version 2.4.2 (2014), http://www.omg.org/spec/SBVR/1.2/

[92] OMG: OMG Object Constraint Language (OCL), Version 2.4 (2014), http://www.omg.org/spec/OCL/2.4/

[93] Parent, C., Spaccapietra, S.: Issues and approaches of database integration. Communications of the ACM 41(5), 166–178 (1998)

[94] Pichler, H., Eder, J.: Business process modelling and workflow design. In: Embley, D.W., Thalheim, B. (eds.) Handbook of Conceptual Modeling, pp. 259–286. Springer (2011)

[95] Pirotte, A., Zimányi, E., Massart, D., Yakusheva, T.: Materialization: A powerful and ubiquitous abstraction pattern. In: Proceedings of the 20th International Conference on Very Large Data Bases. pp. 630–641 (1994)

[96] Polyvyanyy, A.: Structuring Process Models. Ph.D. thesis, Hasso Plattner Institute for Software Systems Engineering, Potsdam, Germany (2012)

[97] Reichert, M., Rinderle-Ma, S., Dadam, P.: Flexibility in process-aware information systems. In: Jensen, K., van der Aalst, W.M. (eds.) ToPNoC II, LNCS, vol. 5460, pp. 115–135. Springer (2009)

[98] Reichert, M., Weber, B.: Enabling Flexibility in Process-Aware Information Systems: Challenges, Methods, Technologies. Springer (2012)

[99] Rinderle, S., Reichert, M., Dadam, P.: Correctness criteria for dynamic changes in workflow systems – a survey. Data & Knowledge Engineering 50(1), 9–34 (2004)

[100] Rolland, C.: Modeling the evolution of artifacts. In: Proceedings of the First IEEE International Conference on Requirements Engineering. pp. 216–219 (1994)

[101] Rolland, C.: A comprehensive view of process engineering. In: Pernici, B., Thanos, C. (eds.) CAiSE 1998. LNCS, vol. 1413, pp. 1–24. Springer (1998)

[102] Rolland, C., Nurcan, S.: Business process lines to deal with the variability. In: Proceedings of the 43rd Hawaii International International Conference on Systems Science. pp. 1–10. IEEE Computer Society (2010)

[103] Rolland, C., Nurcan, S., Grosz, G.: A unified framework for modeling cooperative design processes and cooperative business processes. In:

Proceedings of the 31st Hawaii International Conference on System Sciences. pp. 376–385. IEEE Computer Society (1998)

[104] Rolland, C., Prakash, N., Benjamen, A.: A multi-model view of process modelling. Requirements Engineering 4(4), 169–187 (1999)

[105] Rosemann, M., van der Aalst, W.M.P.: A configurable reference modelling language. Information Systems 32(1), 1–23 (2007)

[106] Sánchez González, L., García Rubio, F., Ruiz González, F., Piattini Velthuis, M.: Measurement in business processes: a systematic review. Business Process Management Journal 16(1), 114–134 (2010)

[107] Scheer, A.W., Thomas, O., Adam, O.: Process modeling using event-driven process chains. In: Dumas, M., van der Aalst, W.M.P., ter Hofstede, A.H.M. (eds.) Process-Aware Information Systems, pp. 119–145. Wiley, Hoboken (2005)

[108] Schrefl, M., Stumptner, M.: Behavior-consistent specialization of object life cycles. ACM Transactions on Software Engineering and Methodology 11(1), 92–148 (2002)

[109] Schütz, C.: Extending data warehouses with hetero-homogeneous dimension hierarchies and cubes: A proof-of-concept prototype in Oracle. Master's thesis, Johannes Kepler University Linz (2010)

[110] Schütz, C.: Multilevel business modeling: From hetero-homogeneous data warehouses to multilevel business processes. Tech. rep., Austrian Marshall Plan Foundation (2012), Marshall Plan Scholarship paper. http://marshallplan.at/images/papers_scholarship/2012/Schuetz.pdf

[111] Schütz, C., Delcambre, L.M.L., Schrefl, M.: Multilevel business artifacts. In: La Rosa, M., Soffer, P. (eds.) BPM 2012 Workshops. LNBIP, vol. 132, pp. 304–315. Springer (2013)

[112] Schütz, C., Neumayr, B., Schrefl, M.: Integration and reuse of heterogeneous information: Hetero-homogeneous data warehouse modeling in the Common Warehouse Metamodel. In: Proceedings of the 18th Americas Conference on Information Systems (2012)

[113] Schütz, C., Neumayr, B., Schrefl, M.: Business model ontologies in OLAP cubes. In: Salinesi, C., Norrie, M.C., Pastor, O. (eds.) CAiSE 2013. LNCS, vol. 7908, pp. 514–529. Springer (2013)

[114] Schütz, C., Schrefl, M.: Variability in artifact-centric process modeling: The hetero-homogeneous approach. In: Grossmann, G., Saeki, M. (eds.) Proceedings of the 10th Asia-Pacific Conference on Conceptual Modelling. CRPIT, vol. 154, pp. 29–38. Australian Computer Society (2014)

[115] Schütz, C., Schrefl, M., Delcambre, L.M.L.: Multilevel business process modeling: motivation, approach, design issues, and applications. In: Proceedings of the 5th Ph.D. Workshop on Information and Knowledge Management. pp. 91–94. ACM, New York (2012)

[116] Schütz, C., Schrefl, M., Neumayr, B., Sierninger, D.: Incremental integration of data warehouses: the hetero-homogeneous approach. In: Proceedings of the ACM 14th International Workshop on Data Warehousing and OLAP. pp. 25–30 (2011)

[117] Schütz, C.G.: Multilevel Business Processes: Modeling and Data Analysis. Ph.D. thesis, Johannes Kepler University Linz, Austria (2015)

[118] Smirnov, S., Reijers, H.A., Weske, M.: A semantic approach for business process model abstraction. In: Mouratidis, H., Rolland, C. (eds.) CAiSE 2011, LNCS, vol. 6741, pp. 497–511. Springer (2011)

[119] Smirnov, S., Reijers, H.A., Weske, M., Nugteren, T.: Business process model abstraction: a definition, catalog, and survey. Distributed and Parallel Databases 30(1), 63–99 (2012)

[120] Stärk, R., Schmid, J., Börger, E.: Java and the Java Virtual Machine. Springer (2001)

[121] Stefanov, V., List, B.: Bridging the gap between data warehouses and business processes: A business intelligence perspective for event-driven process chains. In: Proceedings of the 9th IEEE International Enterprise Distributed Object Computing Conference. pp. 3–14 (2005)

[122] Stefanov, V., List, B.: A UML profile for representing business object states in a data warehouse. In: Song, I.Y., Eder, J., Nguyen, T.M. (eds.) DaWaK 2007. LNCS, vol. 4654, pp. 209–220. Springer (2007)

[123] Stefanov, V., List, B., Korherr, B.: Extending UML 2 activity diagrams with business intelligence objects. In: Tjoa, A.M., Trujillo, J. (eds.) DaWaK 2005. LNCS, vol. 3589, pp. 53–63. Springer (2005)

[124] Steinmann, H., Schreyögg, G.: Management: Grundlagen der Unternehmensführung. Gabler, Wiesbaden, 6th edn. (2005), in German. Management: Fundamentals of business administration.

[125] Stumptner, M., Schrefl, M.: Behavior consistent inheritance in UML. In: Laender, A., Liddle, S., Storey, V. (eds.) ER 2000, LNCS, vol. 1920, pp. 451–530. Springer (2000)

[126] Sturm, A.: Supporting business process analysis via data warehousing. Journal of Software: Evolution and Process 24(3), 303–319 (2012)

[127] Thalheim, B.: Entity-relationship modeling: foundations of database technology. Springer (2000)

[128] W3C: XQuery Update Facility 3.0 – W3C Working Draft 08 January 2013 (2013), http://www.w3.org/TR/2013/WD-xquery-update-30-20130108/

[129] W3C: State Chart XML (SCXML): State Machine Notation for Control Abstraction – W3C Candidate Recommendation 13 March 2014 (2014), http://www.w3.org/TR/2014/CR-scxml-20140313/

[130] W3C: State Chart XML (SCXML): State Machine Notation for Control Abstraction – W3C Last Call Working Draft 29 May 2014 (2014), http://www.w3.org/TR/2014/WD-scxml-20140529/

[131] W3C: XML Schema Definition Language (XSD) 1.1 Part 2: Datatypes – W3C Recommendation 5 April 2012 (2014), http://www.w3.org/TR/2012/REC-xmlschema11-2-20120405/

[132] W3C: XPath and XQuery Functions and Operators 3.0 – W3C Recommendation 08 April 2014 (2014), http://www.w3.org/TR/2014/REC-xpath-functions-30-20140408/

[133] W3C: XPath and XQuery Functions and Operators 3.1 – W3C Candidate Recommendation 18 December 2014 (2014), http://www.w3.org/TR/2014/CR-xpath-functions-31-20141218/

[134] W3C: XQuery 3.0: An XML Query Language – W3C Recommendation 08 April 2014 (2014), http://www.w3.org/TR/2014/REC-xquery-30-20140408/

[135] W3C: XQuery and XPath Data Model 3.0 – W3C Recommendation 08 April 2014 (2014), http://www.w3.org/TR/2014/REC-xpath-datamodel-30-20140408/

[136] W3C: State Chart XML (SCXML): State Machine Notation for Control Abstraction – W3C Proposed Recommendation 30 April 2015 (2015), http://www.w3.org/TR/2015/PR-scxml-20150430/

[137] Wazlawick, R.S.: Object-oriented analysis and design for information systems: Modeling with UML, OCL, and IFML. Elsevier, Burlington (2014)

[138] Weber, B., Reichert, M., Rinderle-Ma, S.: Change patterns and change support features – enhancing flexibility in process-aware information systems. Data & Knowledge Engineering 66(3), 438–466 (2008)

[139] Weske, M.: Business Process Management: Concepts, Languages, Architectures. Springer (2007)

[140] Wirth, N.: What can we do about the unnecessary diversity of notation for syntactic definitions? Communications of the ACM 20(11), 822–823 (1977)

[141] Yongchareon, S., Liu, C., Zhao, X.: A framework for behavior-consistent specialization of artifact-centric business processes. In: Barros, A., Gal, A., Kindler, E. (eds.) BPM 2012, LNCS, vol. 7481, pp. 285–301. Springer (2012)

Printed in the United States
By Bookmasters